Keynes, Coordination and Beyond

Keynes, Coordination and Beyond

The Development of Macroeconomic and Monetary Theory since 1945

Harry Garretsen

Department of Economics
University of Groningen
The Netherlands

Edward Elgar

© Harry Garretsen 1992

Published by
Edward Elgar Publishing Limited
Gower House
Croft Road
Aldershot
Hants GU11 3HR
England

Edward Elgar Publishing Company
Old Post Road
Brookfield
Vermont 05036
USA

A CIP catalogue record for this book
is available from the British Library

A CIP catalogue record for this book
is available from the US Library of Congress

ISBN 185278 620 5

Printed in Great Britain by
Billing & Sons Ltd, Worcester

Contents

Illustrations

Acknowledgements

This study was carried out at the Department of Economics at the University of Groningen between September 1987 and October 1991. I would like to thank the following people:

Professor Th. van de Klundert, Professor A. Nentjes and Professor G.F.W.M. Pikkemaat for their willingness to read the entire manuscript and to provide useful comments.

Professor Jan Pen for many stimulating discussions on economics and for reminding me not to forget the main message of Keynesian economics.

Heleen Nijkamp who provided research assistance and who also completed the list of references.

Mrs. Tijman–Logtenberg who corrected my English.

The editors of *De Economist*, *Metroeconomica* and *The Journal of Post Keynesian Economics* for their permission to let me use articles that have been published in these journals.

Participants at the 1989 convention of the *European Economic Association* in Augsburg for their comments on a first version of the model used in chapter 5; participants at the 1989 convention of the *Eastern Economic Association* in Baltimore for their criticism on a first draft of chapter 6; participants at the 1991 workshop on the emergence and stability of institutions at Louvain–la–Neuve for their remarks on some of the material used in chapters 7 and 8.

I would especially like to thank Hans van Ees, Lex Hoogduin and Maarten Janssen for letting me use (parts of) papers that I have written with them and for many useful suggestions and stimulating discussions that have contributed significantly to the final result of this study. Most of all, I thank Simon Kuipers for his support and supervision.

1 Introduction

1.1 Keynes's theoretical legacy and its inheritants: purpose of this study

It is a commonplace to argue that *The General Theory of Employment, Interest and Money* by John Maynard Keynes (Keynes (1936), hereafter GT)[1] has greatly influenced the post–war development of economic theory and policy. Both mainstream and non–mainstream economists as well as Keynesians and non–Keynesians would probably subscribe to this view. But the agreement stops right there, for as to the question of what Keynes had to say on economic theory and policy there are numerous, often conflicting answers. These answers range from the position that in terms of theoretical insights the GT is much ado about nothing and its sole innovation is to be found in its argumentation in favour of macroeconomic stabilization policy, on the one hand, to the position that the theoretical insights of the GT have largely been misunderstood with the result that what normally goes for Keynesian theory and policy has very little to do with the GT, on the other hand.

Of these two extreme positions the idea that Keynes's main contribution is to be found in his recognition that there is a case for stabilisation policy has dominated the discourse about Keynesian theory and policy both at the academic and the policy levels. After its initial success in the 1950s and the 1960s, this Keynesian view became discredited in the 1970s, the era of stagflation. The mainstream view of Keynesian policy has also been in the defence in the 1980s, the era of *laissez–faire* policies. The policy interpretation of the GT basically assumes that the theoretical differences between Keynes on the one hand and the classical economists of his day and the contemporary neo–classical economists on the other hand were and are not fundamental, respectively. Or, in other words, the GT did not disrupt the theoretical continuity in the development of mainstream economics during this century. According to

1

this view, Keynes's theoretical contributions are his insistence on the role of money as a store of value and his analysis of involuntary unemployment in case of price and/or wage stickiness.[2] The GT therewith became a special case of the more general neo-classical theory, for its conclusions depended on the interest elasticity of money demand and especially on the assumption of price/wage stickiness. The mainstream debate between Keynesians and monetarists and also, to a large extent, the more recent debate between new-Keynesians and new-classicals are cast in an analytical framework in which the Keynesian results vanish if the price mechanism is allowed to do its job.

Adherents of the second above-mentioned position take as their starting point that the GT is not a special case of a more general neo-classical theory and that the GT contains theoretical insights that are very much at odds with the latter. Until recently the idea that the dominant interpretation of the GT is at variance with the contents of the GT has been especially expressed by various strands of non-mainstream economics.[3] In recent years, however, there have also been a growing number of studies that use the general equilibrium framework that underlies mainstream economics in order to show how some of Keynes's ideas can be incorporated in a general equilibrium framework with the result that the unhampered working of the price mechanism cannot be relied upon in bringing about Pareto-efficient outcomes for the economy as a whole. Though the adherents of this second position emphasize very different theoretical aspects of the GT and also make use of rather different analytical frameworks they all have in common the idea that Keynes's GT is foremost an attempt to bring out the theoretical deficiencies in the (neo-)classical notion that the coordinative efficiency of markets is a proper assumption for the economy as a whole. Or, in other words, they conceive the GT as an attempt to show why the *Invisible Hand* does not work for the economy as a whole.

If one neglects the significant differences in the various analytical frameworks it therefore seems an appropriate short cut in our view to categorize the answers to the question of the relevance of the GT in those that focus on the policy implications and consider the theoretical relevance to be rather limited, and in those that stress the theoretical insights.[4] In our view the same distinction between the inheritors of Keynes's theoretical legacy can also be stated as follows. If one takes Keynes's claim seriously 'that the postulates of the classical theory are applicable to a special case only and not to the general case, the situation which it assumes being a limiting point of the possible positions of equilibrium' (Keynes, GT, p. 3) the question becomes whether and how the GT does indeed yield insights that justify this claim. If the answer is affirmative this implies that the classical analysis which focuses on this special case, full–employment equilibrium, will not do for the analysis of the economy as a whole. If the answer is negative, this means that the GT does not challenge the main implication of classical and neo–classical theory that if prices are allowed to perform their coordination enhancing task the alleged special case of full–employment equilibrium becomes the only feasible equilibrium.

One of the aims of this study is to show why Keynes considered his theory to be more general, and above all how subsequent developments in economic theory dealt with the aforementioned question and with Keynes's analysis in this respect.[5] Our analysis does not lead to a definite perspective on the not very interesting issue of what Keynes really meant, but rather we intend to show that much of the muddle and cross talk about the meaning and the relevance of the GT can be traced back to a failure to get the questions right. In our view any analysis of Keynes's GT as such and of its relevance for current economic theorizing should face Keynes's declared objective that his theory is fundamentally different from its classical counterpart. The aforementioned policy interpretation is not able to address this issue (either positively or negatively) because it uses an analytical framework in which Keynes's distinction between a general and a special case simply cannot be made since this framework is basically similar to the classical one that Keynes started out to refute in the first place. In analysing Keynes's theoretical contribution and in elaborating upon this contribution it is therefore essential to start with the main questions involved and not with an attempt to come up with Keynesian answers in a particular analytical framework. In our opinion the main question is whether and how the unhampered working of the price mechanism is able to coordinate economic activities for the economy as a whole to the extent that the full–employment Pareto–efficient equilibrium is the only feasible equilibrium. Keynes's conclusion is that except by sheer coincidence the price mechanism is not able to perform this task, his main criticism against classical theory being that it (implicitly) assumed what had to be proven. Or, in other words, Keynes tried to argue that his theory was a general theory of which classical theory was merely a special case because the former dealt with this fundamental issue for market economies whereas the latter did not. Hence, the first objective of this study is to show that the analysis of the coordination problem in decentralized economies lies at the heart of Keynes's GT (chapter 2).

The main part of this thesis will, however, not deal with an exegesis of Keynes's GT or of related writings by Keynes but will instead focus on the development of macroeconomic theory in which our hypothesis concerning the coordination issue as Keynes's theoretical legacy is used as a benchmark. Given the validity of this hypothesis one of the main themes of this study is that mainstream economics did not take up Keynes's lead. The second objective is to show that especially mainstream economists participating in the so- called microfoundations debate did by and large not address the coordination issue and therefore did neglect Keynes's main theoretical innovation. As a result, this debate has mainly provided the right answers to the wrong questions (chapter 3). This conclusion raises the following two questions. First of all, what is a fruitful extension (if any) of Keynes's GT in a neo-classical or, more accurately, in a general equilibrium framework? (chapter 5) Secondly, given our rather negative assessment of the microfoundations debate it raises the question whether there are alternative approaches that do address Keynes's coordination issue and, if so how these insights can be used to elaborate upon Keynes's analysis of the coordination problem (chapters 4, 6, and 7). In our attempt to answer these two questions, it turns out that an extension of Keynes's analysis does not imply a search for (better) microfoundations for macroeconomics in the first place, but that it is rather the other way around, an extension of Keynes's analysis of the coordination problem calls forth the need for macrofoundations for microeconomics (to be defined in the next section). In our view, this conclusion holds irrespective of whether one tries to extend Keynes's coordination issue in a general equilibrium framework or not (chapter 8). In the absence of a coordinating mechanism that guarantees Pareto-efficient outcomes (like the invisible hand, the Walrasian auctioneer or Robinson Crusoe) or, even more fundamentally, in the presence of uncertainty in the sense of Keynes or Knight, the need for coordination becomes an endogenous one. In case a Pareto-efficient coordination is exogenously imposed upon the economy if only prices are flexible on the one hand and if the formation of expectations boils down to assuming equilibrium on the other hand, economic subjects are faced only with the issue of price flexibility for the well-known allocative reasons. It will turn out that in case the need for coordination is endogenized the analysis should focus on (imperfect) coordinating devices of which money is an outstanding example. More generally, the analysis should focus on the emergence and stability of institutions and conventions. It is important to define an institution and a convention right from the outset. Following Schotter (1981) (who follows Lewis (1986)) a social institution will be defined as 'a regularity in social behaviour that is agreed to by all members of society, specifies behaviour in specific recurrent situations, and is either self-policed or policed by some external authority' (Schotter (1981), p. 11). The main difference with an convention is that a convention is always self-enforcing whereas a institution need not to be self-enforcing. Driving on the right side of the road and money as a medium of exchange are two examples of a convention. A system of property rights and agreements that foster price stability (wage contracts!) are two examples of institutions. Price stability, for instance, may only be possible if some external agency (a central bank) enforces certain institutional arrangements upon the economic agents. Given these definitions, the bottom–line of our study is that, apart from some notable exceptions, the Keynesian revolution never got started because the validity of the central concepts of microeconomics for the analysis of the economy as a whole remained unchallenged.[6]

To sum up, the objectives of this study are threefold.

1) To argue that Keynes's main theoretical innovation in the GT is his analysis of the coordination problem for decentralized market economies.

2) To show that subsequent developments in macroeconomic theory in general and in the microfoundations debate in particular have neglected this problem with the result that they addressed the wrong question.

3) To show what constitutes a (more) fruitful extension of Keynes's analysis of the coordination problem and to argue that this implies a need for macrofoundations for microeconomics.

No doubt, this study raises more questions than it answers. Our emphasis on questions, however, is not without reason. Before answering what the meaning and relevance of the GT and, more importantly, what the main objectives of research for macroeconomic theory are, economists must first make sure what the basic questions are.[7] In order to live up to our own standard in this respect the next section briefly deals with the definition of some concepts and with our methodological position.

1.2 Micro, macro and methodology

In order to avoid confusion, it is important to define the concepts of macro and micro since these concepts will not only be frequently used in the following chapters but the meaning of macro and especially micro varies in the literature. In the standard use of these two concepts, micro is defined as the theory of individual behaviour and macro as the theory which studies the relations between a number of aggregate variables that represent the economy as a whole. Examples of the former are, of course, the theory of the consumer and the theory of the firm and IS/LM–type of models are an example of the latter. So far, so good. But any textbook on microeconomics also deals with the theory of the market and often also with general equilibrium theory. Varian (1984) is a good example. Hence, microeconomics does not only refer to the theory of individual behaviour but also to the theory that analyses the determination of relative prices and the allocation of resources, either on a partial level (theory of the market) or on the level of the economy as a whole (general equilibrium theory). The fact that general equilibrium theory is above all a theory about the economy as a whole is of particular relevance for the purpose of our study because for the analysis of the economy as a whole we now have two theories at our disposal: standard macroeconomic theory and general equilibrium theory which is a microeconomic theory. The attempt in mainstream economics to provide macroeconomics with a microeconomic foundation can be best understood as an attempt to ground important economic phenomena that are the subject of standard macroeconomic theory (e.g. unemployment, inflation, fluctuations in output etc.) upon a general equilibrium framework. The main question underlying the microfoundations debate therefore is how these macroeconomic phenomena can be reconciled with the main assumptions underlying general equilibrium analysis.[8] The need for microfoundations for Keynesian macroeconomics in mainstream economics basically arises because it is assumed in Walrasian general equilibrium analysis that the price mechanism coordinates economic activities in a Pareto–efficient manner whereas in Keynesian macroeconomics this mechanism is somehow not supposed to work. Underneath this there is, however, a fundamental difference in our view: the distinction between theories that assume that the price mechanism ensures a socially efficient degree of coordination and those that do not.

This last distinction lies at the heart of what Keynes had to say on the micro/macro distinction or, more accurately, on what became known as micro and macro after the GT was published. In chapter 21 of the GT Keynes concluded that

> the division of economics between the theory of value and distribution on the one hand and the theory of money on the other hand is, I think a false division. The right dichotomy is, I suggest, between the theory of the individual industry or firm and of the rewards and the distribution between different uses of a *given* quantity of resources on the one hand, and the theory of output and employment *as a whole* on the other hand (Keynes, GT, p. 293).

In Keynes's view, the particular division between micro and macro that started off the microfoundations debate is not very useful to begin with. The question then is whether Keynes's distinction corresponds to the standard use of micro and macro as mentioned at the beginning of this section. In our opinion this is not the case. Keynes's theory of output and employment for the economy as a whole is not the same as what became Keynes's macroeconomics in standard textbook macrotheory as will be explained at length in the subsequent chapters. Again, in our view, Keynes's theory of output and employment is essentially concerned with the issue of coordination in decentralized market economies. As will become clear, the coordination problem in the GT centres around the characteristics of a monetary economy. Especially the role of expectations turns out to be crucial. Chapter 21 of the GT reflects this in Keynes's explanation of the above cited dichotomy. Keynes refers to the theory of the individual industry as being 'not concerned with the significant characteristics of money' which means that it analyses 'what distribution of resources between different uses will be consistent with equilibrium under the influence of normal economic motives in a world in which *our views concerning the future are fixed and reliable in all aspects*' (Keynes, GT, p. 293, emphasis added). The theory of output and employment as a whole on the other hand requires the complete theory of a monetary economy which, according to Keynes, implies the analysis of a system 'in which changing views about the future are capable of influencing the present situation. *For the importance of money essentially flows from its being a link between the present and the future*' (Keynes, GT, p. 293).[9] Hence, we introduce a third definition of the micro/macro distinction. In order to avoid confusion we use quotation marks when referring to this distinction. 'Macro' refers to those theories of the economy as a whole that do not take the coordination issue for granted in the sense of not assuming that the unhampered working of the price mechanism is able to take care of the establishment of a unique, stable Pareto–efficient outcome. 'Micro' refers to all those approaches of the economy as a whole that do take this issue for granted (see also section 3.1). Keynes's GT is an example of a 'macro' theory but the recent coordination failures approach within a general equilibrium framework (see section 3.4. and chapter 5) or some of the alternative approaches of chapter 4 are also examples. Walrasian general equilibrium analysis and new–classical macroeconomics are two examples of 'micro' theories. The definition of 'macro' does not a priori exclude any analytical framework. The interpretation of the phrase 'macro'foundations for microeconomics is now rather straightforward and can be defined as follows: The analysis of the implications of the coordination problem for the behaviour of individual agents.[10]

In our opinion the emphasis on the behaviour of individual agents is in line with the GT. The fact that Keynes at various instances did use an aggregate analytical framework in the GT must be looked upon as a *short cut* in order to be able to illustrate certain insights (After all, Keynes was a Marshallian who knew his way with the *ceteris paribus* clause, see also chapter 2). But as, for instance, the aforementioned explanation by Keynes of the theory of output and employment as a whole illustrates, views concerning the future are crucial for an analysis of the coordination problem. Hence, the role of expectations in the GT can only be understood in terms of the behaviour of individual agents. As to the importance of the behaviour of individual agents in the GT, we agree with Hahn (1984) who concludes that

> about two thirds of the *General Theory* deals with the theory of
> the action of agents, their motives for saving and for holding
> money, their investment and speculative behaviour etc. It is
> a consequence of intellectual coarseness and not of Keynes that
> university syllabuses are so frequently divided into watertight
> macro– and microeconomic courses. Even if it is granted that in
> the manipulative, one might almost say arithmetical, stages of
> Keynesian economics, relative prices play a subordinate role, it
> is after all the case that Keynes argues that the actions of
> agents in markets would not result in the equilibrium posited by
> his predecessors. It is hard to see how this very important
> proposition is to be understood without microtheory. Moreover the
> fundamental postulate that agents will not persist in actions
> when more advantageous ones are open to them plays a central role
> in the Keynesian scheme (Hahn (1984), pp. 64–65).[11]

Many textbook interpretations of the GT conceive the typical
Keynesian situation as deficiencies in aggregate demand causing
aggregate unemployment and suboptimal levels of aggregate output. In
explaining this situation it seems, however, difficult to circumvent
the issue of (a lack of) coordination of individual decisions.

Our definitions of 'macro' and 'macro'foundations lead to the
following two observations about methodology. The first observation
concerns our definition of 'macro'. In our view, the analytical
framework in which the question of coordination is analysed is only
of secondary importance. As will become clear in the subsequent
chapters, the rather broad definition of 'macro' and 'micro' enables
the analysis of mainstream as well as non–mainstream approaches. Or,
in other words, coordination issues can be analysed within a general
equilibrium framework or within an alternative framework. In terms of
methodology this means that we adhere to what is known as
methodological pluralism (Caldwell (1982)).[12] This methodological
approach 'takes as a starting assumption that no universally
applicable, logically compelling method of theory appraisal exists.
(Or, more correctly, even if it exists, we can never be sure that we
have found it, even if we have.)' (Caldwell (1982), p. 245). This
ultimately means that there is no 'right' theory to analyse economic
issues in general and the coordination issue in particular. Hence,
this study deals explicitly with the possibility of analysing the
coordination issue within a general equilibrium framework as well as
within e.g. post–Keynesian and Austrian economics. Following Caldwell
(1982, pp. 248–249) the fact that multiple research programmes are
allowed for implies that external criticism of a particular research
programme is not very useful and that instead internal criticism has
to be advocated. Discussions on a certain topic in a *particular*
analytical framework between opponents that adhere to different

research programmes have to take place in terms of that framework. Debunking of theories for not applying to the standards of an alternative framework has to be ruled out. A good example of applying external criticism, where instead internal criticism is called for, is the discussion concerning the analysis of long-term expectations in the GT (see Dow and Dow (1985) and also chapter 2). As we will argue in chapter 2 in Keynes's analytical framework, it makes perfect sense to treat these expectations as exogenous in order to cope with the fundamental indeterminacy of the GT, the role of uncertainty. Keynes's analysis is cast in a Marshallian framework. This analysis of long-term expectations has been criticized from the point of view of a Walrasian general equilibrium framework as being irrational. The exogeneity of these expectations and, hence, of the fundamental indeterminacy of the economic system in the GT can indeed not be reconciled with a Walrasian general equilibrium framework because 'within such a framework it is logically difficult, as well as antithetical, to leave one set of expectations outside the model. Indeed it is an inherent property of closed, deterministic models, which are designed to represent a complete system, to enforce a strict dualism (between endogeneity and exogeneity, as between rationality and irrationality) which is consistently upheld throughout the system' (Dow and Dow (1985), p. 57). The criticism that Keynes's analysis is based on irrational behaviour is not justified if one sticks to methodological pluralism. [13]

The choice for methodological pluralism can also be explained by referring to Keynes's own methodological position in this respect. Keynes explicitly considered his GT not to be *the* theory for the analysis of the economy as a whole. It depends on the particular problem at hand which variables need to be considered and which theory applies (see chapter 18 of the GT). Hence, different questions call forth different theories. There does not exist a universally applicable economic theory. This point is made forcefully by Keynes in the context of the well-known Keynes-Tinbergen debate (Keynes (1937B), pp. 285-320). Keynes's emphasis on economics being a moral science instead of a physical science (see especially Keynes (1937B), pp. 299-300) can also be interpreted as an argument against the search for an economic theory that can be applied in all circumstances.

The argument of economics as a moral science also reveals that expectations and actions of individual agents are decisive in Keynes's view:

> I also want to emphasize strongly the point about economics being a moral science. I mentioned before that it deals with introspection and with values. I might have added that it deals with motives, expectations, psychological uncertainties ... It is as though the fall of the apple to the ground depended on the

apple's motives, on whether it is worthwhile falling to the ground, and whether the ground wanted the apple to fall, and on mistaken calculations on the part of the apple as to how far it was from the centre of the earth (Keynes (1937B), p. 300).

This leads to the second methodological observation. The definition of 'macro'foundations as the analysis of the coordination problem for the *behaviour of individual agents* implies that we think it to be in accordance with the GT that the issue of coordination and individual behaviour cannot be separated. It does, however, not imply that we stick to the standard interpretation of methodological individualism according to which agents are not only the relevant decision makers but also in making these decisions the outside world is taken as given. In fact, the need for 'macro'foundation precisely concerns the issue that in taking individual decisions the outside world is not just another constraint. The individual agent is at the centre-stage of the GT but due to the implications of the coordination problem individual actions are also partly determined by, for instance, conventions and institutions. In mainstream economics, however, methodological individualism is mostly interpreted as implying that the microfoundations for macroeconomics are fully derived from individual decision making. In fact, in the following chapters we will argue that this interpretation cannot stand close scrutiny and forecloses a full-fledged analysis of the coordination problem. Chapter 3 of our study shows that the microfoundations debate can be characterized as employing methodological individualism in this way (see also Kirman (1989)).[14] This rounds up our discussion of micro, macro, and methodology. Before turning to a brief outline of the various chapters in the last section of chapter 1 it is useful to make a few remarks on what this study is not about. First of all, it is not about methodology. It primarily deals with economic theory. Secondly, it is not about a new interpretation of what Keynes really meant. It deals with an important analytical question raised by Keynes, not with the issue of whether he provided an adequate answer to this question. Following Gerrard (1991), we think that one of the main reasons for the ongoing debate about the relevance of the GT is the failure to distinguish between the meaning of the GT as such, on the one hand, and the significance of the GT for the development of economic theory, on the other hand. This study will primarily focus on the issue of the relevance of Keynes's ideas for the development of economic theory and will therefore only mildly concern the issue of interpretation. Thirdly, this study is not about 'who's right or wrong' in economic theory. The issue at stake is that some theories that may be perfectly consistent in their own right have not much to say about what we consider and what we think Keynes considered to be a central problem of decentralized economies.[15] Finally, the title of our study is not meant to imply that we do a priori reject every invisible hand explanation of economic phenomena as such. The use of the invisible hand assumption is criticized as far as it is used to circumvent the coordination problem.

1.3 Outline of the following chapters

Many interpretations of the GT emphasize one or two outstanding features of the GT. It is our opinion that these interpretations are a specific elaboration of Keynes's method of characterizing his own theory and his version of the classical theory by means of the indeterminacy and the micro–macro issue. The emphasis on the whole *structure* of the GT makes clear that not only many interpretations of Keynes's GT are different variations of these two issues, but that the line between Keynesian and classical theories should be drawn between those theories in which the coordination problem has some role to play and those theories in which this coordination problem is absent. The various interpretations of the GT are typically biased since the analytical framework (partly) determines the answers to the question of what constitutes Keynes(ian) economics. In chapter 2 of our study it is shown that once the debate on what Keynes really meant is stripped from the issue of the proper framework to do economic theory it becomes clear that contrary to *communis opinio* Keynes's line of reasoning in the GT is rather straightforward.

The main differences between Keynes and the Classics can be analysed by focusing upon the following two issues:

1. Keynes's method of analysing the determinants, the determinates and indeterminacy in his theory and his version of the classical theory. This is the indeterminacy issue.

2. The (ir)relevance of the standard demand and supply analysis for the economy as a whole. This is called the micro–macro issue for the following reason. In a demand and supply analysis of a single sector, changes in sector prices do not influence sector income. For the economy as a whole this cannot be the case, since prices are incomes.

Both the fundamental indeterminacy and the importance of the micro–macro issue in the GT are a reflection of the coordination problem. This holds true for, for instance, Keynes's analysis of the labour market (are workers in a position to determine their real wage, the fallacy of composition), the goods market (the coordination of savings and investment, paradox of thrift), the role of money and finally for his analysis of expectations. In the last part of chapter 2 we will argue that Keynes's methodology enabled him to analyse the determination of the level of effective demand and to analyse the fundamental indeterminacy of the economic system at the same time.

Chapter 3 deals with the mainstream microfoundations debate. This debate is set against our emphasis on the importance of the coordination issue for an understanding of Keynes's GT. The early attempts to incorporate Keynes's GT into a general equilibrium framework finally led to what is now known as the microfoundations debate. As mentioned in section 1.2, the need for microfoundations for Keynesian macroeconomics basically arose because it is assumed in (Walrasian) general equilibrium theory that the price mechanism coordinates economic activities well, whereas in (Keynesian) macroeconomics this mechanism is somehow not supposed to work. The so-called disequilibrium analysis was above all an attempt to get rid of *Walrasian* general equilibrium theory in order to be able to analyse situations of non-market clearing. The criticism raised against this approach in particular and the lack of a proper microfoundation for macroeconomics in general gave rise to new-classical economics and after some time to the Keynesian counterattack in the form of new-Keynesianism. These developments, including most of the new-Keynesian work, do, however, only provide a microfoundation of what is called classical macroeconomics in chapter 2. Microfoundations of Keynes's economics in a general equilibrium framework do nevertheless exist. There are two lines of research that are of particular interest, the coordination failures approach (including search equilibrium models) and the research that focuses upon the indeterminacy of equilibria. The question as to whether these two approaches do indeed analyse Keynes's coordination issue is postponed until chapter 5. Finally, chapter 3 addresses the question whether the theories discussed in this chapter really provide a choice theoretic foundation of macroeconomics. This can be seriously questioned with respect to the concept of (rational) expectations and to the market-clearing assumption.

In chapter 4 we look at some alternative approaches and their relevance for microfoundations, coordination, and their connection with the analysis of Keynes in chapter 2. Both post-Keynesian economics and (neo-)Austrian economics address the microfoundations and the coordination issue. In post-Keynesian economics, the microfoundations issue is the most explicit in the post-Keynesian theory of mark-up pricing. Within post-Keynesian economics, the question whether Keynes also adhered to some mark-up rule is much debated but this question seems besides the point. What matters is that, notwithstanding the interesting contributions to what determines the level of the mark-up, these approaches are not fundamentally different from their neo-classical counterparts. Moreover, the models in which these mark-up pricing schemes are used as a foundation for the macro analysis are highly aggregated and are not concerned with coordination as such. The role of indeterminacy in Keynes's GT is neglected since money and uncertainty are only of minor importance. Kalecki himself is a case in point. We do argue, however, that the mark-up may be firmly rooted in post-Keynesian economics (or neo–Austrian economics for that matter) since the mark–up might be looked upon as a buffer of liquidity or, more generally, flexibility. The post–Keynesian analysis of time, money and uncertainty is explicitly concerned with what we will call the fundamental indeterminacy of Keynes's GT. It is here that a striking similarity exists with neo–Austrian economics. Since Austrian economics is microeconomics by definition, the microfoundations debate is simply not an issue. For our present purposes, the Austrian analysis of the process of coordination and the related microanalysis of money are of some importance for the connection with Keynes's analysis on this issue. In fact, there are some clear subjectivistic elements in Keynes's writings. Both post–Keynesian and Austrian economics are (not surprisingly) rather critical of neo–classical economics and vice versa. It is our contention, however, that recent developments in general equilibrium theory (especially those to be mentioned in chapter 5) to some extent (start trying to) cope with the same issues as the alternative approaches which appear in this chapter. This issue is taken up in chapter 8. The discussion in the present chapter clears the ground for the more detailed analysis of money and uncertainty in chapters 6 and 7, just as chapter 3 serves as a prelude to chapter 5.

Chapter 3 ends with the conclusion that a microfoundation of Keynes's economics within a general equilibrium framework should have the following features: strategic interaction (equilibrium coordination failures) and/or indeterminacy of equilibria. Since much of the relevant literature only stresses one of these two features, a multi–sector overlapping generations model is developed in chapter 5 in which both features are dealt with to some extent. It is shown how some important elements of Keynes's GT can be incorporated in such a model. It is obviously not Keynes's model for a number of reasons (but see our plea for methodological pluralism in the previous section). One of these reasons is that the overlapping generations model (OLG) in this chapter is a model of a barter economy. The inclusion of a non–producible good called money would seriously diminish the Keynesian content of the model. Money in Keynes's GT is totally different from money in the kinds of general equilibrium models in which perfect foresight prevails. Notwithstanding the fact that some assumptions in such a general equilibrium model like our OLG model are clearly at odds with Keynes's GT, the main point of our analysis of the OLG model is that essential aspects of Keynes's analysis can be incorporated in a general equilibrium framework as long as it is recognized that the assumption of (real) price or wage rigidities is of secondary importance for an understanding of Keynes's economics and, hence, that the recent literature on indeterminacy and coordination failures is more in the spirit of the GT. The issue of price stickiness and the difficulties of incorporating money are further analysed in chapters 6 and 7. Apart from analysing our specific multi–sector OLG model chapter 5 also briefly summarizes how to use these kinds of models to analyse phenomena such as chaos and sunspots and it briefly relates the results obtained to Keynes's theory.

The main conclusion of this chapter is that the literature under consideration (all those approaches that question the uniqueness and stability of equilibria) does address only the issue of equilibrium coordination. There is no proper place for the analysis of money, which is after all a major coordinating device in Keynes's GT. As it is not clear how to diminish the degree of indeterminateness the analysis in chapter 5 does also lead to the question as to whether the dismissal of the Walrasian auctioneer and its implication of multiple and/or unstable equilibria will appear to be a Pyrrhic victory for general equilibrium theory or not.

Chapter 6 and chapter 7 analyse in somewhat more detail the (ir)relevance of money in a general equilibrium framework and criticize the various manners in which money is thought to be essential. One of the major reasons for the difficulties underlying the incorporation of money in neo–classical economics is the lack of a theory of decentralized exchange. There are, however, some interesting recent theories of decentralized exchange in which money's role as medium of exchange is explicitly analysed in a search equilibrium framework. These attempts can be characterized by saying that they try to endogenize the cash–in–advance constraint. In fact, these theories deal with the dismissal of the second function of the Walrasian auctioneer: the establishment of exchange arrangements. The first part of chapter 7 discusses these theories and it turns out that these theories neglect the implications of their analysis of money as a medium of exchange for price setting behaviour, and hence for the theory of value. From the perspective of Keynes's attempt to integrate the theory of money and the theory of value and given the numerous attempts in the microfoundations debate to link the (non–)neutrality of money and the theory of value this neglect is rather dissatisfying to say the least. In our view an extension of these theories may result in a rationale for nominal price stickiness. Money acts as a coordinating device and the utility of money depends on the variability of nominal prices. Before discussing the compatibility of money and price flexibility in chapter 7, chapter 6 analyses Keynes's theory of the essential properties of money, as outlined in chapter 17 of the GT, in order to arrive at the conclusion that the prerequisite of nominal stickiness for monetary stability is an important, though much neglected, part of the GT.

Money and sticky prices can both be looked upon as coordinating devices as soon as the Walrasian auctioneer and the abovementioned equilibrium assumption concerning the formation of expectations are dismissed. Money is an institutional solution to a coordination problem. The suggested implications of the use of money for the theory of value therefore are an example of a 'macro'foundation for microeconomics. In fact, it will be argued that individual agents face a trade–off between the (dis)advantages of price stickiness and price flexibility. One of the topics of chapter 8 is the more general idea of the existence of a trade–off between coordination and flexibility in a decentralized market economy in which agents face the need to achieve some form of coordination.

This book is concerned with the implications of the coordination problem of Keynes's GT. Mainstream economics either circumvents the question of how individual agents establish a certain degree of coordination (chapter 3) or finds itself in trouble, once indeterminacy and multiplicity are allowed for (chapter 5). The former leads to a classical position in which more flexibility is generally to be preferred. In order to avoid an anything goes position with respect to the latter it is necessary to extend these approaches with attempts that aim at diminishing the degree of indeterminateness. Chapter 8 will briefly discuss some of these attempts (path–dependency, learning behaviour, convergence properties of these models). The analysis in chapters 4, 6 and 7 indicates that non–mainstream economics have taken up Keynes's lead by taking the implications of Keynes's analysis of the indeterminacy issue seriously. In the trade–off between coordination and flexibility the role of conventions/institutions is important. Money is but one example. There are numerous economic and noneconomic examples of how people deal with coordination issues. The importance of conventions can be traced back to Keynes's GT. Neo–classical economics deals with only one institution, the market, and it does so in a peculiar way since the equilibrium assumption excludes the analysis of the process of market exchange. For the economy as a whole the institution of an auctioneer substitutes for the market.

It is interesting to note that recent developments in general equilibrium theory and some of the alternative approaches are at least trying to deal with the same kind of questions though, of course, in a rather different analytical framework. In this respect, the need for 'macro'foundations for microeconomics does also imply that the Keynesian revolution was aborted right from the beginning since at least part of the real challenge for economic theory in elaborating upon the work of Keynes lies in changing microeconomics.

Notes

[1] All references to Keynes's writings in this study are to *The Collected Writings of John Maynard Keynes*, i–xxx, Macmillan, London.

[2] For a long time nominal wage stickiness was thought to be Keynes's assumption in this respect. In more recent years, however, the Keynesian position in mainstream economics has become associated with various forms of price and wage stickiness, see chapter 3.

[3] Loosely to be defined as those strands of economic thought that do not belong to or did not grow out of the neo–classical synthesis. Hence, this label applies to for instance post–Keynesian economics as well as to disequilibrium economics that followed the lead of Clower (1965) and Leijonhufvud (1968).

[4] According to this view the GT is foremost about economic theory and the issue of stabilization policy is not only of secondary importance but the standard view of Keynesian stabilization policy can simply not be found in the GT. For a controversial analysis of the relation between Keynes's policy views and the GT see for instance Meltzer (1988) or Kregel (1985). See also Patinkin (1990) on this issue.

[5] It becomes clear from the preface of the GT that it was at least Keynes's intention to criticize the prevailing economic theory on purely theoretical grounds, as the main purpose of the GT 'is to deal with difficult questions of theory, and only in the second place with the applications of this theory to practice. For if orthodox economics is at fault, the error is to be found not in the superstructure, which has been erected with great care for logical consistency, but in a lack of clearness and of generality in the premisses' (Keynes, GT, p. xxi).

[6]This conclusion holds if one defines microeconomics as the theory of individual behaviour but also if one defines it as the theory of the determination of relative prices and allocation as in general equilibrium analysis. Compare this with Hicks's conclusion that the search for microfoundations for macroeconomics takes for granted that macro should be founded on micro, 'what were the grounds for holding that the one was more solid than the other? We were begging the question but we should have faced it' (Hicks (1979), p. viii).

[7]O'Driscoll and Rizzo (1985, p. 17) rightly stress, following Robinson (1977), that what really characterizes economic theories is not the answers given to particular economic problems but the questions that these theories try to answer.

[8]Following Weintraub (1985, p. 26), see also Janssen (1990), pp. 30–31, general equilibrium analysis has the following features. There are economic agents who have preferences over outcomes. Given these preferences, agents independently optimize subject to certain constraints. This optimization or, in other words, the choices of each agent are made in interrelated markets on the condition that agents have full knowledge. Finally, the objective market outcomes which are the result of the (subjective) optimization of all agents are taken to be situations of equilibrium. As Janssen (1990) observes, this last characteristic (the equilibrium assumption) is different from the other assumptions for it does not deal with rational behaviour of individual agents. Hence, general equilibrium analysis is essentially based upon the assumptions of rational behaviour and equilibrium. The equilibrium assumption for the economy as a whole is, of course, especially relevant for the purpose of this study.

[9]See also our discussion about a shifting and a stationary equilibrium in section 2.6.

[10]See also Boyer and Orléan (1991) who observe that the non–uniqueness or instability of equilibria calls for the endogenization of the coordination problem in terms of the analysis of coordinating mechanisms that individual agents use in decentralized economies.

[11]See also Hahn (1984) pp. 307–327 on the issue of Keynes and coordination.

[12]Also known as critical pluralism, see Caldwell (1991, p. 26).

[13.]This point also applies the other way around; it is too easy to dismiss general equilibrium analysis (as some post–Keynesians and Austrians are inclined to do) beforehand as a useful tool for analysing and extending Keynes's GT merely because it does not incorporate Keynes's version of long–term expectations and hence of uncertainty.

[14]See also de Cecco (1990) who connects Kirman's view as to the uselesness of the search for microfoundations for macroeconomics with Keynes's analysis on the use of the atomic and organic hypothesis in the social sciences (see also section 5.4)

[15]See also the preface of the GT, p. xxi.

2 Indeterminacy in Macroeconomics: On the Structure of Keynes's General Theory

2.1 Introduction[1]

Before we can address the question as to how mainstream and non–mainstream economics dealt with Keynes's coordination issue, it is necessary to be more specific on Keynes's theory in general and the GT in particular. As outlined in the previous chapter we are primarily interested in the theoretical issues raised by Keynes in the GT and not in the question whether Keynes was right or wrong in answering these issues. This emphasis on questions instead of on answers implies that this chapter mainly deals with the analytical structure of the GT. The purpose of this chapter is to illustrate our claim that Keynes's GT is, above all, a theory of the coordination problem in decentralized economies.

Since the publication of the *General Theory of Employment, Interest and Money* in 1936, Keynes's major work has been subject to numerous interpretations. Discussions about the theoretical value of Keynes's GT have greatly influenced the development of macroeconomics. Starting with Hicks's '*Mr. Keynes and the Classics*' (Hicks (1937)), many theoretical debates have had their origin in Keynes's GT. The framework of the neo–classical synthesis, the debate between Keynesians and monetarists within that framework, the development of the non–Walrasian general equilibrium theory, the new–classical counterrevolution, the (new–)Keynesian reaction to this counterrevolution, and the critique of, for instance, post–Keynesian economists and Austrian economists on mainstream economics are all, to a greater or lesser extent, inspired by Keynes's GT. This chapter does not attempt to add another full–fledged interpretation to the existing interpretations of Keynes's theory, nor does this chapter provide a careful exegesis of Keynes's writings. Instead, we focus on Keynes's method in the GT and try to show that Keynes's own theory and his criticism of classical theory centre around the so-called indeterminacy issue and the difference between a partial (micro) analysis and an analysis of the economy as a whole (macro). In our view, both issues are related and are a reflection of the coordination problem in a decentralized monetary economy.

In many interpretations of the GT, the emphasis is on one or two outstanding features of the GT. While we do not wish to deny the validity of any of these interpretations as such, it is our opinion that these interpretations are a specific elaboration of Keynes's method of characterizing his own theory and classical theory by means of what we call the indeterminacy and the micro–macro issue. In our view, the emphasis on the structure of the GT makes clear that not only many interpretations of Keynes's GT are different variations of these two issues but also that the line between Keynesian and classical economics should be drawn between those theories in which the coordination problem has some role to play and those theories in which this coordination problem is absent. In our opinion the various interpretations of Keynes's GT are typically biased since the analytical framework (partly) determines the answers provided to the question of what constitutes Keynes(ian) economics. Once the debate on what Keynes really meant is stripped from the issue of the proper framework to do economic theory it becomes clear that contrary to communis opinio Keynes's line of reasoning in the GT is rather straightforward in our view. The controversy among economists as to what 'Keynes really meant' is, to a considerable extent, due to the various attempts to mould this structure of the GT upon a particular analytical framework. After presenting our view on Keynes's method in the GT we will argue that many interpretations of Keynes's GT are based on an erroneous interpretation of Keynes's methodology in the GT (section 2.6).

The chapter is organized as follows. In section 2.2 a broad outline of the GT and of Keynes's interpretation of classical theory is given. In section 2.3 it is shown that Keynes's analysis of the labour market follows logically from the negation of the second classical postulate (the real wage rate equals the marginal disutility of labour). As a result, Keynes ends up with an indeterminacy in the labour market. This indeterminacy is resolved by the determination of the level of employment on the goods market. However, as we show in section 2.4, this implies that in Keynes's theory the level of investment becomes indeterminate. In order to resolve this second type of indeterminacy, the role of money and uncertainty is introduced. This is the subject of section 2.5. In sections 2.3, 2.4 and 2.5 we show that the indeterminacy and the micro–macro issue, as defined in section 2.2, are two recurrent themes in both Keynes's theory and his version of the classical theory. Many of the different elements of Keynes's argumentation are, of course, well-known. However, we are not interested in these specific elements as such but rather in the connections between those elements. That is to say, we are primarily interested in the *structure* of Keynes's argumentation. Section 2.6 concludes this chapter with a discussion of the relation between determinism and indeterminacy in the GT.

2.2 Basic issues of the *General Theory*

For our present purposes it is convenient to think of the GT as being composed of three rather different, though connected, parts. In the first part Keynes sets out his principle of effective demand. The second part deals with the foundation of the two components of aggregate demand: consumption and investment. In the last part of the book Keynes is, among other things, concerned with the implications of the flexibility of money wages. Money wages are explicitly held constant throughout the analysis in the first two parts.

In all three parts of the GT, Keynes repeatedly confronts his theory with his version of classical theory. Keynes's main criticism of the classical theory is that standard supply and demand analysis does not hold for the economy as a whole. This is especially true for the labour market. Keynes concludes that his theory of effective demand is more general than the classical counterpart, because classical theory only applies to the special case of full employment, whereas his theory also applies to situations of underemployment (see GT, p. 3). The question we are interested in is how the different parts of Keynes's theory are logically connected once it is granted that the second classical postulate (real wage equals the marginal disutility of labour) does not hold for the economy as a whole. Also, we try to make clear, as Keynes does, that the acceptance of the first and second classical postulate logically results in a classical system.

In chapter 2 Keynes sums up the basic assumptions of classical theory as follows (see GT, pp. 21–22) :
1. The real wage equals the marginal productivity of labour
2. The real wage equals the marginal disutility of labour
3. Supply creates its own demand meaning that the aggregate supply price always equals the aggregate demand price.

One can derive the major implications of classical theory from these assumptions. The real wage and the level of employment are determined by the demand for and the supply of labour. The level of output corresponds to this level of full employment. The rate of interest then equilibrates savings and investment. Expectations do not have any impact on these variables and the quantity theory of money holds.

Keynes, on the other hand, criticizes the second and third of these classical assumptions. As a consequence the classical system of determinants and determinates breaks down. In Keynes's theory the level of employment depends on aggregate output for any given level of nominal wages. The level of output depends, in turn, on the marginal propensity to consume and the level of investment; the level of investment on the marginal efficiency of capital and the rate of interest; the rate of interest on the quantity of money and liquidity preference. Finally, the marginal efficiency of capital and liquidity preference are greatly influenced by the lack of knowledge of individual agents as to the future course of the economy. For the economy as a whole, movements in wages influence the level of aggregate income and wage flexibility therefore may not be the appropriate cure for unemployment. In sections 2.3–2.5 of this chapter we analyse the main differences between Keynes's GT and the classical theory by focusing upon two issues that are crucial for an understanding of Keynes's theory:

1. Keynes's method of analysing the determinants, the determinates and indeterminacy in his theory and classical theory. We refer to this as the indeterminacy issue.

2. The (ir)relevance of the standard demand and supply analysis for the economy as a whole. In what follows we refer to this as the micro–macro issue for the following reason. In a demand and supply analysis of a single sector economic agents may assume that a change in the price does not have an impact on their income. For the economy as a whole this cannot be the case. Prices are incomes for the economy as a whole.

It must be emphasized that both issues are nothing but analytical devices which are used, in our view, in the GT to distinguish his theory from his version of the classical theory. As such, these two issues are not Keynesian or classical. The indeterminacy issue can be applied to both Keynes's theory and the classical theory and it is only after this issue is applied on Keynes's theory that the conclusion follows that indeterminacy as such is a crucial feature of Keynes's GT. Using the same line of reasoning it can be observed that the micro–macro issue is neutral in the sense that it does not yield any a priori information on the Keynesian or classical content of a theory. Again, it is only in the application of this issue to Keynes's GT, that the importance of the endogeneity of aggregate output for the analysis of the coordination problem becomes clear.

2.3 The labour market

In accepting the first classical postulate (the real wage rate equals the marginal productivity of labour) and in denying the second, Keynes ends up with an indeterminacy in the labour market: one schedule, the downward sloping marginal productivity of labour (MPL) curve, is available to determine two variables: the real wage and the level of employment. According to the classical position, the real wage and the level of employment are determined by the demand for and the supply of labour. So there is no indeterminacy whatsoever in the classical view of the labour market. The crux of Keynes's criticism of this classical view of the labour market is that

there may be *no* method available for labour as a whole whereby it can bring the wage goods equivalent of the general level of money–wages into conformity with the marginal disutility of the current volume of employment. There may exist no expedient by which labour as a whole can reduce its *real* wage to a given figure by making revised money bargains with the entrepreneurs (Keynes, GT, p.13).

If one assumes a given level of aggregate income an individual worker may indeed assume that he may work more hours by accepting a lower money wage because his real wage will decrease proportionally. For the economy as a whole the endogeneity of aggregate income makes this lower nominal wage offer potentially ineffective if this individual wage cut is part of an overall wage cut. An overall decrease in nominal wages may lead to a fall in aggregate demand and hence to a decline in the general price level. In the end real wages may even have *in*creased. Keynes therefore concludes that workers are perhaps in a position to determine their relative real wage, but they are, generally speaking, not in a position to determine their absolute real wage. In Keynes's opinion the second classical postulate (the marginal disutility of labour equals the real wage) does not hold because for the economy as a whole changes in factor rewards have a feedback on the level of aggregate spending. The indeterminacy in Keynes's labour market is resolved through the determination of the level of employment on the goods market. Given this level and the MPL schedule the real wage can be determined. However, the MPL curve should not be interpreted as the aggregate demand curve for labour. Whereas in the classical view the MPL curve is the demand curve for labour, in Keynes's analysis the MPL curve only implies that real wages and the volume of output are uniquely correlated. For the economy as a whole, the real wage is an endogenous variable and the individual firm therefore is not in a position to determine its real wage.[2]

After analysing the two classical postulates in chapter 2 Keynes turns his attention to the analysis of the factors in the goods market that determine the level of employment.[3] It is only in chapter 19 that Keynes explicitly returns to the analysis of the labour market. In this chapter Keynes addresses the issue of nominal wage flexibility. The distinction between a theory which assumes a given level of aggregate income and a theory in which this variable is endogenous is crucial in this chapter. Throughout chapters 1–18 Keynes assumes nominal wages to be constant since all relevant variables are denominated in terms of the wage–unit. Keynes shows that in case of unemployment falling wages need not necessarily increase the level of employment as it does in classical theory.

Given his assumption of decreasing returns for both labour and capital, an overall fall in wages might lead to an increase in the marginal efficiency of capital and/or a decrease in the rate of interest. Both tendencies would stimulate investment and thereby stimulate employment. However, this argument is only valid for a given level of income. If a single firm reduces its nominal wage it may assume that the demand for its product is not affected. However, if all firms pursue this policy the level of demand of each will be negatively affected so that the level of employment may not increase. Demand and supply are interrelated for output as a whole.

> It follows therefore that if labour were to respond to conditions of gradually diminishing employment by offering its services at a gradually diminishing money wage, this would not, as a rule, have the effect of reducing real wages and might even have the effect of increasing them, through its adverse influence on the volume of output (GT, p.269).[4]

It is not a priori clear whether the cost reducing effect of a fall in aggregate wages will exceed the demand reducing effect or not. In case the positive substitution effect exceeds the negative income effect a policy of nominal wage reduction may increase employment. Keynes's concept of the fallacy of composition is based on the idea that the classical labour demand and supply schedules make sense only if the level of aggregate income is constant. Once it is granted that this level is not given for the economy as a whole the classical system becomes indeterminate.

2.4 The goods market

One of Keynes's central propositions is that fluctuations in the level of effective demand (the point of intersection of the aggregate demand and the aggregate supply schedule) are caused by fluctuations in aggregate demand. It is at this point of Keynes's analysis (Ch. 5 of the GT) that the importance of expectations arises for the first time in the GT. As we will illustrate in the next section the instability of aggregate demand is mainly due to the role of expectations governing investment in Keynes's opinion. In this section we will focus upon Keynes's view as to the equilibrating mechanism between savings and investment. The assumption that people save some part of their current income is made in Keynes's theory as well as in classical theory. The equilibrium condition for the goods market can be written in both theories as savings equals investment: $S = I$. The remainder of this section will show that this apparent similarity hides a crucial difference between Keynes and the classics. This difference can be understood along the lines of both the indeterminacy issue and the micro–macro issue. Keynes argues that savings need not equal investment for an individual agent. For the economy as a whole, however, $S = I$ holds by definition. An individual act of saving or investment is never a one–sided affair. Every such individual act implies a two–sided transaction since 'no one can save without acquiring an asset, whether it be cash or a debt or capital goods; and no one can acquire an asset which he did not previously possess, unless either an asset of equal value is newly produced or someone else parts with an asset of that value which he previously had.' (GT, pp.81–82). According to Keynes, the creation of new assets implies saving and new investment whereas the trade of existing assets implies saving and an equal amount of dissaving. This line of reasoning leads to the conclusion that for the economy as a whole $S = I$ holds by definition.

For an individual agent the decision to save more will, as a rule, not affect his income. For the economy as a whole the level of aggregate income is, however, not fixed as we already saw in the case of the labour market. An attempt to collectively save more (that is to decrease the propensity to consume) may not lead to an increase in aggregate savings because the decrease in the propensity to consume leads to a decrease in aggregate income and thereby to an offsetting decrease in total savings. The attempt to save more is just offset by the decrease in income, hence total savings remain unchanged. In a closed economy, aggregate savings can increase only when aggregate investment increases. This phenomenon has become known as the paradox of thrift. This paradox is another example of a fallacy of composition[5] and hence of the micro–macro issue.

At the end of chapter 7 Keynes summarizes his position with respect to the conceptual difference between savings and investment on the individual and the aggregate level as follows.

> Though an individual whose transactions are small in relation to the market can safely neglect the fact that demand is not a one–sided transaction, it makes no sense to neglect it when we come to aggregate demand. This is the vital difference between the theory of the economic behaviour of the aggregate and the theory of the behaviour of the individual unit, in which we assume that changes in the individual's own demand do not affect his income. (Keynes, GT, p.85).

This quotation illustrates Keynes's position with respect to aggregate savings and investment and the endogeneity of aggregate income. The main implication of this position is addressed in chapter 14 of the GT. As we saw above, goods market equilibrium in classical theory also implies $S = I$. It is with respect to the equilibrating mechanism that Keynes and the classics disagree. According to Keynes the classical theory of the rate of interest amounts to the proposition that, given the level of aggregate income, the amount of investment and savings are solely functions of the rate of interest and that the equilibrium rate of interest is determined by S and I. Under the assumption of a given aggregate income there is no difference between Keynes and the classics with respect to the function of the rate of interest.

Keynes's repudiation of the classical theory of interest again directly follows from his idea that this kind of Marshallian partial equilibrium analysis is ill–suited for the economy as a whole. Once the assumption of a given aggregate income is relaxed this standard supply and demand analysis breaks down and the classical theory of the rate of interest becomes indeterminate. A shift in the investment schedule implies a change in aggregate income and thus, according to Keynes, a shift in the savings schedule. The supply of new capital (S) and the demand for new capital (I) are not independent. Keynes's criticism of the classical theory of the rate of interest can be illustrated as follows.

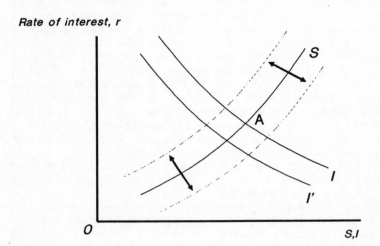

Rate of interest, r

Figure 2.1 The interdependency of savings and investment
(see also Keynes, GT, p. 180.)

The initial equilibrium is given by point A. If an unfavourable shock hits the economy the investment schedule shifts to the left. A decrease in investment lowers the level of aggregate income and this lowers aggregate savings. It is not clear a priori whether the savings schedule will shift to the left or to the right. Once again, it may be appropriate for an individual portfolio holder or investor to assume that the level of aggregate income is given. For the economy as a whole, aggregate income is endogenous and the system is indeterminate, given Keynes's analysis of the labour market: there is only one equation to determine two variables, namely the interest rate r and aggregate income Y, in formula $I(r) = S(r,Y)$. The classical theory 'could be used to tell us what the level of income will be, given (from some other source) the rate of interest; and alternatively, what the rate of interest will have to be, if the level of income is to be maintained at a given figure (e.g. the level corresponding to full employment)' (GT, p.181). In Keynes's theory the equilibrating mechanism for the goods market is the level of aggregate income. This implies that, in contrast with classical theory, the various components of aggregate demand are not substitutes but rather complements. In classical theory a decrease in consumption (an increase in savings) leads to an increase in investment. But, if, as in Keynes's theory, Y is the equilibrating mechanism on the goods market the question arises how the level of investment and the rate of interest are determined. This issue is addressed in the next section.[6]

The above overview of Keynes's theory of savings and investment makes clear that the conclusion of the previous section that the indeterminacy argument and the micro–macro issue are crucial for an understanding of Keynes's theory and for his interpretation of classical theory, also applies to the goods market.

2.5 Investment, the interest rate, money and fundamental indeterminacy

The level of investment is determined by the marginal efficiency of capital and the rate of interest. Both the marginal efficiency of capital (mec) and the rate of interest are to a large extent determined by expectations and the uncertainty governing these expectations. There is an equilibrium if the mec equals the rate of interest. This equality determines the level of investment. What is of particular interest here is the fact that these determinants of investment are themselves determined by expectations. This implies that in Keynes's theory investment and savings are not determined by the same variables, because investment is based on future values of variables whereas savings are not, since savings are based on current income. First, we turn to the concept of the mec. The mec is composed of the expected return on new investment and the supply price of investment. Keynes assumes that the input of capital is subject to diminishing returns. An increasing level of aggregate investment exerts a downward pressure on the mec.[7] The use of a mec schedule as such has some similarities with the classical investment demand schedule (see GT, chapter 14, p. 178). What is important is the fact that Keynes's mec schedule is, to a large extent, based on expectations whereas the classical investment demand schedule is solely based on physical factors like the marginal productivity of capital. In chapter 12, Keynes elaborates upon some ideas of his *Treatise on Probability* (1921). Entrepreneurs need to form expectations about the prospective yield of a new investment. These expectations are made in the light of incomplete knowledge of an uncertain future.[8] Firms do not have a complete knowledge of the future state of the economy, because they simply do not know how much other firms will invest, what part of today's savings will turn up as future consumption or what the future state of technology will be. According to Keynes the fluctuations in the so-called state of confidence may be large and the level of investment may therefore be volatile. Keynes uses the now well-known phrase that investment is governed by animal spirits. Entrepreneurs need to make expectations about other firms' decisions which depend on the latter's expectations. This means that entrepreneurs need to make expectations about the expectations of other entrepreneurs etc. There is a fundamental indeterminacy associated with this kind of expectation.[9] The problem of infinite regress associated with analysing higher order expectations re-emerges in section 3.5 of our study.

According to Keynes, expectations may be self-fulfilling. If all entrepreneurs revise their expectations because they become more optimistic about the future, an increase in aggregate income will come about and the optimistic expectations may be realized. The individual entrepreneur may take, as in classical theory, the expectations of other entrepreneurs as given in deciding upon his production or investment. However, the production of that entrepreneur influences the demand for other products and thereby has repercussion effects on the demand for his own product.

The other variable that determines the equilibrium level of investment is the rate of interest. In an equilibrium the rate of interest equals the mec and this condition determines the volume of investment (see chapter 11 of the GT). But what determines the rate of interest? In chapter 13 Keynes starts his analysis of the determinants of the rate of interest with the assumption that a decision to save consists of two rather different decisions. The first decision is about the amount of non-spending and the second decision concerns the issue in what form the individual saver will hold command over his future consumption (GT, p.166). This second decision is determined by the individual's degree of liquidity preference. Classical theory is primarily concerned with the first decision whereas Keynes emphasizes the importance of the second decision. In his view the rate of interest is the price which equilibrates the desire to hold wealth in the form of money with the desire to hold wealth in other assets.

The fact that subjects do not spend all of their current income on current consumption is not a sufficient condition to crack Say's law. Even the fact that some part of the unspent income will be held in the form of money will not do. Keynes assumes that an act of saving does not imply 'a substitution of future consumption-demand for present consumption-demand' (GT, p. 210; see also the conclusions of chapter 5 of our study) and he further assumes that money possesses some special properties that cause the standard substitution mechanism not to work in the case of money. Both conditions are sufficient to crack Say's law. The assumed special properties of money are analysed at length in chapter 6 of this study. The fact that economic subjects hold an asset that yields no interest is explained by relating the liquidity preference schedule to uncertainty. Since the future is unknown portfolio holders need to form expectations about the future rate of interest. The analysis of the relation between liquidity preference and uncertainty is similar to the analysis of the mec and uncertainty. A decrease in the 'state of confidence' leads to an increase in liquidity preference and thus to an increased desire to hold wealth in the form of money. Given the quantity of money this increased desire exerts an upward pressure on the rate of interest. An increase in the rate of interest has negative implications for the level of investment.

These two determinants of investment, the mec and the rate of interest, are both, to some extent, determined by expectations and uncertainty. This leads to the *fundamental indeterminacy* of the GT, for now the question arises as to what determines this uncertainty or what determines expectations. In the main part of the GT Keynes assumes that, in general, short–run expectations are fulfilled at the level of effective demand so the question reduces to the determination of long–run expectations (for the difference between short–run and long run expectations see section 2.6). The very nature of Keynes's concept of uncertainty makes an answer to that question in terms of economic factors virtually impossible because

> by uncertain knowledge, let me explain, I do not mean merely to distinguish what is known for certain from what is only probable...the sense in which I am using the term is that in which the prospect of a European war is uncertain, or the price of copper and the rate of interest twenty years hence, or the obsolescence of a new invention, or the position of private wealth owners in the social system in 1970. About these matters there is no scientific basis on which to form any calculable probability whatever. We simply do not know (Keynes (1937B), pp. 113–114).

In his analysis of the determination of output and employment for the economy as a whole Keynes therefore assumes the state of long–run expectations to be given. Again, as in our analysis of the labour and the goods market, we end up with an indeterminate system. But in contrast with these previous sections this indeterminacy can be resolved only by assuming the 'state of uncertainty' to be given.[10] We return to this subject in section 2.6.

The portfolio equilibrium condition that the mec equals the rate of interest also holds in classical theory. It is in the explanation of the level at which this equilibrium occurs that both theories diverge. In the classical theory of the rate of interest, investment demand (the mec–schedule) is one of the determinants of the system and the rate of interest falls into line with the mec (see also section 7.5). But as we saw in the previous section this only makes sense according to Keynes, as long as Y is given and perfect foresight prevails. In Keynes's theory, the rate of interest is setting the pace and 'is determined by forces partly appropriate to itself, and prices move until the marginal efficiency of other assets falls into line with the rate of interest' (Keynes (1937A), p.103). As shown above, the factors determining the rate of interest are liquidity preference and the quantity of money.

2.6 Keynes on determinism and indeterminacy

In chapter 18, Keynes gives a summary of the central ideas of the GT. To begin with, Keynes gives an enumeration of those factors that are taken as given, independent and dependent. Any division of the relevant variables is, 'of course, quite arbitrary from any absolute standpoint' (GT, p.247) and depends on the aim of the analysis. The main object of the GT is to analyse what determines the aggregate level of income and the aggregate level of employment. According to Keynes, it is perfectly legitimate to take the level of aggregate income as given if one would choose to analyse a single industry or firm. In that case, expectations may be taken as given too and the role of money and uncertainty does not come into play. Furthermore, in the theory of the individual firm, expectations of other firms may be taken as given. In the analysis of the economy as a whole, expectations of other firms may not be taken as given. Subjects make expectations about other subjects' investment and consumption plans. This makes expectations indeterminate for the economy as a whole. The distinction between the theory of the individual firm (or what amounts to the same in Keynes's GT, classical theory) and the theory for the economy as a whole (Keynes's theory) thus revolves around our micro–macro issue and our indeterminacy issue. In one of the reactions to the early critics of the GT, Keynes sums up his main differences with classical theory as follows:

   1. 'The orthodox theory assumes that we have a knowledge of the future of a kind quite different from that which we actually possess...the hypothesis of a calculable future leads to a wrong interpretation of the principles of behaviour which the need for action compels us to adopt' (Keynes (1937B), p.122).
   2. 'The orthodox theory would by now have discovered the inability to deal with fluctuations in employment, if it had not ignored the need for a theory of the supply and demand of output as a whole.' (Keynes (1937B), p. 123)

   This first difference, the role of knowledge, corresponds with the indeterminacy of expectations and the role of money and uncertainty and hence this difference is related to our analysis of the indeterminacy issue. In the classical theory expectations do not matter, whereas in Keynes's GT the role of expectations is crucial.

The fundamental lack of knowledge about future economic conditions provides a rationale for holding money and this explains the statement in the preface of the GT that 'a monetary economy, we shall find, is essentially one in which changing views about the future are capable of influencing the quantity of employment and not merely its direction' (GT, p. xxii).

The second difference emphasizes the endogeneity of aggregate output. In Keynes's GT, this endogeneity is a reflection of the fundamental difference between Keynes and the classics concerning the role of the price mechanism as a device for coordination between individual agents. In classical theory the price mechanism takes care, or better, is assumed to take care of this coordination and relative prices clear all markets. In Keynes's theory on the other hand the price mechanism may not do the job since for instance savings and investment or the supply of and the demand for labour are not determined by the same variables. Hence the price mechanism may simply not be able to provide the appropriate signals to ensure the full–employment equilibrium. One of the main reasons why the price mechanism may not provide those signals is that some variables, notably the level of investment, are governed by expectations. The two abovementioned differences are thus related for if

> our knowledge of the future was calculable and not subject to sudden changes, it might be justified to assume that the liquidity–preference curve was both stable and very inelastic...In these conditions we might reasonably suppose that the whole of the available resources would normally be employed; and that the conditions required by the orthodox theory would be satisfied (Keynes (1937B), p. 119).

In other words, once we abstract from the role of indeterminacy in the GT and hence from the role of expectations and uncertainty classical theory comes into play. This is, for instance, the case in those theories in which expectations are simply neglected (neo–classical synthesis[11]) or in which rational expectations are assumed (see also section 3.5.). At the other extreme there are attempts in, for instance, (neo–)Austrian economics that elaborate *exclusively* upon Keynes's indeterminacy in their analysis of the GT. The analytical differences underlying the various interpretations of the GT are, to a considerable extent, due to a misunderstanding of Keynes's methodology in the GT. Following Kregel (1976) we may observe that especially the various assumptions made by Keynes about the constancy of expectations generally have been misunderstood. It is to this topic that we turn in the remainder of this section.

Before doing so, it should be emphasized that up till now we have focused (almost) exclusively on the structure of the GT in this chapter. It should be emphasized, however, that the GT did not came out of the blue, so to speak. In his analysis of the role of expectations and uncertainty in a monetary economy for instance

Keynes builds upon his *Treatise on Probability* (1921, hereafter TP). Though there are references in the GT to the TP (see p. 148 and p.240) the importance of the TP for an understanding of Keynes's GT has long gone unnoticed. This neglect is primarily due to the fact that Keynes's analysis of what we called the fundamental indeterminacy for economies as a whole has been submerged in the vast majority of interpretations of Keynes's GT starting with Hicks (1937). The dismissal of Keynes's analysis of indeterminacy and hence the dismissal of the role of expectations and uncertainty forecloses the connection between the TP and the GT. The analysis of expectations is simply neglected as in the case of the neo-classical synthesis or it is moulded upon a fully determinate framework as in the case of rational expectations. Recently, however, the importance of the TP for Keynes's GT has been increasingly recognized (see, for instance, Carabelli (1988), Lawson (1985), Hoogduin (1991) and de Cecco (1990) in his review of Meltzer (1988)). For our present purposes O'Donnell (1990) is important as he shows how the relation between determinism and indeterminacy in the GT has its origin in the TP. According to O'Donnell the two central concepts of the TP, probability and weight of the argument, can be understood only if one conceives the analytical structure of the TP as consisting of two domains: a determinate and an indeterminate domain. In the determinate domain, probabilities are known and comparable and the same holds for the weight attached to an argument. This corresponds fairly well with the treatment of uncertainty in neo-classical economics, in which risk is substituted for uncertainty. In the indeterminate domain probabilities are neither known nor comparable and the same holds for the weight of the argument. It is here that uncertainty prevails and decisions have to be based on inconclusive knowledge. Hence, these two domains are fundamentally different. The transition from the TP to the GT takes place by replacing the determinate domain by the world of short-term expectations of the GT and by substituting the world of long-term expectations (or, in other words, uncertainty) of the GT for the indeterminate domain of the TP. In agreement with our analysis of Keynes's method (see also below, the distinction between the stationary and the shifting model) the analysis of the determination of the level of effective demand in the GT belongs to the first domain and the analysis of the fundamental indeterminacy to the second domain. The transition from the TP to the GT is completed by substituting expectations in general and confidence (liquidity preference) for probability and weight of the argument. The conclusion that it is essential to discriminate decision making in the determinate domain from that in the indeterminate domain will be used in chapter 7 of our study.[12]

Apart from the TP, the *Treatise on Money* (1930, hereafter TM) is also important in the development of the GT. Especially Keynes's use of a Marshallian equilibrium framework and the theory of liquidity preference in the GT have their origins in the TM (see also Nentjes (1977)). The main analytical differences between the GT and the TM arise from Keynes's innovation of the theory of effective demand in the GT. It is illuminating to quote Keynes at some length in this respect.

> My so-called 'fundamental equations' [of the TM] were an instantaneous picture taken on the assumption of a given output. They attempted to show how, assuming the given output, forces could develop which involved a profit-disequilibrium, and thus required a change in the level of output. But the dynamic development, as distinct from the instantaneous picture, was left incomplete and extremely confused. This book [the GT], on the other hand, has evolved into what is primarily a study of the forces which determine changes in the scale of output and employment as a whole; and, whilst it is found that money enters into the economic scheme in an essential and peculiar manner, technical monetary detail falls into the background (Keynes (1936), p. xxii).

This study of the changes in the scale of aggregate output and employment became the theory of effective demand. As the quotation already indicates, the dismissal of the assumption of the TM of a given level of output does not only imply that output and employment became endogenous in the GT but it also implies that the analysis of the determination of the level of aggregate output and employment calls forth the analysis of money and uncertainty and, hence, of the fundamental indeterminacy of the GT. The recognition that the *determination* of the level of output and employment cannot do without the analysis of the *indeterminacy* of the GT may, at first sight, seem paradoxical but it is essential for an understanding of the GT in our view. Keynes's definition of a monetary economy mentioned at the beginning of this section aptly summarizes his position in this respect and it also summarizes the main difference between the GT and the TM.

As our present study is not an exercise in the history of (Keynes's) economic thought we will leave the question of the relation between the GT and Keynes's pre-GT writings at rest. This brief digression on the antecedents of the GT is merely meant as a further illustration of a central theme of this chapter, namely that those interpretations of the GT that are solely based upon the endogeneity of aggregate output and employment miss the main point of the GT. The introduction of the principle of effective demand in the GT called forth the analysis of the determination of the level of effective demand. The exclusion of the indeterminate part of Keynes's theory (the role of money and uncertainty) and its consequences for the analysis of expectations, lead to a position in which one can indeed conclude that there is no fundamental difference between Keynes and the classics. As long as there are no frictions that hamper the working of the price mechanism the main classical conclusions as outlined in section 2.2 hold and there is no coordination problem whatsoever. In our view, this failure to grasp the importance of Keynes's insistence on the fundamental indeterminacy of the economy as a whole in his analysis of the determination of effective demand is mainly caused by:

1. A lack of understanding of the methodological framework in the GT.
2. The alleged necessity to mould the GT upon a analytical framework in which the fundamental indeterminacy of the GT simply could not be addressed.

The second issue is the subject of chapter 3. In this section we focus upon the first issue. In one of the early drafts of the GT (Keynes (1973A), pp.440–441) Keynes tries to set out his theory of effective demand by means of the following equations (see also Kregel (1976), p. 210–211 and Meltzer (1988), p. 129):

$$C_w = f_1 (N, r, E) \qquad (2.1)$$

$$I_w = f_2 (N, r, E) \qquad (2.2)$$

$$D_w = C_w + I_w \qquad (2.3)$$

$$F(N) = D_w \qquad (2.4)$$

in which:

C_w = level of consumption in wage units
I_w = level of investment in wage units
N = level of employment
r = rate of interest
E = state of long–term expectations
D_w = level of effective demand in wage units

Equation (2.4) is defined by Keynes as the employment function which gives the level of employment that the level of D_w calls forth.

At first sight, this set of equations resembles the Keynesian Cross interpretation of Keynes. There is, however, a crucial difference. In Keynes's set of equations and in contrast with this interpretation of Keynes, C_w and especially I_w are governed by the state of long–term expectations E. As has been argued at length in this chapter the incorporation of expectations lies at the heart of the fundamental indeterminacy of the GT.[13] But the exposition of the principle of effective demand along the lines of (2.1)–(2.4) becomes virtually impossible if the impact of E has to be taken into account at every instant. The fact that Keynes did not use anything like (2.1)–(2.4) in the GT indicates that he concluded that his dynamic theory cannot be fully captured within such a static representation. In the neo–classical synthesis, the solution to the issue of dealing simultaneously with the principle of effective demand and the role of expectations consists of *dropping* the E variable so to say whereas the solution of letting E stand for rational expectations (or perfect foresight) circumvents the problem. Keynes, on the other hand, chose to

> make assumptions, not about the absence of false expectations and uncertainty in the economy under consideration, thus creating an economy with perfect information and certainty, but rather to assume that although expectations and uncertainty are always present, yet different assumptions could be made about the constancy of expectations and their effect on the system. It is not the assumptions made about the economy under analysis that are different, but the assumptions made about expectations in an economy in which these play an integral part (Kregel (1976), p. 211).

According to Kregel (1976) and in accordance with our position Keynes makes use of the following three models with respect to the role of expectations in the GT and in the defence of the GT (see also Hoogduin and Snippe (1987)). First of all, there is the *static* model in which short–term expectations are always realized, long–term expectations are constant and both forms of expectations are independent. Secondly, there is the *stationary* model in which short–term expectations may be disappointed but firms are nevertheless to determine the level of effective demand so that in equilibrium these expectations are realized. Long–term expectations are still constant and both forms of expectations are independent. Finally, there is the *shifting* model in which short–term expectations are not realized, long–term expectations are liable to changes and both forms of expectations are no longer independent. Of special relevance for our present purposes is the difference between the stationary and the shifting model. In order to avoid an 'anything goes' position, Keynes employs the stationary model in the main part of the GT and, hence, treats long–term expectations as constant in order to be able to show how a certain level of effective demand (again this is the level at which aggregate demand equals aggregate supply) comes about. But, in contrast with the classical theory, there are infinitely many levels of effective demand, given the particular state of long–term expectations. In mainstream interpretations of the GT, this use of the stationary model has been mistaken for the idea that expectations are not essential for an understanding of Keynes's GT. The inclusion of current income, instead of expected income, in IS/LM models is a case in point. Keynes's definition of a shifting model coincides with his definition of a monetary economy as given in section 2.6 of this chapter (for Keynes's own definitions of a shifting and a stationary model see GT, p.293). The way Keynes deals with the difficulties of analysing both the determination of the level of effective demand and the role of expectations and uncertainty fits in with a Marshallian way of thinking in which it depends on the problem at hand which variables are taken as given and which are not (see also chapter 18 of the GT). Indeed, one of the main reasons why the role of expectations and uncertainty was submerged in most interpretations is that this Marshallian methodology of Keynes is hard to reconcile with the Walrasian general equilibrium framework that underlies neo–classical economics.

Hodgson (1985) criticizes the methodological position of Keynes in the GT as being an unfruitful and even inconsistent marriage of determinism and indeterminacy:

> in some ways the two rival approaches, of the rational expectations school and the Austrian school, are more consistent than that of Keynes. The first erects a kind of holistic determinism, the second the indeterminacy of a mass of colliding individuals. In comparison, Keynes's uneasy juxtaposition of the determinism of his post–Marshallian model of the economy with the indeterminacy of expectations is unlikely to endure. For its apparent inconsistency on these crucial issues it   is likely to be steadily eroded by Austrians and rational expectations theorists from both sides (Hodgson (1985), p. 33).

As a criticism of Keynes's position in the GT this conclusion will not do for Keynes's methodology is perfectly consistent in its own right in our view. We agree with Hodgson (1985), however, as far as the future development of Keynes's theory is concerned. Without a further analysis of how economic agents deal with this indeterminacy of expectations caused by uncertainty, Keynes's economics is prone to a 'take–over' by the deterministic extreme of rational expectations or by the indeterministic extreme of subjectivistic expectations of the (neo–)Austrians. The analysis of the question as to how Keynes's theory can be elaborated upon in this respect is taken up in various subsequent chapters of our study. For the purpose of the present chapter it suffices to note that the lack of understanding of Keynes's analytical framework, on the one hand, and the difference between his Marshallian approach and the Walrasian approach, on the other hand, explain why Keynes's central message (namely that the invisible hand assumption is not a proper assumption for the analysis of the economy as a whole) did not get through. In the deterministic framework of neo–classical economics coordination is assumed beforehand if only prices are allowed to do their allocational job. Keynes's innovation of the principle of effective demand and his analysis of the implications of introducing this principle lead to the opposite conclusion. Keynes's analysis of, what we labelled, the micro–macro issue and the indeterminacy issue shows that there are no a priori reasons (even if prices are fully flexible) why the actual level of employment will correspond to the full–employment level. This is a result of the fact that both the fundamental indeterminacy and the application of the micro–macro issue in the GT are a reflection of the coordination problem. This holds true for, for instance, the analysis of the labour market (are workers in a position to determine their real wage, the fallacy of composition with respect to nominal wage cuts), the goods market (the coordination of savings and investment, the paradox of thrift), the role of money and uncertainty and finally for his analysis of expectations. With respect to the analysis of expectations especially the issue of how in decentralized auctioneerless economies agents succeed in coordinating their expectations (about the expectations of other agents) is an outstanding example of a coordination problem (see also section 3.5).

Many approaches in macroeconomic theory can be characterized by the way they take account of the indeterminacy and the micro–macro issue in their analysis. To a considerable extent, the Keynesian content of these theories is influenced by the choice of the analytical framework. Walrasian general equilibrium theory is a good example in this respect. Both aspects of the coordination problem are irrelevant since the Walrasian auctioneer is assumed to take care of the coordination of individual plans. This is, however, the subject of the next chapter. At the beginning of chapter 3 the main arguments of the present chapter will be briefly summarized. Our inquiry into the basic questions underlying the GT does not come to a halt with the end of this chapter. Chapter 2 merely serves as an input for the forthcoming chapters and, if necessary, Keynes will pop up in these chapters to illustrate our argument. It will turn out that a useful extension of Keynes's analysis within a general equilibrium framework centres around the dismissal of the Walrasian auctioneer as an establisher of unique, stable, and Pareto–efficient outcomes (chapters 3 and 5) and that such an extension in an alternative framework centres around an elaboration of Keynes's fundamental indeterminacy (chapters 4, 6 and 7). Note that the incorporation of fundamental indeterminacy (uncertainty) in the analysis necessarily implies the dismissal of the abovementioned task of the auctioneer but that the reverse is not true.

Notes

[1] Sections 2.2–2.5 of this chapter are taken from Garretsen and Janssen (1989A).

[2] For a similar line of reasoning see Solow (1986) and Davidson (1983). Keynes's argument does not depend on the question whether real wages are anti or pro-cyclical; see also Keynes (1939). The assumption of increasing returns reinforces Keynes's argument but Keynes explicitly assumed the degree of competition to be given (GT, p. 245).

[3] We do not deal with the (relevance of) the aggregate supply curve in this chapter. For our present purposes it is important to point out that the aggregate supply and demand curve are interdependent in the GT. This is in sharp contrast with Keynes's interpretation of the classical theory in which the independency of supply and demand is crucial. The issue whether the foundation of the aggregate supply curve in the GT is compatible with profit maximization along traditional lines or not has been heavily debated in the literature but is beyond the scope of this chapter see; for instance, Brady (1990) for a recent assessment.

[4] Moreover, complete wage flexibility is not compatible with monetary stability (GT, p. 270) as will be argued in chapter 6 of our study.

[5] For an earlier version of the Paradox of Thrift in Keynes's writings see for instance Keynes's well-known example of the thrift campaign in his *Treatise on Money* (1930), pp. 158–160. The idea of the paradox of thrift goes at least back to the eighteenth century economist Barbon who argued that an increase in the propensity to save would depress economic activity and would lead to a decrease in overall savings. Hume criticized this idea, as he argued that the interest rate would equilibrate savings and investment and an increase in the propensity to save should thus be welcomed (see Aschheim and Hsieh (1969), pp. 20–24 and 146–150).

[6]One way of short–cutting this indeterminacy problem is to make investment exogenous. This route was taken by early Keynesians who came up with the Keynesian Cross representation.

[7]We follow Keynes's terminology to the extent that we also use marginal efficiency of *capital* (mec) when referring to investment. It is probably more appropriate to use the concept of the marginal efficiency of *investment* in case of investment projects. Since it is our purpose to analyse Keynes's method in the GT we stick to the use of the concept of the mec.

[8]In Keynes's view basically every expectation consists of two rather different components i.e. the probability of that expectation, on the one hand, and the confidence attached to that probability, on the other hand. Though economic subjects do make expectations about an uncertain future it is important for an understanding of Keynes's theory in chapter 12 to note that Keynes's concept can never be captured by some probabilistic function. This refers to the well–known distinction between risk and uncertainty; see for instance Lawson (1985), Hoogduin (1991).

[9]Compare this with Keynes's example of the Beauty Contest, GT p.156 and section 3.5. There are some interesting similarities between Keynes and Hayek (see for instance Hayek (1967), especially chapter 3 and of course Hayek (1937); see chapter 4).

[10]Note that this does not mean that the role of uncertainty is only relevant in the analysis of the mec and the rate of interest. Since firms are uncertain about the future demand for their products indeterminacy also matters for the goods and hence the labour market. See also Chick ((1983), chapter 2) who convincingly argues that the role of (historical) time, uncertainty and money in the GT are to a great extent different ways of expressing the same fundamental indeterminacy of decentralized economies. In our study (see especially chapter 6) we emphasize money and uncertainty.

[11]For our interpretation of the neo–classical synthesis see section 3.3.

[12]As O'Donnell (1990, p. 259) acknowledges this interpretation of the relation between the TP and the GT depends on the assumption that Keynes's philosophical ideas did not really change between 1921 and 1936.

[13]In a letter to Hicks Keynes criticized Hicks's interpretation of the GT in Hicks (1937) for laying too much emphasis on current income instead of expected income. 'At one time I tried the equations, as you have done, with I [current income, HG] in all of them. The objection to this is that it overemphasizes current income. In the case of the inducement to invest, expected income for the period of the investment is the relevant variable. This I have attempted to take account of in the definition of the marginal efficiency of capital. As soon as the prospective yields have been determined, account has been implicitly taken of income, actual and expected. But, whilst it may be true that entrepreneurs are over-influenced by present income, far too much stress is laid on this psychological influence, if present income is brought into such prominence' (Keynes (1973B), pp.80–81).

3 The Right Answers to the Wrong Question? An Assessment of the Microfoundations Debate

3.1 Introduction[1]

In this chapter we try to assess whether and how the post–war developments in mainstream macroeconomic theory in general and the microfoundations debate in particular have elaborated upon the main issues of Keynes's GT as analysed in the previous chapter. In decentralized economies, economic behaviour of agents is regulated by a system of markets. To develop a truly general economic theory, all the implications of the market process, both with respect to individual behaviour as well as with respect to the performance of the economy as a whole, should be considered. However, the degree of complexity of such a theory is enormous and, given the current state of the art beyond the limits of economic theorizing. A more realistic approach may be the careful application of the *ceteris paribus* clause. As we saw in chapter 2 this Marshallian device is also used by Keynes in his GT in order to keep the analysis tractable given the existence of indeterminacy for the economy as a whole. This use of the *ceteris paribus* clause does not imply a permit for anything goes but rather the use of a methodological device that helps to keep the analysis manageable. An outstanding example of such a research strategy is the familiar distinction between macroeconomic and microeconomic theory (see also section 1.2). In this respect microeconomic theory is often defined as the analysis of economic behaviour of the individual decision unit. Macroeconomic theory analyses the performance of the economy as a whole by means of the developments in and between aggregates or a small number of sectors. However, as noted in the introduction of our study, the analysis of the behaviour of the economy as a whole is also an object of research of general equilibrium theory, which is mostly thought to belong to the domain of microeconomics. This resemblance raises two related observations. The first observation concerns the relationship between general equilibrium theory and macroeconomic theory. This observation

41

lies at the heart of the microfoundations debate. The second and more fundamental observation considers the usefulness of the distinction between microeconomic and macroeconomic theory as such.

Walrasian general equilibrium theory is above all the analysis of the allocation of a natural level of output, *given* that the Walrasian auctioneer coordinates individual activities successfully. In the best developed general equilibrium model, the Arrow–Debreu–McKenzie model (ADM model), a unique equilibrium price vector exists for each set of endowments, preference orderings and technologies that 'reconciles the potentially conflicting choices of all the economic agents' (Weintraub (1977), p. 9). A given set of endowments, preference orderings, and production technologies determine a unique natural level of output. The actual level of output always coincides with this natural level of output since the equilibrium price vector guarantees the full utilization of resources in the economy. The determination of the level of output as a whole is hardly considered an interesting question in this context. On the other hand, the object of research of macroeconomic theory has been the study of the consequences of the failure of the market system to coordinate activities so as to achieve the best possible outcome for the economy as a whole in terms of the levels of employment, output, and welfare. The choice of a *macro*economic, in the sense of highly aggregated, framework to analyse these consequences is only of secondary importance. We do not consider the standard micro–macro distinction to be very relevant in this respect. More fundamental is the recognition that market economies can get stuck at low and suboptimal levels of output for prolonged periods.

For this reason, as outlined in section 1.2, we suggest an alternative distinction ('micro'–'macro') between economic theories, which takes account of different objects of research and discriminates by the alternative application of the *ceteris paribus* clause. On the one hand, we propose to classify micro and macro theories of the economy as a whole in those that assume perfect coordination and in those that do not take this assumption for granted. To the first category we reckon for instance Walrasian equilibrium theory and new classical macroeconomics. As examples of the second category one can think of Keynes's *General Theory* and the new–Keynesian theory of coordination failures. On the other hand, we distinguish economic theories of the economy as a whole from those theories that focus on particular characteristics of individual behaviour (e.g. consumer behaviour, theory of the firm) and of markets (asymmetric information, customer markets). These last two subcategories are referred to as partial economics. Inasmuch as these theories analyse the implications of these characteristics for the performance of the economy as a whole, they belong to the category of theories in which the coordination issue is taken for granted.

It should come as no surprise that in the context of the general equilibrium model deviations from the natural level of economic activity can only result from exogenous shifts in the technological structure of the economy (e.g. technology shocks, preference shocks, or input shocks), on the one hand, or from the *ad hoc* introduction of restrictions (wage and price rigidities) in the exchange process, on the other hand. This general equilibrium approach has served as a benchmark in the theoretical explanations of low levels of economic activity. It has especially served as a benchmark in the debate about the necessity of providing macroeconomics with microfoundations. It is the purpose of this chapter to discuss several conceptual features of the microfoundations debate. In this respect, we will apply the aforementioned analytical distinction between 'micro' and 'macro'. We think that this approach may illuminate our opinion that the recent revival of the microfoundations debate, with its emphasis on peculiar and perhaps more institutional characteristics of markets[2] (partial economics), tends to shift attention away from more fundamental considerations about the workings of a market economy (the issue of coordination). In this chapter we intend to show that the search for microfoundations has probably provided the right answers to the wrong question.

The organization of the chapter is the following. Section 3.2 summarizes some important concepts of Keynes's economics, as outlined in chapter 2, and discusses the neo–classical synthesis and non–Walrasian general equilibrium analysis. Section 3.3 focuses on new–classical macroeconomics, whereas section 3.4 will discuss new–Keynesian economics. New–Keynesian models that incorporate an explanation of price rigidities are analysed in section 3.4.1. In section 3.4.2 the issue of coordination failures is dealt with. Section 3.5 concludes the chapter with some final observations.

3.2 Keynes's economics and general equilibrium theory: the origin of the microfoundations debate

Since Keynes's theory gave rise to the development of modern mainstream macroeconomics and initiated the theoretical debate that still dominates the developments in a large part of economic theory it is reasonable to begin a discussion of this debate with a brief summary of our analysis of Keynes's GT in chapter 2. In the GT, Keynes attempts to show that classical theory is ill–suited for analysing the economy as a whole. Keynes's criticism is directed at the classical analysis of the determination of aggregate output and aggregate employment. In classical theory, the real wage and the level of employment are determined by the demand for and the supply of labour. The natural level of output corresponds to this level of employment. The rate of interest equilibrates savings and investment.

In this context, consumption and investment represent competitive claims on a given quantity of output. Aggregate demand does not have any persistent impact on the level of aggregate output if prices are fully flexible. Expectations are only of minor importance and the Quantity Theory of Money holds in a dichotomized economy. If prices are fully flexible, relative prices clear all markets. In the classical analysis, unemployment is caused by wage or price rigidity.

Keynes's main criticism of classical theory centres around what he considered to be two central classical assumptions, i.e. the assumption of a full–employment equilibrium and the unimportance of expectations. The latter assumption is connected with the role of money and above all of uncertainty in Keynes's theory. The first assumption originates from the fact that classical economists analysed economy–wide phenomena with the theory of the behaviour of the individual unit under the assumption of the perfect coordination of individual activities. In the GT, the endogeneity of the level of output is a consequence of Keynes's rejection of the use of the invisible hand assumption. In the absence of a coordinating device like the invisible hand (or of corresponding metaphors like the Walrasian auctioneer and Robinson Crusoe), economic agents need to make their own decisions with respect to the various prices at which trade takes place. In such a world it is by no means clear why the resulting level of aggregate output should correspond with the natural or full–employment level of output. The dependence of aggregate output on aggregate demand reflects a fundamental conceptual difference between Keynes's theory and his version of the classical theory. In classical theory it is *assumed* that the price mechanism coordinates the decisions of the individual agents perfectly. In Keynes's GT agents need to form expectations about the behaviour of other agents and the issue at stake is precisely whether an individual may neglect the fact that demand is not a one–sided transaction. The crucial question in a decentralized economy is how the price mechanism may establish a degree of coordination that ensures full employment. Keynes concludes that the price mechanism may not do the job. The coordination problem is a consequence of the individual *lack of knowledge* about the behaviour of other agents in the economy. Agents cannot neglect the impact of their activities on the behaviour of other agents in the present or in the future. Supply and demand schedules in the various markets are not only determined by relative prices as in classical theory but by expectations as well. To quote Heller, agents 'condition their expectations of demand [or supply] on some non–price variable of the economic system' (Heller (1986) p. 158).

Immediately after the publication of the GT, Hicks (1937) incorporated Keynes's GT in a general equilibrium framework. Since in this framework the auctioneer is assumed to take care of the coordination issue, Keynes's emphasis on the independent impact of expectations on the decisions of economic agents disappeared. As we saw in the previous chapter the exclusion of expected income and the sole reliance on current income inevitably led to a neglect of the indeterminate part of the GT. In this respect, the Keynesian revolution was aborted right from the start of the neo-classical synthesis. Hicks's analysis led to the original formulation of the well-known IS/LM model. In the 1950s and 1960s the IS/LM model virtually became Keynesian macroeconomics. It was left to Patinkin (1956) to show that in the static, general equilibrium model of his *Money, Interest and Prices* Keynes's unemployment equilibrium eventually rests on the assumption of price or wage rigidity. In contrast with Keynes's GT, IS/LM models do not consider problems of coordination with the result that this issue more or less disappeared as a separate problem. Patinkin's aim was to show that the incorporation of the real balance effect in a Walrasian general equilibrium model, on the one hand, destroys the classical dichotomy but on the other hand, renders the mutual existence of involuntary unemployment and wage and price flexibility impossible in the long run. Patinkin's version of the IS/LM model, combined with a labour market characterized by sticky nominal wage rates, constitutes the core of the neo-classical synthesis. The fundamental characteristics of the classical model remain intact even if the Keynesian innovations (the theory of effective demand and the theory of liquidity preference) are incorporated into the classical model. This comes as no surprise since we showed in section 2.6 that Keynes's analysis of the determination of the level of effective demand cannot be separated from the question of indeterminacy and hence of the coordination issue. Because of low speeds of adjustment it can be argued within the framework of the neo-classical synthesis that Keynesian and classical theories do not exclude one another but focus on different situations (the short run and the long run, respectively). During the 1950s and 1960s economic research was directed towards the elaboration of the basic model, e.g. the microfoundation of the demand for money (Baumol (1952) and Tobin (1956)) and the development of modern portfolio analysis (Tobin (1958) and Markowitz (1959)). Theoretical research focused upon the impact of (monetary) policy on the level of nominal aggregate income, on the one hand, and the decomposition of this last variable into real and purely nominal changes, on the other hand. This last issue initiated the well-known debate about the Phillips curve. However, the debate between Keynesians and monetarists was, above all, an empirical debate. The theoretical framework as such remained undisputed (B. Friedman (1978) and Laidler (1982)). Involuntary unemployment in a Walrasian general equilibrium model became a special case and was explained by referring to the liquidity trap

(Hicks (1937)), price or wage rigidities (Patinkin (1956)), money–illusion or interest inelastic investment.

Blanchard (1987) illustrates the position of the majority of Keynesians during the heyday of the neo–classical synthesis with the following simplified model (in logs):

$$y = \alpha(m - p) \qquad \alpha > 0 \qquad\qquad (3.1)$$

$$y = \beta(W - p) \qquad \beta < 0 \qquad\qquad (3.2)$$

$$W = W^* \qquad\qquad\qquad\qquad (3.3)$$

y = aggregate demand and supply
m = a global shift variable, *e.g.* the log of the money stock
p = the general price level
W = the nominal wage level

Equation (3.1) represents aggregate demand that is a reduced form of IS/LM. Equation (3.2) is a reduced form of aggregate supply on the assumption that aggregate demand equals aggregate supply. Equation (3.3) gives the level of nominal wages. Nominal wages are exogeneously fixed, either by assumption (the wage rigidity case) or by reference to the existence of complete money–illusion. The fact that nominal wages are exogenous ensures the non–neutrality of money since it can easily be shown that

$$\frac{\partial p}{\partial m} = \frac{\alpha}{\alpha - \beta} < 1 \qquad\qquad (3.4)$$

Hence, monetary policy has real effects. In the monetarist version adaptive expectations allow for the non–neutrality of money in the short run. In the long run the classical dichotomy holds and equations (3.2) and (3.3) are replaced by equation (3.2'):

$$y = \beta(w) \qquad\qquad (3.2')$$

w = the real wage level

The real wage equals the marginal productivity of labour and the level of employment is completely determined in the labour market (compare with Keynes's analysis of the second classical postulate!). Given the level of real wages real output is determined by equation (3.2'). Changes in m now only lead to equiproportionate changes in p since y is supply–determined.

In the neo–classical synthesis there is a clear analytical distinction between the analysis of resource allocation based on standard choice theoretic foundations, on the one hand, and the analysis of the determination of the level of aggregate output, on the other hand. This is not to say that macroeconomic models within the tradition of the neo–classical synthesis lack microfoundations (see Patinkin (1956)). The Arrow–Debreu model allows the analysis of both microeconomic and macroeconomic phenomena. However, important phenomena like the level of aggregate output or the level of aggregate unemployment cannot be explained from choice theoretic foundations. In (Walrasian) general equilibrium theory it is assumed that the price mechanism coordinates economic activities well whereas in Keynesian macroeconomics this mechanism is somehow not supposed to work. Underneath this there is a more important difference: the distinction between theories that *assume* that the price–mechanism ensures a socially–efficient degree of coordination and those that do not. Following Weintraub (1979) we may observe that economists in the tradition of the neo–classical synthesis have tried to cut economic phenomena into micro and macro when, in fact, 'the appropriate cut is between models of coordination success and models of coordination failure' as we argued in the introduction to this study, but 'the rules of the ADM modeling game ensure that coordination success will occur' (Weintraub (1979), p.75).

The insight that situations of non–market clearing cannot be analysed adequately with a *Walrasian* general equilibrium model was taken up by and is essential in the work of Clower (1965) and Leijonhufvud (1968, 1981). Eventually this led to the development of the non–Walrasian fixprice general equilibrium approach. In the non–Walrasian general equilibrium theory false trading is allowed which creates the possibility that agents are rationed in their respective demands. As a result excess demand functions should not only include relative prices but quantity constraints as well. This implies the incompatibility of (the notional version of) Walras's Law and the existence of quantity constrained equilibria. In the case that both the nominal wage W and the nominal goods price p are fixed the issue of Keynes vs. the classics is analysed in the context of disequilibrium analysis in the following manner: excess supply on the goods and labour market characterizes the case of Keynesian unemployment whereas excess supply on the labour market and excess demand on the goods market characterize the case of classical unemployment. It is quite straightforward to show that in case of Keynesian unemployment, shocks in aggregate demand influence the level of output and employment since output and employment are completely demand determined. Similarly, demand shocks do not influence realia in case of classical unemployment because output and employment are supply determined. Following Grandmont (1989, p. 272), it can be shown that the disequilibrium analysis becomes very similar to the new–Keynesian theories of section 3.4, once p becomes flexible (and hence clears the goods market) while W remains fixed. It now

depends on the type of wage rigidity that prevails on the labour
market whether Keynesian or classical results occur. If real wages
are fixed, the classical case results because N (the level of
employment) is completely determined on the labour market and
aggregate demand has no role to play. In case of nominal wage
rigidity, the analysis is analogous to Keynes's analysis of the
labour market after the dismissal of the second classical postulate.[3]

According to Leijonhufvud (1968), who elaborates upon the work of
Clower, the analysis of Keynes's GT leads to the following
conclusions. (1) Keynes's GT is perfectly compatible with a standard
choice theoretic framework; (2) price incentives are important in the
GT; (3) the ranking of price– and quantity adjustment is reversed in
Keynes's GT (e.g. quantity adjustment occurs before price adjustment)
and (4) it is by no means clear *how* these price incentives should
lead to a degree of coordination that ensures full–employment. 'The
only thing which Keynes removed from the foundations of classical
theory was the deus ex machina – the auctioneer which is assumed to
furnish, without charge, all the information needed to obtain the
perfect coordination of the activities of all traders in the present
and through the future' (Leijonhufvud (1981), p.15).[4] Hence, despite
the fact that Leijonhufvud emphasized both the coordination failure
argument and the rationing argument, the non–Walrasian general
equilibrium theory focused exclusively on the rationing argument
whereas the coordination failure argument was sidestepped once more.
The weakness of the non–Walrasian equilibrium approach is to be found
in this area. The informational requirements needed to establish
non–Walrasian equilibria even exceed those in flexprice general
equilibrium models like the ADM model. On the other hand, despite the
assumed capacity of information dissemination in the economy, agents
are only allowed to trade on a market by market basis and cannot
signal demand packages concerning more than one market at the same
time. The recognition that agents are unable to communicate across
markets is the starting point for the coordination failure literature
of section 3.4.2 (see also Gordon (1990)). Furthermore, as Hahn
(1978) among others pointed out, these non–Walrasian equilibria are
not Pareto–efficient because there are possibilities for welfare
improving trade that remain unused. Finally, the stickiness in prices
does not originate from the behaviour of individuals but is clearly
assumed *ad hoc* which is the theoretical objection to the fixprice
literature that received most attention. Non–Walrasian general
equilibrium theory (and for that matter, the neo–classical synthesis)
was criticized by new–classical economists for this assumed
non–rationality of price stickiness. The rise of the new–classical
economics meant a return to the classical model that Keynes,
Patinkin, Clower, and Leijonhufvud tried to escape from. It is to
these new–classical theories that we now turn.

3.3 New-classical macroeconomics

From the beginning of the 1970s, a growing dissatisfaction with the weak or missing microeconomic underpinning of the conventional macroeconomic theory of changes in the level of aggregate economic activity eventually resulted in the development of new-classical macroeconomics. This approach was initiated by Lucas (1972, 1973) although Lucas and Rapping (1969) and Phelps (1968), both with adaptive expectations, can be regarded as immediate predecessors. Other important articles include among others Sargent and Wallace (1975, 1976), Barro (1974, 1976), and Kydland and Prescott (1977). The new-classical macroeconomics can be considered as a straightforward application of general competitive equilibrium theory to macroeconomic problems. The assumptions of competitive markets and rationally behaving agents have been maintained. However, the assumption of perfect information was initially relaxed, which enabled Lucas *et al.* to analyse economic disturbances caused by the signal extraction problem individuals face in the new-classical monetary business cycle models.

Barro (1980) distinguishes the following characteristics of new-classical macroeconomic models: (i) Continuous market clearing. Observable levels of transactions, prices, etc. are derived from the intersection points of demand and supply schedules. (ii) Imperfect, but not asymmetric (Buiter (1989)), information. In this respect, the impact of both aggregate-relative and permanent-temporary confusion (Cukierman (1984)) has been analysed. (iii) A natural rate hypothesis. Nominal surprises do not affect realia permanently. On the other hand, perceived nominal shocks do not have any impact at all. (iv) Rational expectations.

Additionally, it can be observed (McCallum (1979), Buiter (1989)) that new-classical macroeconomic models are often identical agent models or carried to the extreme, representative agent models (no heterogeneity of agents). Whatever the merits of new-classical economics it must be emphasized that from the viewpoint of this study they are to be praised for focusing on the need for a theory of expectations.

Blanchard (1987) offers the following simple illustration of the implications of a new-classical model. For the purpose of simplicity, the microfoundation of the relationships is not considered explicitly. Given the equilibrium condition that aggregate demand equals aggregate supply, the economy can be characterized by the following system of equations (in logs).

$$y = \alpha(m - p) \tag{3.5}$$

$$p_i = p + e_i \tag{3.6}$$

$$y_i = \beta(p_i - E_i p) \tag{3.7}$$

$$\alpha, \ \beta > 0$$

$p_i =$ the commodity price in market i

$e_i =$ white noise and uncorrelated across firms (i.e. a relative price shock)

It is assumed that each agent produces output in its own market. Both a global and a local shift variable, m and e_i respectively, are incorporated in the model, reflecting market specific and economy–wide shocks, respectively. Agents only observe local prices. Subjective expectations of p are formulated in line with equation (3.8).

$$E_i p = Em + \gamma(p_i - Em) \tag{3.8}$$

$$0 < \gamma < 1$$

The parameter γ is dependent on the variances of the local and the global shift variables. In the absence of unanticipated shocks $E_i p = Em$. Substitution of (3.8) into (3.7) as well as aggregation over firms (e.g. integration over the unit interval) yields the aggregate supply curve (3.9).

$$y = \beta(1 - \gamma)(p - Em) \tag{3.9}$$

It can be derived from the equalization of aggregate supply and demand and some straightforward calculations that

$$p = \lambda Em + (1 - \lambda)m \tag{3.10}$$

$$y = \alpha\lambda(m - Em) \tag{3.11}$$

with $\lambda = \dfrac{\beta \ (1-\gamma)}{\alpha + \beta \ (1-\gamma)}$

In the absence of nominal surprises money is neutral and output is equal to its natural level. Unanticipated global shocks have a transitory impact on real economic activity through changes in relative prices as can be observed from equations (3.10) and (3.11).

Hence, it is shown that under conditions of general market clearing and rational expectations unanticipated changes affect real economic variables. Subsequent research has been directed for a considerable part towards the sources of propagation of the initial shock, for instance, through capital and inventory accumulation, adjustment costs of factor inputs or consumption smoothing (Lucas (1975) and Blinder and Fischer (1981)), on the one hand, and on the implications for the effectiveness of policy of the derived results (Sargent and Wallace (1975) and Kydland and Prescott (1977)), on the other hand.

It can be argued that the extension of the model above to a full–fledged model of the business cycle contains some serious drawbacks with respect to the persistence of the initial shock. Additionally, changes in the rate of growth of money are non–neutral in case they induce portfolio shifts (Tobin (1978)). Finally, as King (1981) has put forward, information on monetary aggregates is available too promptly to support the assumption about the global ignorance of individuals on empirical grounds. In order to tackle some of these issues, the real equilibrium business cycle approach, following the pioneering articles by Kydland and Prescott (1982) and Long and Plosser (1983), has been expanding very rapidly during the 1980s. Real equilibrium business cycle models are directed towards the explanation of empirical regularities within the context of a stochastic version of the neo–classical model of economic growth. Uncertainty is introduced by unanticipated shocks in technology and preference orderings. The fluctuations in the data are looked upon as following from optimal responses of the choice variables to these random shifts. The basic assumptions underlying the general competitive equilibrium model have been maintained for the remaining part. For the purpose of illustration, it can be observed that fluctuations in economic activity can be derived from the neo–classical macroeconomic model of section 3.2 by modelling the marginal productivity relationship in line with some stochastic process of technological development. In addition, the propagation of the impulse can be generated in a multi–period version of the model from the assumption of normal goods. With normal goods any favourable technology shift changes the intertemporal allocation of leisure because the productivity shock will lead to an increase in real wages and, hence, to the intertemporal substitution of leisure for labour. The latter leads to an increase in personal wealth, which implies that the expenditures on all goods (both for consumption and investment purposes) increase now and in the future, resulting in what is called the comovement and persistence in desired commodity/leisure consumption series. Hence, 'models of this type provide a well–defined benchmark for evaluating the importance of other factors (e.g. monetary disturbances) in actual business–cycle episodes' (Long and Plosser (1983), p. 67).

The analytical structure and the implications of real equilibrium business cycle theory are considered rather controversial. McCallum (1988) offers an excellent and rather critical survey of the essential characteristics of the real equilibrium business cycle approach. In this chapter we intend to focus on the research methodology of the new–classical theories in general. In new–classical macroeconomics, the theory of the performance of the economy as a whole is essentially a microeconomic theory applied to the analysis of aggregates. In this respect, it is simply assumed that the basic principles of the theory of the individual unit are the most suitable for describing all economic problems. Notwithstanding the introduction of the rational expectations hypothesis (see, however, section 3.5) this position essentially implies that new–classical economists adhere to the three classical postulates as set out in section 2.2. This position also takes for granted that the individualistic foundation of microeconomic theory is correct. However, from a theoretical point of view the general competitive equilibrium approach is only legitimate in situations where individual decisions can be considered independently, without reference to the activities intended in other segments of the economy. To put it differently, it is legitimate in situations where the coordination of individual activities has already been achieved or is of no interest to the problem at hand. The assumptions of continuous market clearing and homogeneity among agents do precisely establish these situations. Potentially conflicting individual intentions and aggregate outcomes are reconciled in a unique and individually as well as socially optimal way. The metaphors of the Walrasian auctioneer and of Robinson Crusoe are just alternative examples of assuming a coordinated solution to exist. Because of individual homogeneity, there is no need to analyse the exchange process explicitly since individual homogeneity and exchange are mutually exclusive. Given this representative agent assumption, in a large number of new–classical models the main implication of the theory that different levels of economic activity can result only from either individual misperception or from shifts that are exogenous to the economy itself, is rather straightforward. The sole reference to relative prices as an explanation of economic activities, rests on the assumption that the economic agents can neglect the impact of their activities on other agents. Economy–wide phenomena, such as the levels of aggregate economic activity and employment (but not the general price level), follow *mutatis mutandis* from individual economic activities but they are analysed as if they originate from allocational peculiarities given the endowments and technological characteristics of the economy, which again implies that the coordination of these individual activities does not need a separate theoretical treatment. Note however that the assumption of perfect coordination by itself does not possess an individualistic behavioural foundation. To state the argument more explicitly, in the context of a model where there is no conceptual difference between the representative agent and its multi–person alternative, it is logically impossible to ground the determination of the (market clearing) exchange ratios on individualistic behavioural assumptions. Markets clear by assumption and not by implication of individual behaviour (see, of course, also Arrow (1959)). If the embodiment of this assumption, the Walrasian auctioneer, is no longer part of the analysis, Pareto–inefficient solutions are feasible and it is not clear how an equilibrium will ever get established, let alone a situation of perfect coordination. The existence of a market clearing, Pareto–optimal equilibrium does eventually rest on the assumption that agents behave cooperatively. However, the assumption of cooperative behaviour cannot be derived from the assumptions underlying optimal individual decision making (see also section 3.5 for a more elaborate discussion of this last argument). New–classical macroeconomics does not live up to its own standard. [5] It does not offer a solid foundation of some aspects of individual behaviour (including the formation of expectations), of the determination of market prices, and of the establishment of a unique socially and privately efficient situation of general market clearing. More specifically, it fails to provide a superior microfoundation of the level of economic activity when compared with the analyses of the 1960s.

3.4 New–Keynesian macroeconomics

3.4.1 The microfoundation of price rigidities
The rise of new–classical macroeconomics during the 1970s has caused a recent outburst of analyses with a more Keynesian flavour directed toward the development of a microfoundation for market failures, given the assumption of rational expectations. According to Blanchard (1987) most of these Keynesian imperfect competition theories have taken as a starting point that 'prices do not adjust fully and instantaneously to nominal money and focused on the reasons for and implications of imperfect price adjustment' (Blanchard (1987), p.1). The major aim of these theories is to give a rationale for price rigidities in order to explain the non–neutrality of money and thereby to provide a rationale for stabilization policy. The assumption of imperfect competition is deemed necessary to countervail the classical argument that complete price flexibility ensures a Walrasian equilibrium with full employment and hence ensures the quantity theory of money to hold. In this respect the debate between new–Keynesians and new–classicals takes place within a framework that Keynes described as classical.

Imperfect competition can be explained from increasing returns to scale, on the one hand or from heterogeneity in products on the other hand. In the former context (for instance, Weitzman (1982)) real wages move pro cyclically and have adverse effects on employment. Kaldor (1983) argues that Weitzman's model, which does not rest on the assumption of price rigidity, provides a necessary foundation for Keynes's macroeconomics because perfect competition and Keynes's macroeconomics cannot be reconciled (see Kaldor (1983), pp.12–15). In our view it is hard to disagree with Kaldor on this issue from the point of view of mainstream economics. Within a general equilibrium context, Keynes's coordination issue implies at least dismissing the auctioneer in his role of establisher of a unique, stable Pareto–efficient equilibrium. In doing so, however, agents have to set their own prices which implies the introduction of imperfect competition. Keynes's assumption (GT, p. 245) of a given degree of competition refers to the fact that he considers his theory to be independent from any specific form of (imperfect) competition.[6] However, in contrast with Weitzman (1982), many of the imperfect competition theories are partial equilibrium models (e.g. efficiency wage models, kinked demand curve models, credit rationing models), which rely on price rigidities to derive the desired non–neutralities. On the other hand, it can be argued that the impossibility to enter the market on a sufficiently large scale in Weitzman's model, at least implicitly, hinges on some assumption about missing information or the failure to coordinate activities perfectly (see also van de Klundert (1987)).

In our view, many new–Keynesian models are better characterized as classical rather than Keynesian (some new–Keynesians are quite clear on this issue, see Mankiw (1991) who states that 'with new Keynesians looking so much like old classicals, perhaps we should conclude that the term 'Keynesian' has out–lived its usefulness' (Mankiw (1991), p. 10)) As an independent explanation of deviations from the natural level of output, theories of real stickiness are often inadequate, since cycles may be demand determined (as in Keynes's GT), on the one hand, and nominal shocks cannot be analysed because an adequate theory about the developments in the numeraire (money) does not exist, on the other hand.[7] In this respect we agree with Grandmont (1989) in his conclusion that the new–Keynesian approach of imperfect competition 'yields essentially the same conclusions as, those obtained earlier [in case of disequilibrium analysis, HG] under the assumption of perfect competition on the goods market. The system will react in a Keynesian manner if there are nominal wage rigidities, in a Classical way if the rigidity is real' (Grandmont (1989), p. 274). Grandmont illustrates this conclusion with equation (3.12) which represents the equilibrium condition for a monopolistically competitive firm i ($i = 1,...,b$) with *increasing* marginal costs. [8]

$$\frac{dc}{dy}(y,\ p,\ W) = p(1 - \frac{1}{be})$$ (3.12)

The left-hand side of (3.12) gives the marginal costs and the right-hand side gives marginal revenue. With *b* and *e* (the number of firms and the price elasticity of demand, respectively) fixed prices are set as mark-up over marginal costs. If *be* goes to infinity the usual equilibrium condition for perfect competition results. Under real wage rigidity as in the majority of new-Keynesian theories equation (3.12) determines the level of output and the classical theory comes into play. In case of nominal wage rigidity on the other hand aggregate demand shocks lead to changes in the real wage and thereby to changes in output and employment. As Grandmont (p. 276) notes *y* may, of course, change under real wage rigidity through the usual classical channels of shocks in technology, preferences or changes in the degree of competition (as represented by *be*).[9]

In this chapter we are not primarily interested in the various manners in which the price (or wage) rigidities or fixed cost assumptions, like menu costs, are accounted for. The new-Keynesian analysis that focuses upon a partial equilibrium approach can be summarized by stating that the various imperfectly competitive markets are characterized by some kind of inertial price behaviour and that aggregate demand is typically exogenous. In these theories the dismissal of the Walrasian auctioneer implies that agents do not only have imperfect information but mostly asymmetric information as well. The issue of coordination is not explicitly addressed. The analysis of the endogeneity of aggregate income for the economy as a whole and, hence, of the interdependency of aggregate supply and aggregate demand requires at least a multi-sector economy. Some Keynesian imperfect competition *general* equilibrium models (Blanchard and Kiyotaki (1987), Weitzman (1982)) only allow implicitly the analysis of interdependencies between various firms (workers). However, notwithstanding the fact that in some of the imperfect competition general equilibrium theories externalities may arise, the major aim of *both* partial and general equilibrium theories of imperfect competition remains the explanation of price stickiness and the non-neutrality of money. Since aggregate demand is typically exogenous, shocks in aggregate demand are persistent because of frictions on the *supply*-side of the economy. In fact, many of the Keynesian imperfect competition theories are analytically very similar to the new-classical monetary business cycle model discussed in section 3.3. The extension of imperfect information to include asymmetric information (see Greenwald and Stiglitz (1987)) as a rationale for price rigidities represents an improvement in our opinion. It allows problems of moral hazard and problems with respect to the enforcement of contracts to be analysed. However, although the existence of asymmetric information implies heterogeneity, the heterogeneity concept as such is not used to analyse interdependencies between various agents but is merely used to underpin price rigidities.[10]

Furthermore, new–Keynesian imperfect competition theories do neglect the fact that demand may not be a one–sided transaction. Just as in the new–classical theory, economy–wide phenomena are analysed with the theory of the behaviour of the individual unit. In our view the microfoundation of Keynesian economics should at least start from the fact that for the economy as a whole the dependence of aggregate output on aggregate demand is essential which implies that the coordination issue should not be taken for granted. This means the necessity of a multi–sector economy facilitated by the introduction of heterogeneity among agents. Much of the criticism that applies to the new–classical theory with respect to the assumptions of rational expectations and of instantaneous coordination leading to a *unique* stable equilibrium if and only if prices were fully flexible also applies to the theories in this section. In contrast with the new–classical economics, however, the new–Keynesian theories discussed in this section deal explicitly with the determination of market prices because of the replacement of the Walrasian auctioneer by the assumption of imperfect competition. The existence of imperfect competition is not a sufficient condition for analysing unemployment. Given the assumptions of complete price flexibility and some coordinating device like the auctioneer, only underemployment equilibria can be analysed. To analyse unemployment equilibria the imperfect competition characteristic is supplemented with some example of asymmetric information in order to create the possibility of price rigidities that may explain the existence of unemployment. However, it remains unclear under what conditions a specific form of asymmetric information (as, for instance, efficiency wages or credit rationing) should apply to the economy as a whole. Or, in other words, the majority of contributions to the new–Keynesian literature on the microfoundation of price rigidities are examples of what we called partial economics in chapter 1.

3.4.2 Coordination failures
In the previous section we observed that the Keynesian reaction to the development of new–classical economics initially focused upon the new–classical assumption of market clearing. Attempts were made to rationalize nominal and real rigidities given the assumption of rational expectations. In line with the analysis in chapter 2, we concluded, however, that these attempts often result in a microfoundation of classical macroeconomics instead of Keynesian

macroeconomics. In this section we briefly discuss some *flex*price general equilibrium theories in which Keynesian results may arise because of the existence of many sectors and the indeterminacy of equilibria. In these theories the dismissal of the Walrasian auctioneer leads to coordination failures. The absence of a Walrasian auctioneer implies that not all the available information is revealed to the market. Limitations in information dissemination can exist between agents, between sectors and between periods. In the coordination failures literature these limitations in information dissemination are considered in order to analyse the implications of incomplete information for the exchange process. Whether or not this may result in price rigidities is of secondary importance. Cooper and John (1988) show that there is a variety of general equilibrium models in which social inefficiencies (may) exist despite the fact that all agents behave as maximizers. The existence of macroeconomic inefficiencies implies the existence of coordination failures. A coordination failure implies 'that mutual gains from an all-round change in strategies may not be realized because no individual player has an incentive to deviate from the initial equilibrium' (Cooper and John (1988), pp.442–443). Agents may take as given the prices set by other firms (see Ball and Romer (1987)), the quantities produced by other firms (Heller (1986), Keynes (1936)) or both (Roberts (1987)). In our view this coordination failures literature does provide a starting point for a microfoundation of Keynesian economics in a general equilibrium framework since the use of a multi–sector economy (heterogeneity) in the Cooper and John framework is a prerequisite for the analysis of Keynes's coordination issue. The possibility of multiple Pareto–ranked equilibria does not depend on the constraints imposed upon the exchange process in the general equilibrium model. Keynes's observation that demand is not a one–sided transaction is used as a main building block in the coordination failures literature by means of the concept strategic complementarity. So far, the examples given of the coordination failures literature share the characteristic that they dismiss (part of) the first function of the auctioneer, the establishment of unique Pareto–optimal equilibrium prices. Coordination failures can, however, also arise by dismissing the second function of the auctioneer, the establishment of exchange arrangements. Using the search–equilibrium framework of Diamond (1982, 1984) trade externalities may arise if agents have to make up their own exchange arrangements (see also Howitt (1990)).[11] In chapter 5 the coordination failure literature serves as a starting point for the development of our own multi–sector overlapping generations model. The search equilibrium framework returns in chapter 6 in the analysis of the microfoundations of money.

A second method of analysing some aspects of Keynes's coordination issue in a general equilibrium framework is to change the ADM–model by allowing for an infinite number of goods as well as for an infinite number of agents in order to introduce the indeterminacy of one or more variables in the model. Within any Keynesian–type of overlapping generations (OLG) model these indeterminacies are present and these OLG models underpin the heterogeneity of agents (see Geanakoplos and Polemarchakis (1986)[12]). In new–classical macroeconomics OLG models are not characterized by indeterminacy (Barro (1974)) since the additional assumption of an infinite intergenerational bequest motive leads in fact to a determinate solution. The indeterminacy of one or more variables necessitates the introduction of the process of expectations formation. In Keynes's GT, the role of expectations is essential, specifically the role of those expectations that govern the rate of investment. As is shown in for instance chapter 5 of this study and by John (1988) and Chatterjee and Cooper (1989), the OLG model can be used to amend the coordination failures argument which is essentially static and devoid of expectations. Both the indeterminacy argument and the coordination failure argument may lead to the conclusion that in the absence of the Walrasian auctioneer the assumption of a unique (natural) equilibrium is not a good starting point for analysing economic phenomena.

The endogeneity of aggregate output, combined with the absence of a Walrasian auctioneer, creates the possibility that in the presence of multiple equilibria the economy can get stuck at an equilibrium which is Pareto–dominated by another equilibrium. However, the strength of the multiple equilibria approach is a serious weakness at the same time. Theories of multiple or even of a continuum of equilibria do provide conditions 'for the *existence* of multiple equilibria but do not provide insights into the question which of the equilibria is more or less likely to be observed' (Cooper (1987), p.2; see also chapter 8). This also explains why these theories are not yet very suitable for analysing policy effectiveness. The mere fact that multiple equilibria exist, does not imply that there is any scope for policy, since it is ambiguous if the authorities are able to relieve the limitations on information in the economy. Subsequent research should be directed towards the analysis of these issues and should therefore be especially directed towards the development of theories that shed some light on the question what equilibrium (or what class of equilibria) is more likely to occur.

Some of the arguments that were mentioned in our criticism of the microfoundation of new–classical macroeconomics also apply to those new– Keynesian theories that belong to the coordination failure framework. The assumptions of market clearing (equilibrium) and of rational expectations are not derived from choice theoretic foundations. However, there are also important differences with the new–classical framework. The coordination failure literature and

Keynesian OLG models do not assume a *unique* market–clearing equilibrium to exist. The theories discussed in this section do, however, not really analyse the exchange process. It is only emphasized that the absence of the assumption of perfect coordination implies the possibility that the exchange process may lead to non–cooperative outcomes. But the question how e.g. a non–cooperative Nash equilibrium comes about is left unanswered. It is simply assumed that an individual agent knows that all other agents play Nash (see Bernheim (1984)). The assumption of cooperative behaviour is replaced by the assumption of non–cooperative (Nash) behaviour. In this respect there is a fundamental difference between the concept of coordination failures in the work of Leijonhufvud, Hayek and Keynes for that matter on the one hand and the concept of coordination failures as discussed in this section on the other hand.[13]

Another drawback of the coordination failures literature (and in fact of all general equilibrium theories discussed in this chapter) is that it is essentially concerned with real economies. Money has no proper place of its own in these models. The existence of strategic complementarities or spill–over effects does not depend on the presence of money. Cooper and John (1988, p.462) suggest extending the coordination failure analysis with the introduction of menu–costs in order to arrive at the non–neutrality of money. In line with Buiter (1989) we do not think that this is a fruitful approach because the menu costs approach

> only gives us a theory of nominal stickiness if prices are set in terms of money. If some bundle of real goods were the numeraire and if the cost of changing prices applied to price changes in terms of this real numeraire, there would be no nominal stickiness. The unmotivated assumption that prices are set in money terms is therefore a crucial one. Until we have a theory of money, we are unlikely to see a theory of nominal inertia (Buiter (1989), p.16).

The menu–costs approach also assumes that the costs of changing prices exceed the costs of changing quantities which does not seem a very realistic assumption. The problem is, however, that in general equilibrium theories like the new–classical and the new–Keynesian theories money is in fact inessential. The demand for money is not explained but simply assumed by putting money into the utility function or by some cash–in–advance constraint. We believe that as a possible restriction to the number of alternative equilibria it may be fruitful to incorporate the role of institutions and conventions. Money can be regarded as a convention that reduces uncertainty (see section 6.4). The discussion of the foundations of money and the role of money as an institutional solution to a coordination problem will be postponed until chapters 6 and 7. Anyhow, the coordination failure framework is as yet a rather rudimentary and elementary one. It needs in our view to be extended in a number of directions to incorporate more (institutional) characteristics of modern economies. In this respect, the analysis may benefit from insights that have been developed outside the scope of mainstream economic theory.

Despite the fact that in a number of ways the theories discussed in this section are closer to Keynes's original coordination problem than the new–classical theories or the new–Keynesian theories of the previous subsection, the microfoundations of the theories discussed here are open to similar criticism as these other theories with respect to the market clearing and the (rational) expectations assumption. In that respect both new–classical theories and new–Keynesian theories cannot claim to provide a superior choice theoretic foundation of economics compared with those theories, for instance (neo–) Austrian and post–Keynesian economic theory, that do not belong to mainstream economic theory (see chapter 4).

3.5 Summary and conclusions

In this chapter, we have argued that the mainstream literature on microfoundations can be criticized for a number of reasons. Our arguments refer to the inherent drawbacks of the mainstream microfoundations attempts as such, on the one hand, and specifically to the neglect of the essential feature of decentralized economies, the coordination issue, on the other hand. We will first briefly digress on the former issue.

The choice theoretic foundation as such contains some flaws since important implications of the formation of expectations and the competitiveness of markets cannot be derived from individualistic, behavioural foundations. In particular, new–classical economics can be criticized in this respect. Apart from the assumptions of general market clearing and the hypothesis of rational expectations, the new–classical application of the homogeneity postulate does not allow the determination of exchange values on the one hand, nor the separation between privately and socially efficient equilibria, on the other hand. Although new–Keynesian economics does consider these possibilities, it is open to similar criticism. Both new–classical and new–Keynesian theories fail to provide a superior microfoundation of macroeconomics when compared with non–general equilibrium theories. In the context of a general equilibrium framework, macroeconomics cannot do without microfoundations. In this restricted meaning, the quest for microfoundations of macroeconomics is a legitimate one and a useful object of subsequent research (see also Janssen (1991)). The assumption of general market clearing is needed in (classical/Keynesian) theories that are based on a general equilibrium framework because the existence of a Pareto–efficient general equilibrium depends on the assumption that agents take prices as given (and thus that perfect competition prevails). In answering the question how such an equilibrium will ever get established, one has to fall back on the auctioneer assumption because in the exchange process that should lead to this general equilibrium prices necessarily change and this is at odds with the aforementioned assumption of given prices. The issue of the necessity of a coordinating device like the Walrasian auctioneer was forcefully raised by Arrow (1959). Hahn (1989) aptly summarizes this point: 'The fictitious auctioneer is also consequence of theoretical lacunae and indeed of certain logical difficulty. If prices are to be changed by the economic agents of the theory, that is either by households or firms or both then it is not easy to see how those same agents are also to treat prices as given exogenously as is required by the postulate of perfect competition' (Hahn (1989), p. 65). The standard auctioneer assumption enables the circumvention of the question how out–of–equilibrium trade should be analysed. Moreover, it forecloses the analysis of strategic considerations.

The assumption of rational expectations that underlies new–classical and new–Keynesian theories also turns out to be an equilibrium assumption. Much of the work in the seminal Frydman and Phelps (1983) collection centres around the theme that rational expectations can only be reconciled with individualistic behaviour if it is assumed that 'every individual agent knows the behavioral parameters of the other agents' (Frydman and Phelps (1983), pp. 15–16). But since this same requirement also applies to the other agents concerning the behaviour of that particular agent this raises a logical difficulty *unless* it is assumed that it is rational to expect for every single agent that the expectations of all other agents coincide with the average expectation as predicted by the particular model that the analyst has picked out for this economy. It is only in a state of equilibrium, however, that these average expectations are equal to the rational expectations as predicted by the model. This means that the rational expectations hypothesis is not solely based on individualistic behaviour but also on the fact that the economy is always in a state of expectational equilibrium.[14] The assumption that the rational expectations hypothesis is a *behavioural* hypothesis is thus incorrect since it turns out that it tells nothing about individual behaviour apart from the fact that agents are supposed to behave rationally (see also our discussion of Iwai (1981) in chapter 7). The assumption is warranted in order to avoid the necessity of analysing higher–order expectations. The logical difficulties that arise in analysing these higher–order expectations are described by Keynes in his well-known example of the Beauty Contest (GT, p. 156, but see also, for instance, Keynes, 1937B).

It is not a case of choosing those which, to the best of one's judgment, are really the prettiest, nor even those which average opinion genuinely thinks the prettiest. We have reached the third degree where we devote our intelligences to anticipating what average opinion expects the average opinion to be. And there are some, I believe, who practice the fourth, fitfh and higher degrees (GT, p. 156).[15]

It appears that if the rational expectations hypothesis is no longer used as an equilibrium assumption and agents thus face the problem of coordinating expectations of expectations convergence to a rational expectations equilibrium will result only if the resulting learning processes are based on very stringent assumptions concerning information dissemination (see also Hoogduin (1991), p. 115 and chapter 8 of our study). For our present purposes the main implication of the conclusion that the coordination of expectations should be explicitly analysed and not merely assumed is that economic theory is in need of 'a macrotheoretical foundation for microeconomic behavior' (Frydman and Phelps (1983), p. 28). This is in accordance with our definition of a 'macro'foundation for microeconomics as being the analysis of the implications of the coordination problem for individual behaviour. This ends our brief digression on the conceptual flaws of the mainstream microfoundations literature.

Given the objectives of this study, we are especially interested in the second essential feature of the microfoundations debate mentioned at the beginning of this section: the neglect of the coordination issue. The search for microfoundations is quite often not only an attempt to provide macroeconomics with an individualistic foundation but also an attempt to legitimize the assumed exogeneity of some variables, with the result that the coordination issue is circumvented. In our discussion of new–Keynesian and new–classical macroeconomic theories, we emphasized that it is mostly assumed that aggregate demand cannot be influenced by a single agent. This assumption does, in fact, imply that aggregate demand is exogenous. Furthermore, the perfect coordination of economic activities (in the sense that unique, stable Pareto–superior equilibria are established) is often taken for granted in the microfoundations literature. The analysis of the economy as a whole in terms of microeconomic principles is most obvious in new–classical representative agent models where macroeconomics is nothing more than the economics of a single agent, Robinson Crusoe, blown up to economy–wide proportions. However, also a number of models with a more Keynesian flavour (section 3.4.1) analyse economy–wide phenomena with an apparatus that essentially belongs to what we defined in the introduction of this chapter as partial economics since aggregate demand is exogenous. This approach is only legitimate in situations where the coordination of individual activities has already been achieved or is of no interest to the problem at hand.

The mere assumption that coordination is perfect, implies a denial of an essential feature of market economies. For that reason, the development of microfoundations for macroeconomics should not start from the proposition that coordination is perfect. In agreement with Hahn we may conclude that the main message from Keynes's GT is that even if there are no restrictions imposed upon the workings of the price mechanism 'there are available co–operative strategies which lead to outcomes which are superior to the non–co–operative outcomes' (Hahn (1983), p. 74). The analysis of the economy as a whole should start from the dependence of aggregate demand schedules on aggregate supply schedules and vice versa and therefore from the recognition that variables that may be taken as given in partial economics do not have to be exogenous in analysing the economy as a whole. The difference between what we dubbed partial and coordination economics, among others, concerns the legitimacy of the *ceteris paribus* clause of a given level of output for the economy as a whole. On the other hand, ceteris paribus clauses are not a permit for anything goes. '*Ceteris paribus* clauses are part of almost all science. Rather than condemning them all, one needs to distinguish when one may legitimately employ them and to recognize that rough generalizations can have worth and content despite their vagueness and imprecision' (Hausman (1989), p.118). As has been argued in chapter 2 this strategy is compatible with the methodology employed by Keynes in the GT. In our view, the analysis of the coordination issue in a general equilibrium framework requires the introduction of heterogeneity among agents and of the possibility of indeterminacy as in OLG models. However abstract and imperfect that may be, a sound analysis of the performance of the economy as a whole and, hence, theories that deal with the microfoundation of macroeconomics should discard the assumption of perfect coordination and thus discard the auctioneer, the invisible hand, and Robinson Crusoe. In this respect, the coordination failure literature despite its highly abstract character at least starts from the recognition that the economy consists of different individuals, which opens the possibility of realized non–cooperative outcomes and unrealized superior cooperative outcomes. On the other hand, in the context of the microfoundations debate it is mostly assumed that Walrasian general equilibrium theory should serve as a benchmark in analysing the economy as a whole. Since Walrasian general equilibrium theory does not allow the analysis of the coordination issue, in our view, the microfoundations debate has mainly provided the right answers to the wrong questions. The analysis in this chapter leads to the following two observations. First of all, the microfoundation of Keynes's economics within a general equilibrium framework should deal with the micro–macro issue and the indeterminacy issue through the incorporation of strategic considerations and/or indeterminacy of equilibria in order to become a 'macro'theory as defined in chapter 1. This observation will be elaborated upon in chapter 5. Secondly, the microfoundations of Keynesian and classical mainstream theories contain some serious flaws. It is, therefore, necessary and worthwhile to investigate the microfoundations and the coordination issue in other approaches. This is the subject of the next chapter.

Notes

[1] This chapter is based upon van Ees and Garretsen (1990).

[2] In his survey of the state of the art in macroeconomics, Fischer (1988) also concludes that the focus in the microfoundations debate has primarily been upon specific features of various markets but on the whole his verdict about the microfoundations literature is rather positive.

[3] This does not mean that we consider $W = \bar{W}$ to be a necessary condition for Keynes's theory to hold, see chapter 5 on the fallacy of composition.

[4] In his analysis of the coordination issue Leijonhufvud refers to the work of Hayek (1937, 1945); see chapter 4.

[5] In this restricted sense, we are willing to consider new classical macroeconomics as a dismal science (Peeters (1987)).

[6] Following Chick (1983), we may observe that Keynes did not make any assumption concerning the market structure but changed the standard assumptions concerning the knowledge that firms are supposed to possess in the classical theory, market power is not an issue in the GT.

[7] Under specific assumptions a multi-market model with sticky prices in more than one market may do the job (e.g. Akerlof and Yellen (1985), Buiter (1989) and van Ees (1989) and (1990); for a survey of these models of price stickiness see Rotemberg (1987)).

[8] The assumption that marginal costs are *increasing* over the relevant range of production is important for the necessity of nominal wage rigidity disappears if marginal costs are constant. In the case that supply is completely elastic any demand shock has, of course, an impact on realia. See also the discussion on nominal wage rigidity and the slope of the marginal cost curve in Blanchard and Fischer (1989), pp. 376–388.

[9]The issue of monopoly power will return in our discussion of the post–Keynesian theory of mark–up pricing in chapter 4.

[10]In his discussion of the marginal efficiency of capital (Ch. 11 of the GT) Keynes explicitly refers to problems of moral hazard in his analysis of risks that influence the level of investment. Apart from the standard entrepreneur's risk associated with the uncertainty surrounding the future return on investment there is also a lender's risk. The latter arises because of the possibility of default on the part of the borrower. This type of risk is 'a pure addition to the cost of investment which would not exist if the borrower and the lender were the same person' (GT, p. 144). Problems of moral hazard thus exist because of this separation of the supply and demand for credit. This comes close to the new–Keynesian theories of credit rationing. The main difference with the GT, however, is that the issue of asymmetric information in determining investment in the GT is explicitly linked with uncertainty and hence with the fundamental indeterminacy of the GT. The new–Keynesian approach of credit rationing contains only half of the story so to speak. As the above quotation illustrates, the existence of lender's risk increases the costs of investment. These costs create a difference between the social and private costs of investment. According to Meltzer (1988) this insight and the link with uncertainty are the main theoretical contributions of the GT. Meltzer's interpretation is interesting because his analysis of Keynes's theory is based to some extent on the micro–macro issue (the private versus the social return of investment) and the indeterminacy issue (the importance of uncertainty in determining investment). In his view, in decentralized economies the capital stock, and hence the level of output and employment are below the social optimum because of uncertainty. The existence of the latter leads to a divergence between the private and the social return on investment. Or in the words of Meltzer 'fluctuations in output impose social costs that cannot be removed by private action. Variability imposes a premium for bearing risk and uncertainty that raises the market rate of interest above the social productivity of capital and holds the capital stock below the social optimum' (Meltzer (1988), p.15).

[11]The problem of the establishment of exchange arrangements comes to the fore in a search model because of the lack of a system of markets in these models. Agents who wish to trade therefore need to search for a trading partner.

[13]This is also a major theme of Hoogduin and Snippe (1987, pp.430–431) and of Peeters (1987, p.447) in the microfoundations issue of *De Economist*.

[14]The same point was raised by Hayek (1937) in his criticism of perfect foresight; see section 4.3.1. For a similar conclusion as to the incompatability of Austrian and new–classical economics on this issue see Hoover (1988), pp. 231–248.

[15]In this respect there is an important similarity between Keynes and Hayek; see also chapter 4.

4   Alternative Approaches

4.1 Introduction

In the previous chapter we concluded that the mainstream microfoundations debate mainly gives the right answers to the wrong question. This debate or, in other words, the attempt to ground Keynes upon Walras has led to a state of the art in macroeconomic theory in which both the majority of (new-)Keynesian and (new-)classical analyses are cast in a framework that is similar to the classical one that Keynes criticized in his GT. As we tried to show in chapter 2 of this study, Keynes's GT ultimately centres around the coordination problem for the economy as a whole. Keynes's way of dealing with, what we called, the micro–macro and the indeterminacy issue in the GT is a reflection of this problem. Keynes's coordination issue is either neglected or assumed away in the majority of contributions to the microfoundations debate. This gives two options to elaborate upon Keynes's coordination issue. The first option is to try to incorporate essential features of Keynes's analysis of the coordination issue in the general equilibrium framework on which the mainstream microfoundations debate is based. This route will be taken in chapter 5 of our study in which we focus upon the relevant features of those general equilibrium approaches that have something to say on the multiplicity, indeterminacy or instability of equilibria. Or, in other words, chapter 5 deals with (some of) the approaches mentioned in the second part of section 3.4 of the previous chapter. The second option is to dismiss the general equilibrium framework as a useful tool for analysing the economics of Keynes. This implies that one must look for alternative[1] approaches that have something to say on microfoundations, coordination, and Keynes. This route is taken in the present chapter. The main objective of this chapter is to show that these approaches do indeed deal with these issues to a greater or lesser extent, with the result that these approaches challenge or complement the mainstream analysis as discussed in chapters 3 and 5. The first part of chapter 4 deals with post–Keynesian economics and the second part with Austrian economics.

The analysis and conclusions of this chapter serve as the main input for chapters 6 and 7 on money and uncertainty. Chapter 4 is organized as follows. In the next section we start with a discussion of the basic features of the various strands of post–Keynesian economics. In the second part of section 4.2 we analyse the relation between these strands and the three aforementioned issues: microfoundations, coordination and Keynes. In order to illustrate how some post–Keynesian insights into pricing and uncertainty can be combined to shed some light on our search for 'macro'foundations for microeconomics in a post–Keynesian setting we try to give an alternative foundation for an important element of post–Keynesian microeconomics, the theory of mark–up pricing in the appendix at the end of this chapter. In section 4.3, the basic features of Austrian economics that are relevant for the purpose of this study are briefly discussed. The second part of this section deals with the relation between these features and the abovementioned three issues. Section 4.4 compares post–Keynesian and Austrian economics. The connection between the alternative approaches and the attempts to deal with the coordination issue in a general equilibrium framework is one of the topics of chapter 8.

4.2 Post–Keynesian economics

In our view, the idea as expressed by for instance Hamouda and Harcourt (1989) that it is perhaps easier to describe what post–Keynesian economics is *not* about than to list the essential features of this approach already indicates that post–Keynesians form a rather heterogeneous group. Our purpose in this section is not to give a full–fledged survey of post–Keynesian economics but rather to discuss some basic features of the main strands within post–Keynesian economics in order to establish the relevance of post–Keynesian ideas from the perspective of this study.[2]

4.2.1 Some basic features of post–Keynesian economics.

In what follows we distinguish three main directions in post–Keynesian economics: the Kaleckians, the monetary post–Keynesians, and the neo–Ricardians. Other classifications are no doubt possible but this classification covers the bulk of the post–Keynesian literature in our view. There are important analytical differences between these three strands and even within these strands. But all post–Keynesians are critical of neo–classical economics in general and of general equilibrium theory in particular. The basic criticism is directed at the lack of realism of mainstream economics in their analysis of decentralized market economies. In accordance with Hamouda and Harcourt (1989) we can observe that the agreement stops right there and that the difference between for instance Shackle and the neo–Ricardians is almost as great as between, for instance, post–Keynesian and neo–classical interpretations of Keynes. Before turning to the three abovementioned strands it should be emphasized, that to some extent, the Kaleckian and the monetary post–Keynesian approach overlap (for instance, in the analysis of income distribution).

Recurrent themes in post–Keynesian economics that are *more or less* agreed upon are the following.

Market economies are characterized by instability. There is no reason why a Walrasian general equilibrium should ever be attained even if the market mechanism works smoothly.[3]

Connected with the previous point is the critique that the neo–classical concept of equilibrium assumes away the difficulties of incorporating time in the analysis through their use of logical or mechanical time, as opposed to the post–Keynesian concept of historical time. It is instructive to quote Joan Robinson on this matter

> Equilibrium is described as 'the end of an economic process'; the story is usually told of a group of individuals each with an 'endowment' of ready–made goods or a productive capacity of some kind. By trading and retrading in a market, each ends up with a selection of goods that he prefers to those that he started with. If we interpret this as a historical process, it implies that, in the period of past time leading to 'today', equilibrium was not established. Why are the conditions that led to a non–equilibrium position 'today' not going to be present in the future? (Robinson (1974), p. 2).

Choice–theoretic models base their analysis upon (maximizing) individual behaviour. Following economists like Ricardo, Marx, and more recently Sraffa and Kalecki, post–Keynesians often emphasize the analysis of social groups. As will become clear below, this is especially important in their theory of income distribution. Connected with this and in accordance with the recent new–Keynesian theories in this respect is the importance attached to rules and institutions like trade unions, legal agreements, government agencies, the banking system, etc.

In neo–classical theory (see chapter 6 of our study) money is just another commodity with the result that (apart from some exceptions) a monetary economy is not fundamentally different from a barter economy. In post–Keynesian theory, especially in the work of for instance Davidson (1978), Minsky (1975), Weintraub (1978), Kregel (1982A,B) and Rogers (1989), the use of money in relation to the role of uncertainty in a decentralized economy is emphasized.

The abovementioned criticism of neo–classical theory is specifically made by those post–Keynesians interested in short–run analysis emphasizing the role of money and uncertainty. However, according to other post–Keynesians the analysis should focus essentially on the long–run analysis of growth in a capitalist economy. This latter group of post–Keynesians, more inspired by the work of Ricardo and Sraffa than by the work of Keynes, strongly criticizes the neo–classical theory of value and distribution.

On the issue of methodology post–Keynesian and neo–classical views differ substantially. The neo–classicals use a unified, axiomatic framework whereas post–Keynesians apply different theories to different real world situations (see Dow (1985) and Caldwell (1989)).

Though it is obvious that post–Keynesian economic theory owes much to the ideas of Keynes, his work is only one of many influences. Quite often it is argued that the ideas of Kalecki and Sraffa are at least equally important. Kalecki for instance not only developed a theory of effective demand but also offered a class–oriented analysis of pricing and distribution (see Kriesler (1987)) based on the notion of imperfect competition. Together with the classical surplus approach of Ricardo and Sraffa and Marshall's concept of a normal price, Kalecki's work is as at least as important to some post–Keynesians as Keynes's writings are.

The Kaleckians

Post–Keynesian price theory builds upon Sraffa (1926) not only in its emphasis on imperfect competition but also by dismissing marginalistic analysis of price setting behaviour. The post–Keynesian approach to price setting under imperfect competition was initiated by Kalecki (1938). Kalecki divided the economy into two sectors: the raw materials sector and the manufacturing sector. The latter is characterized by cost–determined prices. In this case, Kalecki postulated constant average and marginal costs up to the level of full capacity utilization and the existence of planned excess capacity as day–to–day practice. Given these assumptions, manufacturing firms with some degree of market power will set a mark–up on their direct costs (wage and raw material costs) to determine their selling price. This mark–up reflects the amount of price discretion an individual firm has and constitutes the profits per unit of output of the firm. The greater the degree of market power of a firm the greater the mark–up (and thus profits per unit) will be. In the competitive raw materials sector marginalistic pricing is assumed. For firms (or industries) applying mark–up pricing changes in demand will not change prices, because supply is perfectly elastic, but rather shift resources among industries by influencing profit expectations.

The question is, of course, what determines the level of the mark-up. For Kalecki, the mark-up was solely determined by the degree of market power a firm (or on a more aggregated level, an industry) possesses. The degree of market power or, to use Kalecki's terminology, the degree of monopoly, is determined by all kinds of structural (supply-side) variables like the concentration ratio in an industry, the degree of product differentiation and the power of trade unions, to mention a few. Though Kalecki is not always quite clear whether his degree of monopoly is equal to the mark-up or not, it is argued by most post-Keynesians (see Asimakopulos (1977)) that the mark-up is just a reflection of the degree of market power. In this view the mark-up is determined by the factors influencing the degree of competitiveness. Cowling (1983) tries to formalize this by making the degree of monopoly a function of the concentration ratio, the (industry wide) demand elasticity and the degree of collusion. Andrews (1964) has also had a major influence on post-Keynesian price theory. His critique of the theory of monopolistic competition, as developed by Chamberlin and Robinson, led him to formulate his own mark-up theory. In the neo-classical theory of monopolistic competition, Andrews argued, producers were supposed to show short-sighted behaviour. Their pricing policy, based on maximizing short run profits, would lead to excess capacity in the long run. This would be a result of the entry of new firms attracted by (too) high short-run prices. In Andrews's analysis, firms are aware of the possibility of entry and therefore try not to charge prices that induce entry. Excess capacity is not the result of short-sighted behaviour but is necessary to preserve the goodwill of customers. Sawyer (1985) sheds light on a difference within post-Keynesian theory with respect to the question as to what determines the mark-up by arguing that, on the one hand, there is, what he calls, the Kaleckian approach where the degree of competitiveness determines the mark-up. On the other hand, post-Keynesians like Eichner (1976, 1983), more in line with the work of Andrews, define the mark-up as the amount of internal funds required by the firm (in Eichner's terminology the megacorp) to finance its planned investment expenditures.

As an aside, it should be noted that the meaning of competition in post-Keynesian theory is different from that in neo-classical theory. In line with the classical economists post-Keynesians view competition as a process (see also section 4.3) with investment as the key variable while competition in a neo-classical sense mostly has a static meaning with price as the key variable.

It is through its analysis of income distribution that the Kaleckian micro-analysis on mark-up pricing is connected with its macro-analysis of the determination of investment. Investment plays a central role in all versions of post-Keynesian economics. Not only because as in Keynes's GT investment determines the level of economic activity but also because it determines the distribution of income and the growth rate of the economy. The rejection of marginalistic analysis implies that factor prices need not to be equal to their respective marginal productivities. The question is then how income distribution is determined. Keynes's General Theory contains no explicit theory of income distribution but it can easily be adapted according to some post–Keynesians so as to incorporate an income distribution theory (see Kaldor (1956)).[4]

To gain some insight in the post–Keynesian theory of income distribution the following highly simplified example, may prove useful (see Kalecki (1971) and Kriesler (1987)):

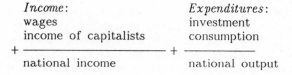

Kalecki assumes that the economy consists of two groups, i.e. workers and capitalists. In his initial analysis, he further assumes that workers do not save but spend their income on consumption and that capitalists do not spend any of their profits on consumption. Given these assumptions, it can be shown that total savings equal profits and that the latter, in turn, equal investments. 'Thus the value of investment goods produced is just equal to the total profits in the system. Since only, and all, profits are saved this is just another way of capturing the S=I relation' (Kregel, 1977, p. 427).

Given Keynes's theorem that investment determines savings, it becomes clear that under these strict assumptions, the level of investment determines the level of profits. The higher the share of investment in national income, the higher the share of profits and by definition the lower the share of wages. This simple model led Kalecki to the well–known conclusion that workers spend (consumption) what they get (wages) and capitalists (firms) earn (profits) what they spend (investment).[5] Allowing for consumption out of profits and for saving out of wages complicates the matter but leaves the basic conclusion unaltered that investment determines the share of profit recipients in national income and thereby the share of wage recipients in national income.

Given a model of mark–up pricing (see Harcourt (1985) and Kriesler (1987), chapter 7) it was possible for Kalecki to combine two theoretical revolutions of the 1930s: the theory of effective demand and the theory of imperfect competition. If, for instance, the profit margins increase (that is if as a result of changes in the degree of market power the mark–up increases relative to the (wage) costs) this may lead to higher prices and therefore, a fall in real wages. The latter will cause a fall in real effective (consumption) demand. Given a certain level of investment these two tendencies i.e. an increase in the profit margins and a fall in effective demand, will offset each other, leaving the level of profits unaltered. By the same reasoning it is possible that a sudden decrease in effective demand will at least in the short–run not lead to a corresponding fall in (factor) prices but to a further contraction as a result of the market power of firms and trade unions and the corresponding rigid prices and/or wages. We will come back to this Kaleckian approach in the next subsection.

The Monetary Post – Keynesians
This group of post–Keynesians extends Keynes's methodology as outlined in section 2.6 of our study by using Keynes's framework of chapters 2–5 of the GT on the principle of effective demand, on the one hand, and by elaborating upon the fundamental indeterminacy in the GT in their analysis of money and uncertainty, on the other hand. We start with the former.

In neo–classical theory the price on the labour market (the real wage rate) is determined in a marginalistic manner: under perfect competition the real wage equals the marginal productivity of labour. The schedule of the latter is in monetary post–Keynesian theory not the demand for labour function (see Davidson (1983)). The money wage is exogenously determined through bargaining between trade unions and the firms. The neo–classical analysis of supply of and the demand for labour is considered to be irrelevant in determining the level of employment. Using the framework of Weintraub (1958) and Davidson and Smolensky (1964), this can be illustrated as follows

The point of intersection of the aggregate supply function (*AS*) and the aggregate demand function (*AD*) is the effective demand. Effective demand is the equilibrium level of output and thereby determines the level of employment. The level of employment and the marginal productivity of labour determine the real wage. Any gap between the level of employment (determined on the product market) and the supply of labour at the going real wage measures the level of unemployment.

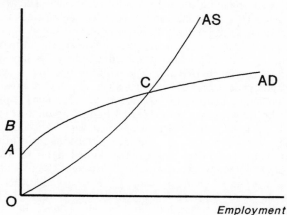

Figure 4.1 The determination of the level of effective demand

The marginal productivity of labour function is not the aggregate demand function of labour. This analysis is based on Chapter 2 of the General Theory. Adherents to the neo–classical synthesis use the downward slope of the MPL function to argue that wage flexibility will ensure full employment in the long run. Monetary post–Keynesians reject such a price/wage stickiness interpretation of Keynes's work because this interpretation is incomplete and incorrect in their view. Incomplete to the extent that it does not incorporate monetary factors and the role of uncertainty (see below) and incorrect to the extent that it contains a fallacy of composition that results from confusing the micro and the macro implications of falling real wages or, in other words, from the fact that the *AD* and the *AS* curve are interdependent for the economy as a whole. Monetary post–Keynesians claim that this aggregate supply and demand analysis does not rest on price rigidities or some form of imperfect competition.[6] At the point of intersection of *AS* and *AD*, the point of effective demand, price adjustments have already taken place. If, for instance, producers expect sales proceeds to be *OA*, when in reality demand is *OB*, there will be an excess demand of *AB*. A process of price adjustment will eventually bring about equality between *AS* and *AD* and an increase in employment. But there is no a priori reason why this process should result in an equilibrium that secures full employment (compare this with our remarks on the realization of short–period expectations in the GT in section 2.6). According to the monetary post–Keynesians, this is mainly due to the instability of the *AD* function and in particular to the instability of one of the components of aggregate demand, aggregate investment and the malfunctioning of the neo–classical price mechanism with respect to one crucial price: the rate of interest. This malfunctioning in turn is caused by the role of money and uncertainty to which we now turn.[7]

As has been mentioned before, post–Keynesians and particularly those focusing on the implications of uncertainty assign a key role to money in economic theorizing. The role of money is rationalized through the incorporation of uncertainty in the analysis.[8] People hold money and use money in exchange just because the future is unknown and holding money provides a hedge against this uncertain future. A lack of knowledge with respect to the future course of the economy and with respect to (future) decisions of other agents results in the substitution of money for knowledge, so to speak. If the degree of confidence in the future changes, the willingness of people to hold money changes too. A decrease in the degree of confidence leads to a greater willingness to hold money. The use of money may reduce the uncertainty at the micro level but it does not do so at the macro level. From a macroeconomic point of view the use of money enlarges the uncertainty and the instability of expectations. Expectations are crucial in determining the level of investment. The inherent instability of capitalism is caused by the volatility of investment which in turn is determined by volatile (long–run) expectations concerning profitability, growth, the financial/banking arrangements etc. Adverse expectations lead to an increase of liquidity preference and a fall in investment. This part of the analysis of monetary post–Keynesians builds especially upon chapters 12 and 17 of the GT.[9] The role of expectations and the surrounding uncertainty with respect to future developments imply that in a monetary economy Say's Law no longer holds and full–employment cannot be guaranteed.

The development of the monetary post–Keynesian approach owes much to the work of, for instance, Davidson (1978, 1982) and Minsky (1975, 1986). Financial institutions play a very distinct role in this approach. The banking system in a modern economy forms a crucial link in the investment process through its ability to provide credit money to firms. Expectations (and the resulting possibility of speculation) on financial markets determine whether firms will continue to succeed in the external financing of their cash deficits. This is particularly clear in Minsky's financial instability hypothesis which extends Keynes's analysis of chapter 17 of the GT, see Minsky (1986), in which business cycles are endogenously determined. An investment boom leads inescapably, through the increasing amount of speculative (bank) finance of investments, to increasing interest rates which in their turn lead to decreasing profit expectations and ultimately falling investment. In the next subsection we will try to assess the relevance of this direction in post–Keynesian economics for our study. In chapter 6 we elaborate upon the post–Keynesian insights as to the relevance of Keynes's analysis of the essential properties of money in chapter 17 of the GT.

Neo – Ricardians

The neo–classical theory of value states that the value of a means of production can be expressed by its price. This theory of value as opposed to the classical theory of value is based on the concept of utility functions and production possibility functions. The classical theory of value emphasizes the physical aspects of the means of production. This observation lies at the heart of the long–run analysis of those post–Keynesians who are often labelled as neo–Ricardians or Sraffians. Following Ricardo, they recognize that land and labour can be treated as homogeneous factors of production but consider this logically impossible with respect to the factor capital. This is in contrast with the neo–classical theory of value. Ricardo already dealt with the problem of valuing heterogeneous capital and this point was taken up by Sraffa (1960) who claimed that marginal productivity theory is useless because there is no simple monotonic relation between the quantity of capital and its price. Sraffa (1960) instead elaborated on the classical surplus approach and reasoned that the crucial relationship in neo–Ricardian economic theory is the distribution of this surplus between workers and capitalists. The distribution of this surplus determines the technical coefficients, the relative prices and the demand for goods and services and thereby the allocation of resources. The neo–Ricardian theory is supply–driven. So if the rate of profit or the wage rate is exogenous, then this determines like a causal chain the wage rate (or the rate of profit), the production technique, the relative prices and the demand for goods.[10]

The neo–classical concept of a production function, for instance the well-known Cobb–Douglas production function, can value only the quantity of capital in homogeneous (money) terms by assuming its price, the rate of interest beforehand, while the purpose of a theory is to determine this price (this was, of course, the main issue at stake in the Cambridge controversy in which the neo–classical opponents argued that the determination of the rate of return on capital and the valuation of capital occurs simultaneously). Neo–Ricardian economists are primarily interested in long–run tendencies of real variables and play down the influence of money and uncertainty. Monetary variables play no essential role. This branch of post–Keynesian economics replaces the neo–classical theory of value by their own objective theory of value which is directed at the explanation of normal prices instead of market prices as the relevant measure of value. Neo–classical value theory does not start with the production decisions but analyses the production and consumption decisions of individuals simultaneously: 'The consumer was assumed to act rationally. This meant that given his income and the supply of goods available at given prices the consumer would seek the greatest possible utility from the expenditures of his income on consumption. The value of each good purchased is thus determined subjectively by the individual utility function' (Kregel, 1973, p. 27).

Value equals market price and there is no surplus whatsoever. Consumers are sovereign, assuming given income, prices and supplies. This is replaced in the neo–Ricardian approach by producers' sovereignty in which the theory of distribution of income is essential in explaining the working of a capitalist economy. Taking either the wage rate or the interest rate as given,the production technique is determined by the former or the latter and it can be shown that the determination of relative prices is independent of the composition of demand. This conclusion is only valid as long as the neo–classical substitution theorem holds or, in other words, as long as there are constant returns to scale and no composite goods (see Eijgelshoven (1982)).

4.2.2 Microfoundations, coordination, Keynes and post–Keynesian economics

It should be emphasized that our discussion of post–Keynesian economics in the previous subsection covers only the main features. A detailed analysis of this approach is beyond the scope of this book. The analysis of section 4.2.1 serves mainly as a means to assess the relevance of post–Keynesian economics for the objectives of our study. Hence, the analysis of the present subsection sets the Kaleckians, the monetary post–Keynesians and the neo–Ricardians against the issues[11] of microfoundations, coordination and the economics of Keynes. It will appear that our approach has much in common with the monetary strand of post–Keynesian economics with respect to microfoundations, coordination, and Keynes. At the end of this chapter an example explains how the alleged necessity of 'macro'foundations for microeconomics can be addressed in a post–Keynesian setting. This is done by analysing the implications of the existence of uncertainty for price setting behaviour.

With respect to the *neo–Ricardian* approach, the following observations are relevant, in our view. As to the issue of microfoundations the answer is rather straightforward. The reliance on the analysis of long–period equilibrium in which the average rate of profit in the economy equals the normal rate of profit implies that short–run behaviour of individual entrepreneurs is of little or no relevance to the analysis. The behaviour of individual agents or, in this case, of individual firms is not considered the appropriate unit of the analysis. The analysis can be conducted in terms of aggregates (or groups) and what really counts is not the individual rate of profit but the *average* rate of profit. This also has a bearing on the issue of coordination. The fact that the analysis of the economy as a whole can be thought of as the analysis of groups (workers and capitalists) in which these groups are conceived as representative agents means that the coordination issue in neo-Ricardian terms only refers to the coordination on this aggregated level. In this respect, we agree with Hodgson (1989) who concludes that 'the Sraffian approach does not offer a theory of human agency and interaction. It simply suggests that the long period positions will somehow reflect and affect the expectations and actions of agents, without explaining how the average rate of profit and long-period prices are attained'[12] (Hodgson (1989), p. 100). Given the definition of the issue of 'macro'foundations for microeconomics as the analysis of the implications of the coordination problem for the behaviour of individual agents this conclusion is not surprising. Within post-Keynesian economics the question whether Keynes developed a long-period theory of employment in the GT is much debated. Neo-Ricardians like Garegnani (1978) answer this question in the affirmative. Given the analysis in chapter 2 of the present study it should be clear that such an interpretation is untenable in our view. Both Keynes's analysis concerning the principle of effective demand and the analysis of what we called the fundamental indeterminacy can not be reconciled with a long-period analysis. In our opinion the principle of effective demand as outlined by Keynes is explicitly based on the motives and decisions of individual agents and the neglect of the role of money, and uncertainty in neo-Ricardian economics implies that this branch of post-Keynesian economics is open to similar criticism as general equilibrium based theories in this respect. We will return to this issue in chapter 6 of our study. This is not to say that Keynes's GT lacks Sraffian elements. Keynes's analysis of the peculiarities of money in chapter 17 of the GT starts off with an analysis of the own-rates of interest that is explicitly based on Sraffa (1932).[13] Despite this last remark, the neo-Ricardian approach is in our view at odds with the three benchmarks of this section, microfoundations, coordination and our analysis of Keynes.

The microfoundations issue is explicitly addressed in the *Kaleckian* approach. The question that arises is whether this foundation of the (macro) analysis of the determination of aggregate investment and output upon the micro analysis of price setting behaviour under imperfect competition differs fundamentally from the recent new-Keynesian attempts in this direction as discussed in section 3.4.1. Or, in other words, are mark-up pricing schemes as advocated in the Kaleckian approach compatible with standard short-run profit maximization or not? In our view, the neo-classical approach and the Kaleckian approach are in this respect not fundamentally different.

It can be shown that the Kaleckian theory is often either indirectly or even directly based on short–run profit maximization. The former is forcefully shown by Marglin (1984), see p. 228 and chapter 14)[14] who shows that Kalecki's degree of monopoly theory is compatible with neo–classical approaches of imperfect competition. The latter is, for instance, argued by Carson (1990) who shows that Kalecki's own formulation of the price equation equals the standard marginalistic formulation in which the mark–up is a function of the price elasticity of demand and in which the degree of monopoly is represented by the inverse of this elasticity. In fact, Kalecki's price equation is equivalent to the price equation given in section 3.4.[15] Also note that Kalecki's analysis of the (macro)effects of changes in wages and the mark–up depends on the assumption of price rigidity (see also Kriesler (1987), p. 88). This enlarges the similarity with the new–Keynesian approaches of section 3.4.1. With respect to the issue of microfoundations we are therefore led to the conclusion that the recent new–Keynesian attempts to build macro upon imperfect competition are a somewhat belated reply to those post–Keynesian economists who, elaborating upon the work of Kalecki, have time and again emphasized the necessity of combining the principle of effective demand with imperfect competition.[16] But for our present purposes it is not only relevant that the Kaleckian approach concerns itself with microfoundations, the coordination issue is more important. In our view, the question as to how to analyse the impact of the coordination problem for the individual agent and the related question how agents react to the existence of this problem are not at home in the Kaleckian approach. As with the neo–Ricardians, the analysis remains on a highly aggregated level in which in terms of coordination only the conflict of interest between, say, a representative employee and a representative entrepreneur matter. Institutions and expectations are not absent but are of minor importance as compared to the nexus prices–income distribution–accumulation. This also implies that the Kaleckian approach differs in at least one important aspect from our analysis of Keynes's GT in chapter 2 as it does not deal with the indeterminate part of the GT. The importance of expectations, the influence of uncertainty on expectations and the role of money, and hence Keynes's insistence on incomplete knowledge, are not fundamental in the Kaleckian approach. It is this difference in the relative importance of the determinate and the indeterminate part of the GT that sets the Kaleckians apart from the monetary post–Keynesians and it also explains their different views as to the necessity to incorporate imperfect competition into the analysis. The former emphasize the necessity to link Keynes's macroeconomics analysis with imperfect competition whereas the latter argue that the inclusion of monopoly elements is not necessary, for what matters is not the specific market structure but the fact that Keynes changed the assumption concerning the knowledge that individual agents possess (see Chick (1983), p. 25).

The *monetary post–Keynesians* do, however, in the determinate part of their analysis, not exclude the possibility of mark–up pricing. In terms of microfoundations the Kaleckian approach and the monetary post–Keynesian approach are not incompatible. The aggregate demand and aggregate supply framework can be easily amended to incorporate mark–up pricing as is shown by Wells (1978) following Weintraub (1961).[17] The feature of the Marshallian aggregate demand–supply framework that is important for our present purposes is the interdependency of the aggregate demand and the aggregate supply function. This interdependency is a reflection of the micro–macro issue of chapter 2. The instability of especially the *AD* function reflects the influence of the fundamental indeterminacy of the GT. The instability of the *AD* function is caused by the instability of aggregate investment which in turn is due to the volatility of expectations and the role of uncertainty (and hence of money) in Keynes's analysis. In emphasizing the necessity to analyse Keynes's principle of effective demand and the implications of the fundamental indeterminacy at the same time, monetary post–Keynesians not only elaborate upon Keynes's framework as outlined in chapter 2 but also (should) address the coordination issue for it is in the *combination* of the principle of effective demand and the fundamental indeterminacy that the central feature of the GT, the importance of the coordination problem for the economy as a whole, comes to the fore. In chapter 6 we will elaborate upon some insights of this branch of post–Keynesian economics in our analysis of the peculiarities of money. In the appendix to this chapter we will give two examples of how the issue of 'macro'foundations for microeconomics can be analysed in a post–Keynesian setting in which uncertainty prevails. These two examples point out that in the post–Keynesian analysis of mark–up pricing it is possible to extend the standard imperfect competition type of argumentation by taking the implications of uncertainty for price setting behaviour into account. This is illustrated by means of a brief discussion of some post–Keynesian ideas on pricing under uncertainty.

This rounds up our discussion of the basic features of post–Keynesian economics. The fact that we consider the monetary branch to be the most useful one in terms of the objectives of this study does not mean that we agree with all of its features or that we conclude that the monetary post–Keynesian approach has the right answers to Keynes's coordination issue, as chapter 5 and chapter 6 will illustrate.

In the next section we will discuss the main elements of the second alternative approach, Austrian economics, with respect to the issues of microfoundations and coordination. In this discussion the economics of Keynes, as has been outlined in chapter 2, will again be used as a benchmark.

4.3 Austrian economics

We will show in this section that there exists a second alternative approach, Austrian economics, that is of some interest in our investigation into the issue of coordination, the quest for microfoundations, and the economics of Keynes. In order to be able to assess the relevance of Austrian economics for the subject of this study the first part of section 4.3 briefly summarizes some important features of Austrian economics. The second part of this section deals with the relation between these features and the objectives of this study.

4.3.1 Some basic features of Austrian economics

Within mainstream economics the influence of Austrian economics is rather limited. In microeconomic theory the work of early Austrians like Menger has been influential in the development of the neo-classical marginalistic theory of value. The reliance on a *subjective* theory of value can be traced back to Menger. In macroeconomic theory the Austrian monetary business cycle theory as developed by Hayek is sometimes thought to be an important predecessor of the new-classical monetary equilibrium business cycle theory as developed by Lucas (1973). This representation of Austrian economics in the mainstream literature is, however, seriously incomplete and incorrect. Incorrect to the extent that it rests upon an erroneous interpretation of Austrian subjectivism. It is incomplete because it neglects important developments in Austrian economics that were especially initiated by Hayek's seminal paper *Economics and Knowledge* (Hayek (1937)). The core concept of Austrian economics is subjectivism. In their excellent survey of Austrian economics O'Driscoll and Rizzo describe subjectivism as follows

> subjectivism refers to the presupposition that the contents of the human mind, and hence decision making, are not rigidly determined by external events. Subjectivism makes room for the creativity and the autonomy of individual choice. Dealing as it does with the individual mind and individual decision making, it is also intimately related to methodological individualism. This is the view that overall market outcomes ought to be explained in terms of individual acts of choice. Thus, for Austrians, and for subjectivists generally, economics is first and foremost about the thoughts leading up to choice, and not about things or the interaction of objective magnitudes (O'Driscoll and Rizzo (1985), pp. 1–2).

This interpretation of subjectivism is rather different from its meaning in the neo–classical theory of value. In the latter the analysis focuses primarily upon the objective consequences of individual choices in terms of (changes in) relative prices on the aggregated level of the market. The individual agent is nothing but a starting point of the analysis whereas the individual agent is the focal point in the Austrian approach. This Austrian view of subjectivism has important implications for economic theorizing. First of all, the uniqueness of individual choice means that the concept of equilibrium only has a meaning on the level of the individual agent. Given the assumption of rational behaviour each agent is always in individual equilibrium.[18] Secondly, equilibrium on any other level, market equilibrium or equilibrium of the economy as a whole, is therefore not as relevant for the Austrian analysis as it is in the neo–classical analysis of equilibrium states. One of the main criticisms of Austrians (following Hayek (1937)) of neo–classical economics is that the latter somehow assumes that the transition of individual equilibrium to a market equilibrium poses no analytical difficulties. According to this criticism the analytical difficulties are either directly assumed away (the invisible hand, the auctioneer) or indirectly assumed away (the use of the rational expectations hypothesis, see section 3.5). Thirdly, the autonomy of individual choice implies that for every agent the knowledge about the (planned) actions of other agents is necessarily incomplete and this knowledge changes as time unfolds. The incompleteness points to the importance of uncertainty and the fact that the amount of knowledge may change as time goes by points to another important concept of Austrian economics, historical time. Finally, the Austrian view on subjectivism implies that in terms of determinacy and indeterminacy as introduced in section 2.6, in our discussion of the structure of the GT Austrian economics focuses upon indeterminacy and rejects the neo–classical emphasis on equilibrium states and the resulting emphasis on wholly determinate outcomes.

Given these implications of subjectivism, the question arises how the analysis of decentralized market economies proceeds from thereon. In a nutshell the answer is that in Austrian economics the concept of market process substitutes for the neo–classical concept of market equilibrium. What does the focus upon market process (which is by definition indeterminate) imply for the analysis of the actions of individual agents? Given the assumption of rational behaviour agents use (imperfect) price signals as a guide in their attempt to improve their position. Knowledge of present and future market conditions is inevitably dispersed. Past individual decisions can always be improved upon in the present period either by changing your own actions or by alert behaviour by other agents. The actual realization of this opportunity implies a tendency towards a market equilibrium but a particular market equilibrium will never be established, for as time goes by new information will become available, creating scope for additional improvements. The role of prices as a transmitter of information is essential in the market process. Given the dispersion of knowledge, prices (imperfectly) disseminate information and provide incentives which improve economic performance in the sense that misallocations are reduced.

The consequences of changes in monetary variables for the functioning of the market process in terms of changes in the general price level as compared to changes in relative prices are at the heart of Hayek's monetary business cycle theory. It is here that Lucas (1981) concludes that his theory (as outlined in section 3.3, equations (3.1)–(3.7)) is similar to Hayek's.[19] This interpretation of Austrian monetary business cycle theory overlooks (at least) two important features of Austrian economics. First of all, Austrian monetary theory also deals with the origin of money. In mainstream economics, the existence and relevance of money is merely assumed (see chapter 6). Secondly, Lucas's interpretation underrates the importance of subsequent developments in Austrian economics in general and in Hayek's own work in particular as to the amendment of the equilibrium concept.

To begin with the first issue, the foundation of money as a medium of exchange has a longstanding tradition in Austrian economics (see especially Menger (1892) but also von Mises (1953)). The role of money is rationalized as the outcome of a process in which self–interested agents somehow recognize that their well–being can be improved by introducing a commonly accepted medium of exchange. It is probably the best example of a naturally evolved institutional solution to a particular coordination problem, the well–known double coincidence of wants. In our view, this important Austrian contribution to the foundation of money has unduly been neglected in the literature. Recent literature on money as a medium of exchange (see chapter 7), however, takes Menger (1892) explicitly as its starting–point. The idea that money is not an invention of the government and that monetary policy hampers the functioning of the market mechanism have in recent years led to a revival of the debate about free currency competition (see Hayek (1976A)). The dismissal of the state monopoly of money supply would, according to the proponents of the privatization of money, put an end to the problems of inflation and instability, for in the case of private money the market process will ensure that only currencies with a stable exchange value are used as money. Ultimately the Austrian argument in favour of free currency competition rests upon the beneficial effects of competition in the market process. A detailed analysis of the free currency debate is beyond the scope of this section (but see Vaubel (1984), White (1984) and Laidler (1990B)). The role of competition, however, leads us to the second abovementioned issue, the development of Hayek's ideas following the original formulation of the monetary business cycle theory. Of particular relevance is Hayek (1937) in which Hayek has become fairly critical of equilibrium theory as employed in his own business cycle theory. The aim of Hayek (1937) is to analyse 'the role which assumptions and propositions about knowledge possessed by the different members of society play in economic analysis' (Hayek (1937), p. 33). It is here that the aforementioned distinction between individual and market equilibrium arises.[20] According to Hayek it is in the transition from an individual equilibrium to a general equilibrium that it is assumed that every agent somehow knows the objective facts that correspond to a state of general equilibrium whereas for individual equilibrium *subjective* knowledge of the facts is relevant. Hence, the essential question arises how this knowledge on the level of the individual agent, subjective knowledge, is transformed into a situation of general equilibrium in which each agent must have the same, objective knowledge. In equilibrium theory, Hayek continues, this problem is avoided by assuming that each agent possesses the necessary amount of objective knowledge. Or, in other words, it is avoided by assuming perfect foresight.

> The statement that, if people know everything, they are in equilibrium is true simply because that is how we define equilibrium. The assumption of a perfect market in this sense is just another way of saying that equilibrium exists but does not get us any nearer an explanation of when and how such a state will come about. It is clear that, if we want to make the assertion that, under certain conditions, people will approach that state, we must explain by what process they will acquire the necessary knowledge (Hayek (1937), p. 46).

Note that Hayek's argument that perfect foresight is an equilibrium assumption is very similar to our discussion of the rational expectations hypothesis in section 3.5.[21] Also note that by assuming that equilibrium prevails it becomes difficult to discriminate between a decentralized economy and a centrally guided economy. The auctioneer in the former becomes the central planner in the latter and there is no fundamental difference between the two systems (see also O'Driscoll (1977), p. 24). In Hayek (1937) the question about the acquisition of knowledge is raised but not really answered. In Hayek (1945) and Hayek (1946) an attempt is made to answer this question. Or, in other words, how is a coordinated outcome for the economy possible despite the fact that knowledge is dispersed. 'Fundamentally, in a system in which the knowledge of the relevant facts is dispersed among many people, prices can act to co-ordinate the separate actions of different people in the same way as subjective values help the individual to co-ordinate the parts of his plan' (Hayek (1945), p. 85) with the result that 'the whole acts as one market, not because any of its members survey the whole field, but because their limited individual fields of vision sufficiently overlap so that through many intermediaries the relevant information is communicated to all' (Hayek (1945), p. 86). Prices are a transmitter of information and the price mechanism is therewith an (imperfect) institutional solution to the coordination problem caused by the fact that knowledge is dispersed. The coordinating role of prices in the market process is enhanced by the (dynamic) forces of competition.[22] In the next section we return to the alleged coordination enhancing function of the price mechanism. Our emphasis on Hayek in this section is caused by the fact that his writings, and specifically Hayek (1937), (1945) and (1946) contain the main features of modern Austrian economics that are relevant for the purpose of our study.

The emphasis on process instead of on equilibrium states can, as has been mentioned before, be seen as Austrians favouring indeterminacy instead of determinacy. If one takes the pervasiveness of indeterminacy literally, however, logical difficulties may arise. In modern Austrian economics it is also recognized that complete indeterminacy and human action are hard to reconcile. Why take any action as an individual agent if the environment is totally unstable and uncertain? Human action can only be rationalized if the environment is to some extent determinate. This calls forth the issue of how individual agents try to shape their environment by means of rules, conventions and institutions, etc. This will be analysed in more detail in chapter 8.[23] This rounds up our brief discussion of some basic features of Austrian economics. Again as in the case of section 4.2 the contents of this section serve as an input for our evaluation of Austrian economics in terms of microfoundations, coordination, and Keynes to which we now turn.

4.3.2 Microfoundations, coordination, Keynes and Austrian economics

Given our previous remarks on the significance of subjectivism in Austrian economics, it is hardly a surprise that the research programmes of providing macroeconomics with a microeconomic foundation is not only not at home in Austrian economics but is also criticized. Macroeconomic theory, defined as the theory of the relation between aggregated variables, does not and cannot have a place in Austrian economics, as all economic theorizing should be cast in terms of the individual agent. All knowledge is subjective and this forecloses a theory of objectively measurable aggregate variables as in mainstream macroeconomics. Economic theory is by definition microeconomic theory (in the standard definition of the theory of individual behaviour). This also implies that economy–wide phenomena, like large–scale unemployment, that are typically analysed in macroeconomic terms must instead be analysed in microeconomic terms.

What is called 'unemployment' equilibrium is a manifestation of *micro*economic discoordination. Macroeconomic phenomena can be analysed properly only by microeconomic analysis. *There are macroeconomic effects of economic disequilibrium, but there is no distinct macroeconomic theory.* That is, there is no consistent theory of macro–aggregates that can be couched solely in terms of these aggregates or that consistently relates aggregates to each other (O'Driscoll and Rizzo (1985), p. 190).

This emphasis on microeconomic theory combined with the aforementioned role of prices does not only make a distinct theory in terms of aggregates obsolete, it also implies that any policy (notably monetary policy) directed at some macroeconomic goals is necessarily flawed as it disrupts the working of the price mechanism and inevitably leads to misallocations: 'there is a presumption that whatever the level of aggregates, they are the outcome of a harmonious process; the important object of study is thus the market process which generates the aggregates, not the aggregates themselves.' (Dow (1985), p. 86).

From the analysis in section 4.3.1, the relevance of the coordination issue can be derived as follows. The dispersion of knowledge on the individual level creates the fundamental coordination problem how despite this dispersion a tendency towards a general equilibrium may come about. As emphasized by Caldwell (1988, pp. 514–515) the main objection of Hayek (1937) against neo–classical theory was its inability to analyse this coordination problem (see also chapter 3 of our study). It is clear that the coordination problem as such is at home in Austrian economics. But our search for 'macro'foundations for microeconomics also concerns the implications of this problem for the behaviour of individual agents. It is here that Austrian economists following Hayek (1946) often merely assume that the price mechanism and the dynamic forces of competition (somehow) take care of the solution of this coordination problem.[24] On the one hand, the coordination problem is at the heart of the analysis whereas, on the other hand, the price mechanism is assumed to migitate this problem at the same time. Dow (1985) summarizes this duality in Austrian economics with respect to the coordination issue as follows. 'There is no theoretical necessity for individuals whose expectations have been disappointed to adjust their behaviour in such a way as to allow more rather than less co–ordination of their actions. The only possible solution is to focus all analysis on the subjectively determined behaviour of individuals, at the expense of reaching any aggregative conclusions. Where such conclusions have been reached, the theoretical leap has been made of *assuming* that individuals' actions are co-ordinated harmoniously' (Dow (1985), p. 85). In our view this supposed efficiency of markets in coordinating individual economic activities follows directly from Hayek's discussion of the role of competition in the market process in, for instance, Hayek (1946): 'competition is essentially a process of the formation of opinion: by spreading information, it *creates* that unity and coherence of the economic system which we presuppose when we think of it as one market' (Hayek, (1946), p. 106, emphasis added). How this creation comes about is, however, left unanswered. In the next section we return to this important issue in discussing the (dis)similarities between post–Keynesian and Austrian economics.

In section 2.6. of our study it was stressed that much of the debate about the meaning of Keynes's GT fails to take account of the (Marshallian) methodology employed by Keynes in the GT. This methodology enabled Keynes to analyse the determination of the level of effective demand on the one hand and to emphasize that the analysis of the economy as a whole is necessarily indeterminate on the other hand. The overlap between the basic features of Austrian economics, as outlined in section 4.3.1, and the GT consists of the indeterminate part of Keynes's analysis. Keynes's analysis of the role of uncertainty and its implications for, for instance, the analysis of money and expectations formation has no doubt similarities with the Austrian approach. This similarity has long gone unnoticed. It has only been in recent years that the subjectivistic elements of the GT start to receive serious attention.[25] Keynes's analysis of the beauty contest in chapter 12 of the GT (see section 3.5) makes the same point about expectations formation as Hayek's analysis of the crucial difference between data that are objectively or subjectively given in his *Economics and Knowledge*. Another example can be found in the well–known Keynes–Tinbergen debate on the use of econometrics (see also section 5.4) as compared to Hayek's verdict of econometrics in his Nobel lecture (Hayek (1976), pp. 270–271). A third example is the role of money or, more generally, of liquidity in a world characterized by uncertainty and historical time. It can be argued that the crux of Keynes's liquidity preference theory is that the need for money arises because the knowledge of individual agents as to the future course of the economy and hence as to the future actions of other agents is not only incomplete but also subject to change as time goes by. Hicks (1974) and Shackle (1974) are two prominent examples of this interpretation of Keynes's liquidity preference theory.[26] As O'Driscoll (1986) shows this analysis of uncertainty and liquidity is close to the analysis of Menger (1892) on this issue. Ultimately Menger's analysis of money as a medium of exchange rests upon the idea of the existing differences in saleability between various goods. The good that is most saleable will become money. The rationale for using a highly saleable good as medium of exchange is essentially the same as the rationale for using money as a flexibility enhancing device in Hicks (1974) (see also O'Driscoll and Rizzo (1985), pp. 193–194).

> What therefore constitutes the peculiarity of a commodity which has become money is, that the possession of it procures for us at any time, *i.e.* at any moment we think fit, assured control over every commodity to be had on the market, and this usually at prices adjusted to the economic situation of the moment: the control, on the other hand, conferred by other kinds of commodities over market goods is, in respect of time, and in part of price as well, uncertain relatively if not absolutely (Menger (1892), p.79).

Despite these examples of similarities between Keynes, in terms of our emphasis on the indeterminacy issue in chapter 2, and the Austrians the differences remain, of course, significant and should certainly not be overlooked. The subjectivistic elements in Keynes's GT should not be overemphasized (see also Lawson (1985). Again, given our hypothesis that the coordination issue is inextricably bound up with Keynes's GT we are not primarily interested in Keynes's economics as such but rather in the (dis)similarities between the issue of coordination and Austrian economics. Two of these differences are especially important for our present purpose. First of all, though indeterminacy is an essential part of Keynes's GT it should again be stressed that much of the analysis in the GT is conducted in terms of (Marshallian) equilibrium states. As outlined in chapter 2, the assumption that (long–term) expectations are given implies that Keynes's position is different from the position of complete determinacy of expectations (rational expectations hypothesis) as well as of complete indeterminacy of expectations (Austrian position). In Keynes's view, uncertainty does not rule out determinate behaviour but this determinacy is not based on objective facts as in the theories that use rational expectations but on subjective facts (beliefs) that are the foundation of norms, conventions, etc. (see also Carabelli (1988), pp. 218–222). Secondly and even more importantly, there is an essential difference between Keynes and the Austrians in general and Hayek in particular on the implications of the coordination problem. It remains basically unclear in the Austrian approach what the implications of the coordination problem are for the behaviour of individual agents or, in other words, how agents are supposed to act upon the existence of this coordination problem. Furthermore, and opposed to Keynes, Austrians by and large do not address the question as to what makes a monetary economy fundamentally different from a barter economy. The Austrian position is that the price mechanism takes care of the coordination problem and that it is possible for money to be neutral in which case the monetary economy functions as if it were a barter economy. Keynes's position, on the other hand, is that the unhampered working of the price mechanism will not solve the coordination problem basically because a monetary economy is fundamentally different from a non–money using economy. The unhampered flexibility of prices may even aggravate the coordination problem. In chapters 6 and 7 we elaborate upon this second difference between Keynes and the Austrians in the analysis of chapter 17 of the GT and the implications of the role of money in a world in which uncertainty prevails.[27]

4.4 (Dis)Similarities between the alternative approaches

This section will use the foregoing discussion on post–Keynesian economics and Austrian economics to compare these alternative approaches. Both approaches are critical of mainstream economics and are neglected by mainstream economists. In chapter 8 we will argue that this neglect tends to overlook some interesting similarities between recent theoretical developments in mainstream economics and the alternative approaches of this chapter on the issue of coordination. In fact, the attempts to deal with Keynes's coordination issue in a general equilibrium framework (chapter 5) (start to) try to answer the same questions [28] as those which are at the heart of the analyses of some post–Keynesian and Austrian economists and which were essential in the writings of Keynes and Hayek in the 1930s.

A comparison of post–Keynesian and Austrian economics should start with the recognition that both approaches are characterized by heterogeneity. There is no such thing as *the* post–Keynesian or *the* Austrian approach. Apart from their mutual criticism of neo–classical economics, neo–Ricardians and Kaleckians, on the one hand, and Austrian economists, on the other hand, have next to nothing in common. The emphasis of the former on the analysis of aggregates (groups) and their use of the equilibrium concept are hard to reconcile with the subjectivistic approach of the latter. Matters are different if one compares the monetary post–Keynesians with the Austrians. As noticed in section 4.2, the former emphasize the importance of uncertainty and historical time and hence the importance of issues of coordination in their analyses. The coordination issue is also of prime importance in Austrian economics.[29] In both the analyses of monetary post–Keynesians and Austrian economics, the role of uncertainty and expectations are not only substituted for the corresponding neo–classical assumptions of risk and perfect foresight but they are also used to argue that the way neo–classical economics deals with expectations formation is incompatible with individual decision making. In emphasizing this incompatibility both approaches draw upon the same sources to some extent. One such example is Richardson (1960) in which the inconclusiveness of individual decision–making under perfect foresight is demonstrated for the case of investment decisions of individual firms under perfect competition.[30] The bottom line of this mutual criticism is the same as that of our criticism of the rational expectations hypothesis in chapter 3: the assumption of perfect foresight precludes the analysis of individual expectations formation with the result that expectations are in fact irrelevant for the analysis.[31] The dismissal of perfect foresight and its replacement by the role of uncertainty ultimately means that the coordination issue is at the heart of both the monetary post–Keynesian and the Austrian argument. But the similarity stops right there. The reaction of monetary post–Keynesians to the necessity to address the analytical *implications* of the coordination problem is to build upon the monetary analysis of Keynes's GT in which money, monetary commitments and institutions in general fulfil the role of partly determining economic activity in the absence of the invisible hand. As argued in the previous section the Austrian analysis of the implications of the coordination problem builds upon the role of prices as a transmitter of information and upon the (dynamic) forces of competition. It remains unclear, however, how prices and competition influence the acquisition of individual knowledge and, hence, how individual decisions lead to coordination improvements.[32] In our view, and here we agree with monetary post–Keynesians, the importance of the role of uncertainty in the GT is not so much that it substitutes indeterminacy for determinacy as is the case in Austrian economics. Rather the implications of uncertainty for analysing individual behaviour and the determination of economic activity are at stake. For instance, in his analysis of long–term expectations in chapter 12 of the GT, Keynes therefore remarks that

> we should not conclude from this [the analysis of long–term expectations–HG] that everything depends on waves of irrational psychology. On the contrary, the state of long–term expectations is often steady, and even when it is not, the other factors exert their compensating effects. We are merely reminding ourselves that human decisions affecting the future, whether personal or political or economic, cannot depend on strict mathematical expectation, since the basis for making such calculations does not exist; and that it is our innate urge to activity which makes the wheels go round, our rational selves choosing between the alternatives as best we are able, calculating where we can, but often falling back for our motive on whim or sentiment or chance. (Keynes, GT, pp. 162–163).

In practice, the steadiness of the state of long–term expectations is a result of the existence of conventions and institutions (see GT pp.

152-153[33]). Since these conventions or institutions are not only responsible for the steadiness of long-term expectations,[34] but are also the consequence of the existence of uncertainty (thus of indeterminacy) this steadiness may be subject to unpredictable and sudden changes. Or, in other words, conventions and institutions are only imperfect coordinating devices. In chapter 6 we elaborate upon the implications of uncertainty in our analysis of what is probably the best example of an institutional solution to the coordination problem, money. In that chapter we build upon insights that are discussed in the present chapter on (monetary) post-Keynesian and Austrian economics. As will be clear by now, the former are of more relevance for the subject of our study than the latter. It was stated in the introduction of this chapter that, apart from the alternative approaches under consideration, Keynes's coordination issue would also be analysed from a general equilibrium point of view. It is to this subject that we turn in the next chapter.

This rounds up our discussion of mainstream economics (chapter 3) and some alternative approaches (chapter 4) with respect to microfoundations, and the coordination problem. Our way of characterizing Keynes's GT by means of his analysis of the micro-macro and the indeterminacy issue can also be used to characterize the two forthcoming chapters. In the next chapter we will mainly elaborate upon those general equilibrium approaches in which the micro-macro issue and the indeterminacy issue are represented through the dismissal of the Walrasian auctioneer as an establisher of unique, stable Pareto-efficient equilibria. The emphasis in chapters 6 and 7 is on the consequences of the fundamental indeterminacy of the GT, the role of uncertainty, in terms of its implications for the usage of money and price-setting behaviour. Finally, it must again be stressed that the discussion of post-Keynesian and Austrian economics in the present chapter is not meant as a full-fledged survey of these theories. Our goal has been more modest, the discussion was meant to illustrate the claim that these theories have something to say as well on the objectives of our study as stated in chapter 1. The question whether post-Keynesian or Austrian economics constitute alternative paradigms in economic theory as well is beyond the scope of this study. Besides, given our plea for methodological pluralism in chapter 1, the search for the most appropriate theory to study the coordination issue is not considered to be very fruitful.

Appendix: Liquidity and mark-up pricing: two examples[35]

In monetary post-Keynesian economics, uncertainty as opposed to mathematical calculable risk is conceived as an outstanding feature of decentralized economies. This emphasis on uncertainty is admittedly of less importance in the Kaleckian or the neo–Ricardian version of post–Keynesian economics. But, an extension of the Kaleckian imperfect competition type of analysis or the Eichnerian internal funds argumentation with a justification of the mark–up based on a Bayesian framework as in Agliardi (1988) does not seem very fruitful. It substitutes the concept of risk for the concept of uncertainty. In this appendix we will briefly discuss two (related) theories in which the relation between the theory of value and uncertainty are at the heart of the analysis.

As has been mentioned above, in the post–Keynesian literature Keynes's aggregate supply and demand framework can be extended in order to incorporate mark–up pricing. From a microeconomic point of view the mark–up in Keynes's framework can indeed be thought to be determined by the degree of competition or by the need to generate internal funds for future investments. In that case one gets a microfoundation of macroeconomics along the lines of Kalecki and Eichner, respectively. However, it is also possible to take Keynes's monetary analysis, with its emphasis on the role of expectations and uncertainty in decentralized economies and, hence, the indeterminate part of the GT, as a starting point for a post–Keynesian theory of value. This line of reasoning leads to what might be called an example of 'macro' (monetary) foundation of microeconomics.

In the latter approach the mark–up can be conceived of as a variable measuring the degree of liquidity or, in other words, flexibility. In a world in which production takes time and in which today's decisions (for instance, how much to invest) have to be based on estimates or mere guesses of uncertain, future decisions by other agents, individual agents deliberately choose not to spend all of their current income, not to produce at full capacity etc. 'Choices that have to be made now are a part of a sequence of choices and this is where the concept of liquidity comes in' (Hicks (1974), pp. 38–39, we will return to this issue in chapter 7). Financial and non–financial liquidity increase the adaptability of economic subjects for it leaves open a broader range of choices as time goes by and more of what is now unknown becomes known. Just as saving is a form of financial liquidity and a hedge against an uncertain future excess capacity and inventories are examples of non–financial liquidity increasing the speed of adjustment when market conditions change.[36] Excess capacity and inventories are both examples of quantity variables that may enhance the liquidity or, in other words, the flexibility of a firm when uncertainty prevails. Following the same line of reasoning, mark–up pricing might be looked upon as an example of a *price* instrument that enhances the flexibility of an individual firm in a world of uncertainty. The mark–up might be looked upon as a buffer of liquidity. Anticipating the discussion on nominal stickiness in chapter 7, it can be argued that price adjustments are not without their costs. These costs may arise for various reasons but in this study it is argued that full price flexibility is not compatible with the existence of money and that therefore some degree of nominal price stickiness is warranted for money to fulfil its functions. In the case that full price flexibility is not necessarily to be preferred by firms, the mark–up may act as a buffer against shocks because it provides firms flexibility as they need not change their prices every time a shock occurs. The existence of a mark–up increases the adaptibility of firms in terms of price–setting behaviour. Firms confronted with their average (labour) costs and their expected proceeds choose the level of the mark–up in order to arrive at a level of employment and output that allows them to adapt to yet unforeseen contingencies. Given the reluctance of firms to change nominal prices in the presence of costs of price adjustment a mark–up supplies room to manoeuvre and to postpone price adjustments.

In this approach mark–up pricing is based on Hicks's interpretation of Keynes's liquidity preference theory in Hicks (1974). This view of pricing under uncertainty has the important implication that one of the central issues of the debate about determining the mark–up loses much of its relevance for there is no such thing as a calculable optimum degree of the mark–up in case of uncertainty. 'Both Keynes and Hicks seem to be arguing that one's choice of liquidity, be it financial as Keynes discussed or non–financial as Hicks noted, is not a variable that is amendable to Marshallian optimization analysis. The type of flexibility or liquidity that is appropriate for any conceivable situation always depends on the value of variables that cannot easily be determined. However, knowledge of the variables affecting the choice of an optimum plan would be essential for the usual neoclassical explanation even when those variables are thought to be merely stochastic disturbances.' (Boland (1986), p.152). Agents can influence the need to remain liquid (or, equivalently, flexible) by fixing nominal commitments. Contracts or, more general, institutional arrangements increase the possibility of predicting the future value of money and hence decrease the need for liquidity since the environment becomes more predictable for the individual firm. In other words, this view on uncertainty and liquidity results in what Shackle (1972) called the role of prices as conventions.

The idea that Keynes's monetary analysis also contains a theory of relative prices has a long–standing tradition in post–Keynesian economics. This leads us to the second example of pricing under uncertainty. Immediately after the publication of the GT, Townshend (1937) pointed out that Keynes's theory of liquidity preference has important consequences for the theory of value. More recently, Kregel (1982A,B, 1987) has time and again emphasized the importance of chapter 12 and especially chapter 17 of Keynes's GT in order to explain the relation between prices, liquidity preference and uncertainty. In chapter 17 of the GT (see, for instance, Davidson (1978), Minsky (1975) and again Shackle (1972)) Keynes explains why a market economy may not automatically tend to full–employment. It is argued that ultimately two essential properties, a zero substitution elasticity and a zero production elasticity of money, cause a policy of *laissez – faire* to be inimical to a return to full–employment. The neo–classical substitution argument would therefore apply to all goods but money. An analysis of these essential properties is beyond the scope of this example and has to wait until chapter 6. What is important in the context of this example is the way in which Keynes sets out his portfolio theory in chapter 17. In Keynes's theory as opposed to the neo–classical theory, the rates of return on the capital assets adjust to the liquidity premium (the rate of return on money) in order to establish a portfolio equilibrium. This liquidity premium[37] is determined by the degree of liquidity preference and hence by uncertainty. The rate of return on money sets a standard for the profitability of the production of new assets (and hence for investment). Keynes's analysis in chapter 17 is based upon Sraffa's concept of the own rates of interest and hence the analysis is cast in terms of spot and forward prices. In a long–term portfolio equilibrium the various rates of return are equalised and spot and forward prices on any asset are equal, which implies that prices are equal to the costs of production. Whenever spot and forward prices diverge prices do not equal the costs of production (see Kregel (1987), pp. 528–531). The difference between prices and costs might be referred to as a mark–up. Since the rate of return on money sets the standard for all other assets in this approach prices and costs (and thus the mark–up) are influenced by the degree of liquidity preference. In this way prices and uncertainty are connected (see also Rymes (1989)). The details of both examples need not concern us here since these examples are only meant to illustrate that, apart from the imperfect competition type of argumention, a post–Keynesian explanation of the mark–up might also result if the role of money and uncertainty is taken into account.

Notes

[1]For want of a better name, we use the word 'alternative' to set these approaches apart from mainstream economics as discussed in chapter 3.

[2]For a survey of post–Keynesian economics see, for instance, Eichner and Kregel (1975), Reynolds (1987), Harcourt (1985), Carvalho (1985) and Hamouda and Harcourt (1989).

[3]It is important to point out that the use of equilibrium concepts in post–Keynesian economics should be distinguished from the use of this concept in a general equilibrium framework. In the latter, equilibrium is related to the question of market clearing. In post–Keynesian economics either a Marshallian concept of equilibrium is employed (e.g. the monetary post–Keynesians) or a classical concept in which a (long–run) equilibrium is established if rates of return (the profit rate) are equalized.

[4]For an assesment of these theories of income distribution see Pen (1971).

[5]Compare with Keynes's analysis of the Widow's Cruse in Keynes (1930).

[6]According to Kregel (1987) 'Keynes did not make *any* assumption concerning the degree of competition except that it was constant' (Kregel (1987), p.490 and the GT, p. 245); see also section 3.4.1.

[7]'it is thus not an imperfection in the operation of the flexible price mechanism in determining which is at the basis of Keynes' unemployment equilibrium, it is rather the imperfection of agents' knowledge causing uncertainty over the propositions determining the return of investment projects. Neither is the absence of a sufficient microfoundation the cause of the macroeconomic result of unemployment equilibrium; it is rather due to (...) *the determination of one crucial price, the rate of interest, by convential factors because of the existence of uncertain knowledge*' (Kregel (1987B), p. 531, emphasis added). Rogers (1989) gives a fairly detailed account of post–Keynesian monetary theory along these lines; see also Rousseas (1985).

[8]Though the importance of uncertainty for an understanding of the GT in general and for explaining the role of money in particular is emphasized by monetary post–Keynesians it has only been in recent years that the theoretical foundation of Keynes's concept of uncertainty and especially the relation between *The Treatise on Probability* and the GT in this respect starts to get analysed. Our discussion of O'Donnell (1990) in section 2.6 illustrates that the recent literature on the foundation of Keynes's concept of uncertainty centres around the determinacy/indeterminacy distinction that is also at the heart of the monetary post–Keynesian literature. See also *e.g.* Carabelli (1988) and Hoogduin (1991) for an analysis of Keynes's concept of uncertainty and its implications for the usage of money.

[9]Though the influence of Keynes (1937B) is also important; see *e.g.* Shackle (1967, 1972). In chapter 6 we will elaborate upon the connection money–uncertainty and upon chapter 17 of the GT. In post–Keynesian monetary theory, the interest rate is a monetary phenomenon determined by the supply of and demand for liquidity. This in contrast with neo–classical theory where the interest rate is (at least to some extent) a real variable determined by savings and investment (see also section 7.5). One way to handle uncertainty is through forward contracting (the money wage contract!; see also section 4.2.2.) but a complete system of forward markets, eliminating uncertainty, cannot exist since it implies a denial of the very existence of uncertainty .

[10]An influential study in this respect is Pasinetti (1977).

[11]As in our discussion of mainstream theories in chapter 3 this does not imply a verdict of these theories as such. Our assessment only sheds some light on the relevance of these approaches for the purpose of this thesis.

[12]This criticism also applies to Marxian theory in our view. Here also macro (aggregated) variables are the focal point of the analysis since micro (individual behaviour) is thought to be determined by macro. Issues of coordination only arise between these macro variables. It will be clear that this is at odds with our search for 'macro'foundations for microeconomics since we are concerned with the implications of coordination problems for individual behaviour.

[13]See the note on p. 223 of the GT. This connection has been used by some post-Keynesian authors, for instance, Nell (1983) to argue that Keynes's analysis in this chapter should be based upon Sraffian foundations, see also section 6.3. For an attempt in this direction see Panico (1988).

[14]See also Tarshis (1980) on this issue.

[15]This also holds for the conclusion of excess capacity that goes along with this price equation. Note that this equivalence in the formulation of the price as a mark-up over costs does *not* imply that the conclusions that follow from the Kaleckian micro-macro connection are equivalent to their neo-classical counterpart. The fact that marginal costs are assumed to be constant in the former and are (often) assumed to be rising in the latter implies that both theories reach for instance opposite conclusions as to the role of demand factors in determining output.

[16]Blanchard (1989) in describing the main elements of new-Keynesian economics recognizes this for he refers to Kaldor (1972) in his assessment that many of the new-Keynesian themes 'are hardly new and one cannot help feel that history of thought repeats itself' (Blanchard (1989), p. 258).

[17]Whether the aggregate supply curve is based on short-run Marshallian profit maximization, as Keynes claims, is much debated in the literature. For a negative assessment see Patinkin (1976, 1982) and for a support of Keynes's claim see Casarosa (1981), Dickson (1983), Brady (1990), and also Davidson and Smolensky (1964) and Weintraub (1958). For an analysis of the fact that Keynes did adhere to some variable cost pricing rule see also Rotheim (1981).

[18]Note that this does not imply that each agent is also in expectational equilibrium. Individual equilibrium does not exclude that expectations are disappointed.

[19]In our view it is more appropriate to link Lucas (1973) with Wicksellian monetary theory in general of which Hayek's theory is just one example. What really connects Lucas's approach with the Wicksellian approach is the natural rate property.

[20]Our analysis of Hayek (1937) follows Caldwell (1988) and O'Driscoll (1977).

[21]This implies that Lucas's comparison of his theory with Hayek's monetary business cycle theory is really off the mark.

[22]See Hayek (1946), pp. 105–106. For a very good analysis of the Austrian view on competition see Kirzner (1973). Competition ensures that the working of the market process leads to coordination improvements, Austrians envisage competition as dynamic and oppose their view on competition to the static interpretation of competition in neo–classical theory.

[23]The influence of Austrian ideas on the so–called new–institutionalist economics (see Langlois (1986)) is therefore not very surprising. Note that Hayek has (somewhat) turned away from the original explanation of the coordination issue (role of prices and competition) and has instead also emphasized the importance of rules and norms (see chapter 8 of this thesis).

[24]Hence, in terms of Hayek's analysis as outlined in section 4.3.1 it remains unclear how the process that gives agents the required knowledge for a general equilibrium should be conceived. The price mechanism appears to be a coordinating device that is imposed on the market process without making clear how the price mechanism changes individual knowledge. (see also Snippe (1987)). For a similar observation see Hahn (1984), p. 128.

[25]There are, of course, notable exceptions. The post–Keynesian Shackle and the Austrian Lachmann, for instance, have always had an eye for the subjectivistic part of the GT. Among the reasons that the relation between this part of the GT and Austrian economics has not been recognized from the outset is also Hayek's refusal to react to the GT. In later years (see Hayek (1976A) and (1976B)) Hayek's criticism of Keynesianism and its inflationary bias did not concern the analytical structure of the GT but was directed at mainstream Keynesianism in which (see chapter 3) solely the determinate part of the GT is taken seriously.

[26]In the neo–classical interpretation of Keynes's liquidity preference theory, mainstream portfolio theory, money becomes just another store of value and the relation between uncertainty (knowledge) and money goes unnoticed. In chapter 6 (see especially section 6.2.) the role of money in an economy where uncertainty prevails will be analysed at length.

[27]For a similar view of this difference between Keynes and the Austrians see e.g. Snippe (1987).

[28]Of course, in a rather different analytical framework, but as we argued in chapter 1, our plea for methodological pluralism implies that it is worthwhile to strip these questions from the particular framework in which they are cast.

[29]For a similar observation see O'Driscoll and Rizzo (1985), p. 9. The fact that Keynes's, the post–Keynesian and Austrian interpretation of uncertainty are not one and the same need not concern us here, but see Hoogduin (1991), pp. 48–50.

[30]For an Austrian example of the use of this study see O'Driscoll and Rizzo (1985) and for a post–Keynesian example see Earl (1983).

[31]See Bausor (1983) as to the incompatibilty of the rational expectations hypothesis and the concept of historical time as employed by (some) post–Keynesians and Austrians. 'Rational expectations analysis is equilibrium analysis. The actual contracting, producing and accumulating that people accomplish, as well as macroeconomic stabilisation policy, do not, on average matter. Tethered to its preordained equilibrium the model is trapped in logical time' (Bausor (1983), p. 9).

[32]Within Austrian economics there are some differences as to the (assumed) coordinating capacities of markets. Sticking solely to subjectivism implies that the analysis reduces to the analysis at the level of the individual agent or more aptly the individual entrepreneur. In this situation the coordination issue loses much of its relevance. Indeterminacy reigns in that case. Emphasizing the coordinating function of markets implies that the coordination problem becomes relatively more one of the interaction of agents and of the various ways of dealing with coordination through rules and institutions. Note that in his more recent writings Hayek also emphasizes the role of rules and institutions in his analysis of pattern coordination; see chapter 8.

[33]In *The General Theory of Employment* (Keynes, 1937B, pp. 114–115) Keynes reaches a similar conclusion. The need to act in a world characterized by uncertainty leads to the prevalence of conventional judgements. See also Carabelli (1988) and Hodgson (1988) on this issue.

[34]This steadiness enables Keynes to take long–term expectations as given in the main part of the GT (see chapter 2) and therefore enables the analysis of the *determination* of the level of effective demand. It also explains why Keynes and monetary post–Keynesians still adhere to a standard (Marshallian) equilibrium concept as opposed to Austrian economists.

[35]This appendix is based upon Garretsen (1990) which was intended as a comment upon Agliardi (1988). Agliardi (1988) analyses some post–Keynesian theories of mark–up pricing. In particular the author elaborates upon two prominent contributions to the post–Keynesian theory of value namely the pricing models of Kalecki and of Eichner. The theoretical foundation of the mark–up model is thought to be weak and Agliardi therefore formulates a model in which the mark–up is explained by the fact that risk–neutral firms are 'uncertain' about the demand conditions for their products. In Agliardi's model the concept of uncertainty is not used in the sense of Keynes or Knight since each firm is able to attach a probability distribution to the respective demand functions. Our comment on Agliardi was not intended as a dismissal of the analysis as such; rather it was meant to illustrate that the explanation of the mark–up by means of uncertainty in the sense of Keynes is also in line with post–Keynesian economics.

[36]Note that this demand for liquidity is a *micro* demand for liquidity. It provides the individual agent flexibility in case uncertainty prevails but it enlarges the degree of uncertainty for the economy as a whole at the same time.

[37]This liquidity premium is the rate of return on money and should as such be distinguished from the concept of liquidity or flexibility in our first example.

5 Indeterminacy and Multiplicity

5.1 Introduction

The assessment of the mainstream microfoundations debate in chapter 3 led to the conclusion that the foundation of Keynes's economics in a general equilibrium setting has to be based upon the analysis of strategic behaviour (multiplicity) and/or the indeterminacy of equilibria (indeterminacy). In this way a general equilibrium foundation of Keynes's economics that does *not* a priori rely on a specific price or wage stickiness assumption is possible. This is important because, as has become clear in chapter 3, the majority of attempts to incorporate the economics of Keynes in a general equilibrium framework has focused upon the necessity of imposing frictions on the working of the price mechanism. In this chapter we argue that the longstanding tradition in mainstream economics to associate Keynesian economics solely with price or wage rigidities does not suffice as a foundation of the economics of Keynes and that in terms of the coordination problem the inclusion of strategic behaviour or indeterminacy are more fruitful in this respect. Both the inclusion of strategic behaviour or, more general, of complementarity as well as of the indeterminacy feature can be looked upon as illustrations of our micro–macro and indeterminacy argument of chapter 2 in a general equilibrium framework. From the analysis in the preceding chapters it will be clear, however, that any foundation of Keynes's ideas within a general equilibrium framework is necessarily flawed and incomplete. But this does not imply that the question as to whether and how these ideas can be incorporated in a general equilibrium framework does not deserve any further attention. On the contrary, the main objective of the present chapter is to argue that Keynes's analysis of the micro–macro and the indeterminacy issue has its counterpart in the general equilibrium approach of analysing the implications of strategic behaviour and the indeterminacy of equilibria in overlapping generations models.

From the outset it should be made clear that the main part of this chapter deals with the implications of the indeterminacy argument. The coordination failures framework which is based on strategic complementarity is used only in sections 5.2 and 5.3 as far as the ideas of complementarity and heterogeneity of agents are concerned.

This chapter is organized as follows. In section 5.2, which constitutes the main part of this chapter, we develop a multi-sector overlapping generations (hereafter OLG) model in order to show how some elements of the GT can be captured once indeterminacy and the heterogeneity of agents are allowed for. OLG models are characterized by the indeterminacy of equilibrium and this serves as a proxy for Keynes's fundamental indeterminacy, the role of uncertainty. From the coordination failures literature we use the idea that a one-sector analysis is qualitatively different from an aggregate analysis. The model in this section is real and the implications of incorporating money in our model will be discussed in section 5.3. It turns out that money in an OLG model is quite a different thing from money in Keynes's GT. In section 5.3 the issue of money in a general equilibrium framework is only briefly touched upon since chapters 6 and 7 of our thesis also deal with this topic. Section 5.4 deals with three issues. First of all, we briefly discuss how our OLG model relates to the coordination failures framework. Secondly, we analyse how e.g. an OLG model may give rise to expectations driven business cycles. Finally, we briefly address the Keynesian content of these theories. Do these approaches, including our own model, really imply an extension of Keynes's analysis of the coordination problem or not? Section 5.5 concludes this chapter.

5.2 Indeterminacy in a Keynesian OLG Model

5.2.1 Introduction

OLG models emphasize the indeterminacy of equilibrium;[1] the theory of coordination failures elaborates upon Keynes's distinction between a one sector (micro) and an aggregate (macro) analysis. But in this section we want to make clear that both approaches only stress a part of the argument. Cooper and John (1988) already suggested to extend their analysis of coordination failures to a dynamic setting in which one could focus upon the role of expectations. In this section we build a multi-sector OLG model in which both arguments are combined.

Our discussion of the OLG model is organized as follows. First of all, a brief overview of the basic elements of Keynes's GT is presented and the incorporation of these elements in the subsequent developments in general equilibrium theory is discussed. Secondly, we show that equilibrium quantities are undetermined in our model and we discuss the most natural way in which the indeterminacy can be resolved from a Keynesian perspective. Thirdly, we develop a multi–sector extension of the model. The multi–sector model gives rise to multiplier effects, because of demand externalities between sectors.

5.2.2 Keynes and the classics in a general equilibrium framework

The theoretical foundation of Keynes's denial of the validity of the second and the third classical postulate (see chapter 2 of our study) for analysing the economy as a whole constitutes the heart of the *General Theory*. In chapter 2 we showed how the structure of the GT can be explained once the analytical importance of the dismissal of the second (real wage equals the marginal disutility of labour) and the third (Say's Law holds) classical postulate is recognized. The discussion of the structure of Keynes's GT and of his version of classical theory in chapter 2 illustrates the following two analytical points of this section. The first point is that the main differences between Keynes and the Classics arise from two essential features of Keynes's analysis. First of all, the significance of money, uncertainty and expectations in Keynes's economics is a result of the fact that the economic system in the GT, as opposed to the classical theory, is characterized by what we have called a fundamental indeterminacy. A second crucial feature of the GT is the recognition that variables that may be taken as given on the level of the individual agent are no longer given for the economy as a whole. The second point is that subsequent developments in macroeconomic theory in which an attempt has been made to incorporate Keynes's ideas into a general equilibrium framework are characterized by a general neglect of these two features. Recent developments in general equilibrium theory focus, however, precisely on the consequences of incorporating these two analytical features in a general equilibrium framework. Two types of recent research are particularly important in this respect: the indeterminacy of equilibrium in overlapping generations (OLG) models (see e.g. Geanakoplos and Polemarchakis (1986) and Woodford (1988)) and the coordination failures literature (see e.g. Cooper and John (1988) and Roberts (1987)).

Indeterminacy of equilibrium is essential to Keynesian type OLG models. In the standard Walrasian general equilibrium model there is no indeterminacy, because in that model economic activity has a definite beginning and end. We agree, however, with Geanakoplos and Polemarchakis (1986) who argue that 'for some purposes economic activity is better described as a process without end. In a world without definite end, there is the possibility that what happens today is underdetermined, because it depends on what people expect to happen tomorrow, which in turn depends on what people tomorrow expect to happen the day after tomorrow, etc.' (Geanakoplos and Polemarchakis (1986), p. 755). The indeterminacy of equilibria in OLG models directs attention to the role of expectations in general equilibrium economics. The indeterminacy of equilibrium can be resolved by choosing the variables that are not determined within the model and by specifying rules by which these variables are fixed.

The theory of coordination failures essentially argues that representative agent models may be misleading for macroeconomic analysis. If multiple individuals or sectors are distinguished in an economy, Keynesian phenomena can be understood as resulting from the difficulty individual agents or sectors face to coordinate their activities. Representative agent models typically assume some sort of coordination. The indeterminacy of equilibria and the heterogeneity of agents are used in this section to illuminate the idea that the incorporation of Keynes's indeterminacy and micro–macro issue in a general equilibrium model[2] do not solely depend on some fix price assumption. One of the limitations of the general equilibrium framework should be made clear before we present our model. General equilibrium theory does not offer a full–fledged monetary theory (see also Hahn (1988)). The role of money and uncertainty in Keynes's analysis is clearly at odds with general equilibrium theory. Instead of introducing money by means of a rather artificial cash in advance constraint as in most OLG models (and as in our model in section 5.3) we have chosen to abstract from the introduction of money in this section. The main reason is that the introduction of money in our model would imply that the non–producible good money would act as a perfect vehicle for the intertemporal substitution of purchasing power. We will return to this point in section 5.3. in our discussion of the monetary version of our model.

5.2.3 The one sector OLG model[3]
Mainly for didactic purposes we start our analysis by considering a one sector version of our OLG model which uses the framework as initially developed by Diamond (1965).[4] The basic structure of our model is as follows. In each period one generation of households, consisting of identical agents, is born that lives for two periods. In period t two generations of households are alive in our economy: those born in period t (the young) and those born in period $t-1$ (the old). Households are endowed with a quantity of labour (l_0) only in the first period of their lives. Income from labour $W(t)l(t)$ can be spent on consumption goods or it can be saved. Labour is the numeraire so the price of labour $W(t)$ is equal to one. Savings in period t take the form of new capital in period $t+1$, which in period t is a perfect substitute for the consumption good. The price of the consumption good in period t is $p(t)$ in terms of labour. Capital $k(t+1)$ produced in period t becomes productive in period $t+1$. For simplicity it is assumed that capital does not have a resale value and that it lasts only one period. Productive capital is not a substitute for consumption goods. The nominal rental rate for holding

a capital good (depreciation included) is $\rho(t+1)$.

Households derive utility from consuming goods in the two periods of their life. Leisure does not enter the utility function. Households of generation t are assumed to solve the following problem. (Subscripts refer to generations; the relevant time period is placed between brackets: $c_t(t+1)$ thus refers to the consumption of generation t in period $t+1$). Again, since labour is the numéraire, $W(t) = 1$.

$$\max \ U_t = \gamma_1 ln \ c_t(t) + \gamma_2 ln \ c_t(t+1) \qquad \gamma_1, \gamma_2 > 0$$

$$\text{s.t.} \quad p(t)c_t(t) + p(t)k(t+1) \qquad \leq l(t)$$

$$p(t+1)c_t(t+1) \qquad\qquad \leq \rho(t+1)k(t+1)$$

$$c_t(t), c_t(t+1), k(t+1) \qquad \geq 0$$

The two budget constraints can also be written in real terms. We define $w(t) \equiv 1/p(t)$ and $1+r(t+1) \equiv \rho(t+1)/p(t+1)$. $1+r(t+1)$ is the real rental rate on capital in terms of goods. The budget constraints can then be rewritten as

$$c_t(t) + (\frac{1}{1+r(t+1)})c_t(t+1) \leq w(t)l(t).$$

Demand functions for consumption goods by generation t become

$$c_t(t) = \frac{\gamma_1}{\gamma_1+\gamma_2} \ w(t)l(t) \quad \text{and} \tag{5.1}$$

$$c_t(t+1) = (1+(r(t+1))k(t+1) = \frac{\gamma_2}{\gamma_1+\gamma_2} (1+r(t+1))w(t)l(t) \tag{5.2}$$

In each period $t+1$ firms transform $k(t+1)$ units of capital goods produced in period t, together with $l(t+1)$ units of labour into

$$y(t+1) = [k(t+1)]^\alpha [l(t+1)]^{1-\alpha} \tag{5.3}$$

units of the consumption good in period $t+1$. Firms demand goods for investment purposes and labour in order to maximize profits. Investment becomes productive capital with a delay of one period. Firms obtain the funds necessary to finance the investment activities by issuing bonds in period t that pay $\rho(t+1)$ per unit in period $t+1$. Demand for investment purposes depends on the expectations firms hold with respect to the following period. As we assume perfect foresight these expectations are equal to the realized values. Under competitive conditions these demand functions read as

$$k(t+1) = \alpha \frac{y(t+1)}{(1+r(t+1))} \qquad \text{and} \qquad (5.4)$$

$$l(t) = k(t)\left[(1-\alpha)\ \frac{1}{w(t)}\right]^{1/\alpha} \qquad (5.5)$$

The demand for labour determines, together with the available capital, the supply of goods. Alternatively, the demand for labour can be inferred from the supply of goods. Supply of goods can be written as

$$y(t) = k(t)\left[(1-\alpha)\ \frac{1}{w(t)}\right]^{(1-\alpha)/\alpha} \qquad (5.6)$$

Note that firms should make their investment decision in period t on the basis of their *expectations* of $r(t+1)$ and $y(t+1)$. Without an expectation about the quantity variable $y(t+1)$ the demand for capital would be indeterminate. This can be easily checked by substituting equation (6) applied to period $t+1$ in equation (5.4): $k(t+1)$ drops out and one obtains the factor price frontier. This observation becomes particularly relevant if multiple sectors are distinguished.

Equilibrium

There are three markets in the economy: a goods market, a labour market and a bonds market. In chapter 2 we have argued that in Keynes's analysis workers may be off their supply curve of labour and hence that the level of employment is not determined on the labour market and households may be rationed. We assume that the demand for labour $l(t)$ is less than or equal to the inelastic labour supply l_0. The assumption that the labour market does not clear is a main difference with Geanakoplos and Polemarchakis (1986). As a labour market clearing condition is lacking there is only one independent market clearing condition left. Equilibrium on the goods market in period t takes the following form.

$$\frac{\gamma_1}{\gamma_1+\gamma_2}\ w(t)l(t)\ +\ (1+r(t))k(t)\ +\ \alpha\frac{y(t+1)}{(1+r(t+1))}\ =\ y(t).$$

From the production structure of the economy and from the assumption that expectations are realized it follows that

$$y(t) = w(t)l(t) + (1+r(t))k(t).$$

We can thus rewrite the goods market equilibrium equation as

$$k(t+1) = \frac{\gamma_2}{\gamma_1+\gamma_2} \, w(t)l(t) = \frac{\gamma_2(1-\alpha)}{\gamma_1+\gamma_2} \, y(t). \tag{5.7}$$

Assuming that $k(t)$ is historically given we have one equation to determine three unknowns ($y(t)$, $y(t+1)$ and $r(t+1)$).[5] The degree of indeterminacy is thus equal to two. There is a variety of ways by means of which the system can be described. Perhaps the most transparent one is the following. Assume that $l(t)$ and $l(t+1)$ are determined outside the context of our model. Then we can express the system as

$$k(t+1) = f\left[k(t), \begin{pmatrix} l(t) \\ l(t+1) \end{pmatrix}\right]. \tag{5.8}$$

In this representation $y(t)$ is determined, via equation (5.3), by $k(t)$ and $l(t)$, whereas equation (5.7) determines $k(t+1)$. The interest rate $r(t+1)$ is determined by the fact that $1+r(t+1)$ must equal the marginal efficiency of capital $\alpha[k(t+1)/l(t+1)]^{\alpha-1}$ (see equation (5.4)) and $w(t+1)$ is determined by equation (5.5). If $l(t+2)$ is chosen exogenously, then the same argument determines the values of the variables in period $t+2$.

Equation (5.8) reveals that the dimension of the family of equilibria increases with one for each subsequent period. In case we consider the model for T periods the dimension of the set of equilibria thus equals $T+1$. This is stated in the proposition below. The degree of indeterminacy increases with the number of periods, because a market clearing condition for the labour market is missing. Adding labour market equilibrium conditions brings the dimensionality of equilibria back to one.

In fact, we only analyse the behaviour of the model for period 0 for we are only interested in the indeterminacy features of our model and not in the steady–state solution. In section 5.4 we will show how the analysis of the dynamic behaviour of these models like our OLG model can be used to create Keynesian phenomena. Given the (comparative) static nature of the analysis in this section it is, however, important to know whether the model is consistent over a larger number of periods.

Proposition 1 Let $k(0)>0$ be historically given. If the economy described above is considered for T subsequent periods there is a $T+1$–dimensional family of equilibria which can be indexed by the employment levels $l(t)>0$, $t=0,..,T$.
Proof For any $k(0)>0$ any $l(0)$ can be chosen such that $y(0)>0$ (see equation 3). According to equation (7), $k(1)$ is then positive as well. Choose a $l(1)>0$ and the same argument establishes that $k(2)>0$,

etc. So, if $l(t) > 0$, $t = 0,1,2,...$, is chosen exogeneously $k(t)$ and $y(t)$, $t = 0,1,2,...$, are both positive. Equations (5.4) and (5.5) show that $1 + r(t)$ and $w(t)$, $t = 0,1,2,...$, are also positive.

The indeterminacy is resolved by choosing the variables that are not determined within the model and by specifying rules by which these variables are fixed (see also Geanakoplos and Polemarchakis (1986)). Depending on the choice of exogenous variables Keynesian and classical results can be obtained in our model. We concentrate on the Keynesian results. In chapter 2 we argued that in Keynes's GT, as opposed to classical theory, the level of employment is determined on the goods market. The level of employment and the marginal productivity of labour determine the real wage rate. Keynes considered the level of nominal wages as being determined outside the context of the model and used labour as a numeraire in most of the GT. Therefore and also because there does not exist a rigorous theory of nominal rigidities, we take $W(t)$ as equal to unity as labour is thus the numeraire.

The fact that aggregate income clears the goods market implies that the rate of interest does not equilibrate savings and investment. Savings depend on the level of aggregate income and the level of investment is determined by expectations with respect to the real rate of return on investment and the future demand for goods. In what follows we take the return on investment $\rho(t+1)/p(t+1)$ and the demand for goods in the next period $y(t+1)$ instead of $l(t)$ and $l(t+1)$ (see equation (5.8)) as exogenous in our Keynesian OLG model.

In order to derive classical results the indeterminacy can be resolved by choosing the real wage rate $w(t)$, which equals $1/p(t)$, and the demand for goods $y(t+1)$ as exogenous variables. In that case the level of employment is determined by aggregate supply (equation (5.6)) and the rate of return on investment clears the goods market and hence equilibrates savings and investment.

5.2.4 A multi-sector extension and two fallacies of composition

Above we emphasized the indeterminacy of equilibria as an important element of Keynes's economics in a general equilibrium framework. The present subsection elaborates upon the micro–macro issue by focusing upon the distinction between a micro and a macro analysis through a multi–sector extension of the model. Each generation consists of a large number of identical individuals per sector. For convenience behaviour is modelled in terms of representative agents *per sector*. It is further assumed that households possess sector–specific labour so that there is no labour mobility between sectors. There is one firm per sector and each firm issues its own bonds. Households regard bonds from different sectors as perfect substitutes.

First of all, it is probably illuminating to devote some attention to the notation we have chosen. Subscripts i, j and h refer to the sector from which goods are demanded; a subscript t refers to the generation; n is the number of sectors. A superscript i denotes the sector that demands: $c^i_{jt}(t+1)$ denotes the demand for consumption goods of sector j in period $t+1$ by sector i's generation t. Where no confusion is possible, sub– and superscripts are dropped to facilitate reading. The utility function of the household in sector i belonging to generation t is of a generalized Cobb–Douglas form.

$$U^i_t = \gamma_1 ln \; c^i_t(t) + \gamma_2 ln \; c^i_t(t+1),$$

where $c^i_t(t) = \prod^n_{j=1} c^\lambda_{jt}(t) \quad \lambda = 1/n.$

Budget constraints can be written as:

$$\sum^n_{j=1} p_j(t)c^i_j(t) + \sum^n_{j=1} p_j(t)k^i_j(t+1) \leq W^i(t)l^i(t)$$
$$\sum^n_{j=1} p_j(t+1)c^i_j(t+1) \leq \sum^n_{j=1} \rho_j(t+1)k^i_j(t+1)$$

In this multi–sector version of our model labour from sector 1 is assumed to be the numeraire so $W_1(t) = 1$. This means that $W_i(t)$, for i is unequal to 1, is endogenous. So $W_2(t)$ is the price of labour of sector 2 in terms of labour of sector 1. A final remark as to labour concerns the abundancy of labour. It is assumed that for every sector the supply of labour is greater than the demand for labour.

Utility maximization leads to demand functions for period t of the following form.

$$c^i_{jt}(t) = \frac{\lambda \gamma_1}{\gamma_1 + \gamma_2} \; \frac{W^i(t)l^i(t)}{p_j(t)} \tag{5.1'}$$

$$c^i_{j,t-1}(t) = \frac{\sum^n_{h=1} \lambda \rho_h(t)k^i_h(t)}{p_j(t)} \tag{5.2'}$$

On the part of the behaviour of firms we have to specify the way a firm's capital stock is composed. For simplicity we assume that the capital stock of sector i is composed of all *other* goods and that the productive capital stock is $(n-1)$ times the minimum of all the other goods available for investment purposes. We also assume that goods from different sectors are identical in order to enable aggregation of capital goods as in equation (5.3').

$$k^i(t) = (n-1) \min_{j \neq i} k_j(t) \quad \text{and}$$

$$y_i(t) = [(n-1) \min_{j \neq i} k_j(t)]^{\alpha} l^i(t)^{1-\alpha} \tag{5.3'}$$

This implies that (compare with our one–sector model)

$$k_j^i(t+1) = \alpha \frac{y_i(t+1) \, p_i(t+1)}{1 + r_i(t+1)(n-1)p_j(t+1)} \quad \text{and} \tag{5.4'}$$

$$l^i(t) = k^i(t) \left[(1-\alpha) \frac{p_i(t)}{W_i(t)} \right]^{1/\alpha}. \tag{5.5'}$$

The equilibrium equations take on the following form. Demand for a sector's production stems from the young and old consumers of *all* sectors and the firms of *all other* sectors. Hence, equilibrium on the n goods markets can be written as $(j = 1,..n)$

$$\Sigma_{i=1}^n \left\{ \frac{\lambda \gamma_1}{\gamma_1 + \gamma_2} \frac{W^i(t)l^i(t)}{p_j(t)} + \frac{\Sigma_{h=1}^n \lambda \rho_h(t) k_h^i(t)}{p_j(t)} \right\} + \Sigma_{i \neq j}^n \frac{\alpha p_i(t+1) y_i(t+1)}{(n-1) \rho_i(t+1)} =$$

$$y_j(t) \tag{5.9}$$

The left–hand side of equation (5.9) shows the level of consumption (consumption of the young and dissavings of the old, respectively) and the level of investment in this period. Using $\Sigma_{h=1}^n \rho_h(t) k_h^i(t) = \alpha p_i(t) y_i(t)$ [6] and $W^i(t) l^i(t) = (1-\alpha) p_i(t) y_i(t)$ and finally $k_j^i = k_j/n - 1$ this equation can be rewritten as $(j = 1,..,n)$

$$\lambda \Sigma_{i \neq j}^n \left\{ \left[\frac{\gamma_1(1-\alpha)}{\gamma_1 + \gamma_2} + \alpha \right] \frac{p_i(t) y_i(t)}{p_j(t)} + \frac{n}{(n-1)} k_i(t+1) \right\} =$$

$$\left\{ \frac{(1-\lambda)\gamma_1 + (1-\alpha\lambda)\gamma_2}{\gamma_1 + \gamma_2} \right\} y_j(t) \tag{5.10}$$

Equation (5.10) reveals a complementarity (positive interdependence) between sectors: an increase in production in sector i leads to higher demand for sector j products (see also Cooper and John (1988)). The complementarity between sectors gives rise to multiplier effects. To see this, assume that prices are equal across sectors, $p_i(t) = p_j(t)$ and also assume that $r_i(t+1)$ and $y_i(t+1)$ $i = 1,..,n$ are determined outside the context of the model. Equation (5.10) can then be rewritten as

$$\mathbf{y(t)} = \mathbf{A} + \mathbf{By(t)},$$

where $\mathbf{y(t)} = (y_1(t),..,y_n(t))'$ is a $n \times 1$ vector and $\mathbf{A}$ is a $n \times 1$ vector and $\mathbf{B}$ is a $n \times n$ matrix of constants and exogenous variables.

The diagonal of **B** has zero elements and the off–diagonal elements are all equal and less than 1 (iff $n>2$). **A** contains e.g. the exogenous variables $y_i(t+1)$. If a change in $y_i(t+1)$, with $i=1,..,n$, has an impact of Δ**A** on the matrix **A** it has the same immediate, or first order, impact on **y(t)**. The total effect of Δ**A** on **y(t)** is

$$\Delta\mathbf{y(t)} = \Delta\mathbf{A} + \mathbf{B}\Delta\mathbf{A} + \mathbf{B}^2\Delta\mathbf{A} + .. = (\mathbf{I}-\mathbf{B})^{-1}\Delta\mathbf{A}.$$

This is the multi–sector version of the familiar multiplier in our model. Note that this multiplier only arises under our choice of the exogenous variables ($W_i(t)$, $r_i(t+1)$ and $y_i(t+1)$). In the classical case with the wage rate $w_i(t)$ and $y_i(t+1)$ as exogenous variables there is no complementarity on the goods market and hence no multipli e r. [8] The emphasis in the classical case is on the substitutability between sectors. This difference between Keynes and the classics in our model with respect to the existence of a demand–multiplier corresponds with Grandmont (1989, p. 273) who also observes that the fixing of real wages forecloses the existence of demand multipliers and that nominal rigidities are needed for a demand multiplier.[9]

If appropriate we will restrict ourselves to the case of symmetric sectors and symmetric equilibria. The symmetric equilibrium equation on the goods market is of the following form (if $k_i = k_j$).

$$k_i(t+1) = \frac{(1-\lambda)\gamma_1+(1-\alpha\lambda)\gamma_2-(1-\lambda)(\gamma_1+\alpha\gamma_2)}{\gamma_1+\gamma_2}y_i(t) = \frac{\gamma_2(1-\alpha)}{\gamma_1+\gamma_2}y_i(t)$$

Hence, in a symmetric equilibrium the following relations hold.

$$y_i(t) = k_i(t)\left[(1-\alpha)\frac{p_i(t)}{W_i(t)}\right]^{(1-\alpha)/\alpha} \qquad i=1,...,n \qquad (5.6')$$

$$k_i(t+1) = \frac{\gamma_2(1-\alpha)}{\gamma_1+\gamma_2}y_i(t) \qquad i=1,...,n \qquad (5.7')$$

These equations (the aggregate supply equation (5.6') and the aggregate demand equation (5.7') respectively) correspond exactly with the equilibrium relations that hold in the one sector model. Thus, in case we analyse the impact of an economy–wide change in parameters or variables, it is justified to use the one–sector model.

The fallacy of composition.
We will now investigate whether and how our model may give rise to a fallacy of composition. As we explained in chapter 2 the idea of a fallacy of composition is central in our reading of the GT for it

illustrates the importance of the micro–macro issue. In chapter 2 we discussed two examples of a fallacy of composition, namely the paradox of thrift (section 2.4) and the fallacy of composition on the labour market (section 2.3). Our analysis of the fallacy of composition is meant to illustrate the Keynesian features of our multi–sector OLG model, for it combines the indeterminacy and the micro–macro issue of Keynes's GT *in a general equilibrium framework*.

The paradox of thrift says that if all households increase their propensity to save, total savings do not increase because in equilibrium total savings must equal total investment and the investment decision is independent of the decision to save. In the classical case, the paradox of thrift does not arise, because the real interest rate (a price variable) equilibrates savings and investment. In the Keynesian case, the real interest rate is determined outside the model by (long term) expectations about uncertain events. This means that it cannot equilibrate the demand for and the supply of goods. In Keynes's view, the level of production (a quantity variable) serves as equilibrator. The paradox of thrift depends, therefore, crucially on the choice of exogenous variables or, what amounts to the same thing, on the choice of equilibrating factors.

So, crucial to Keynes's view on savings and investment is the fact that investment is largely based on expectations of future variables, which are determined outside the context of the model. This is indicated by the choice of $r(1)$ and $y(1)$ as exogenous variables. An increased propensity to save can be represented in our model by an increase in γ_2. This leads to an increased preference of future consumption at the expense of present consumption. The situation is depicted in Figure 5.1. The downward sloping curve represents equation (5.6) and the vertical curve represents equation (5.7).

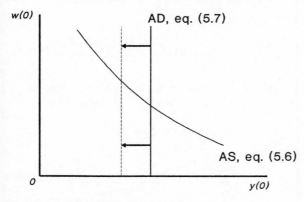

Figure 5.1 The paradox of thrift

Investment is determined directly by the exogenous variables and thus remains constant. The whole burden of adjustment has to be accounted for by $y(0)$. The increased propensity to save is completely offset by a reduction in output so that the total amount of savings remains at the same level as in the old equilibrium. Associated with a decrease in output is an increase in the real wage rate and a decrease in employment.

Note that the paradox of thrift is a typical economy–wide phenomenon. It only occurs if the propensity to save of *all* households increases to the same extent. In the case the propensity to save in only one sector increases savings in this sector increase too. The argument with respect to a change in the propensity to save in one sector is formalized in the rest of this section by using the multi–sector model and the Keynesian assumption that $r_i(t+1) = r_j(t+1)$ and $y_i(t+1) = y_j(t+1)$ are determined outside the context of the model. Suppose that only the propensity to save in sector 1, γ_2^1 increases. Using these assumptions (and the fact that $p_i = p_j$) equation (5.10) can be rewritten as

$$C + \lambda \sum_{i=2}^{n} \frac{\gamma_1 + \alpha \gamma_2}{\gamma_1 + \gamma_2} y_i(t) = \left\{ \frac{(1-\lambda)\gamma_1 + (1 - \alpha\lambda)\gamma_2^1}{\gamma_1 + \gamma_2^1} \right\} y_1(t) \qquad (5.11)$$

$$C + \lambda \frac{\gamma_1 + \alpha \gamma_2^1}{\gamma_1 + \gamma_2^1} y_1(t) + \lambda \sum_{i \neq 1, j}^{n} \frac{\gamma_1 + \alpha \gamma_2}{\gamma_1 + \gamma_2} y_i(t) = \\ \left\{ \frac{(1-\lambda)\gamma_1 + (1 - \alpha\lambda)\gamma_2}{\gamma_1 + \gamma_2} \right\} y_j(t), \quad j \neq 1 \qquad (5.12)$$

where $C = \dfrac{\alpha y_j(t+1)}{1 + r_j(t+1)}$ which under the above assumptions is the same for all j.[10] Equation (5.12) can be rewritten as

$$C + \lambda \frac{\gamma_1 + \alpha \gamma_2^1}{\gamma_1 + \gamma_2^1} y_1(t) + \lambda \sum_{i \neq 1}^{n} \frac{\gamma_1 + \alpha \gamma_2}{\gamma_1 + \gamma_2} y_i(t) = y_j(t), \qquad (5.13)$$

Combining equations (5.11) and (5.13) gives $y_j(t) = y_1(t)$ for all j. The output level is thus the same across sectors and equal to

$$\bar{y} = C / \left\{ \frac{(1-\lambda)\gamma_1 + (1 - \alpha\lambda)\gamma_2^1}{\gamma_1 + \gamma_2^1} - \frac{n-1}{n} \frac{\gamma_1 + \alpha \gamma_2}{\gamma_1 + \gamma_2} \right\} \qquad (5.14)$$

As the denominator of (5.14) is increasing in γ_2^1, output decreases in all sectors. Savings thus also decrease in all sectors $i \neq 1$. The argument can be completed by noting that investment (a component of

C) is not affected by the change in γ_2^1 so that savings in sector 1 have to increase in order to restore equilibrium on the goods market.

We now turn to the question as to whether the multi–sector version of our model may give rise to a second fallacy of composition that has been distinguished in chapter 2, namely the fallacy of composition in the labour market. The fallacy of composition argument in the labour market is simply that in the case nominal wages are reduced in only one sector there is hardly any impact on the demand for goods of that sector so that labour demand (hence, employment) in that particular sector increases. If there is an overall nominal wage cut, demand for goods is affected to the same extent as wages are decreased and labour demand is not affected at all because for the economy as a whole prices are incomes.

The main difference with the paradox of thrift is that in case of the paradox of thrift we are concerned with a change in a parameter, the savings parameter γ_2, whereas the fallacy of composition in the labour market revolves around the idea of changes in a nominal price, the wage rate $W_i(t)$. Since our OLG model is a general equilibrium model the budget constraints are homogeneous of degree zero. This means by definition that an economy–wide change in $W(t)$ has no real effects in terms of output and employment because only changes in relative prices matter. This is immediately obvious in the one–sector version of our model since a change in the price of the numeraire is of no importance to the issue of allocation. Or, in other words, it makes no difference if we define $W(t) = 2$ instead of $W(t) = 1$. Things are rather different in case of a change in $W_i(t)$, with $i=2,...,n$ and $W_1(t) = 1$. A change in $W_i(t)$ does now imply a change in relative prices and must have real effects in terms of changes in the output and employment of sector i. Note that since we have picked labour as the numeraire, it is not possible to manipulate $W(t)$ and $W_1(t)$ in our one–sector model or multi–sector model, respectively.[11]

5.2.5 Conclusions

In this section we tried to give an example as to how the indeterminacy issue and the micro–macro issue of chapter 2 can be analysed within a general equilibrium framework. In the current literature on OLG models and coordination failures, both issues are essential. However, both branches of modern general equilibrium theory present only a part of the overall argument. In our multi–sector OLG model, the indeterminacy argument is combined with the idea of complementarity on the goods market and hence with the micro–macro issue. The fact that our model does not describe a monetary economy stems from the fact that general equilibrium theory does not offer a full–fledged monetary theory. In our view (see chapter 6), this is ultimately due to the fact that Keynes's concept of uncertainty and hence the fundamental indeterminacy of the GT have not (yet) been captured in a general equilibrium model. Of course, as will be clear from the preceding chapters and from what will become clear in the remainder of this chapter, the incorporation of Keynes's ideas within a general equilibrium framework has its limitations. But, and this is the main point of the preceding discussion, important aspects of Keynes's analysis and, hence, of the coordination problem can be incorporated within a general equilibrium framework as long as it is recognized that the assumption of price or wage rigidities is insufficient to grasp the meaning of Keynes's economics. In our view the recent literature on OLG models and coordination failures is more in line with the spirit of Keynes's GT than the attempts (see chapter 3) that solely give an explanation of real or nominal price rigidities. As Keynes set out in the GT the existence of the fallacy of composition is a consequence of the fact that demand and supply are interdependent at the aggregate level. We extended this result in this section by showing that this interdependency is connected with the indeterminacy of equilibria. Besides, if equilibrium is not unique (perfect foresight) expectations sustain any equilibrium, given the initial conditions on the state variables. In such a world it becomes particularly troublesome that perfect foresight expectations do not represent a theory of expectations formation. This conclusion will be elaborated upon in section 5.4. Before doing so, however, we turn to the monetary version of our model.

5.3 The inclusion of money in the model

In this section the analysis of the previous section is extended through the inclusion of money. The aims of this section are twofold. First of all, we will investigate whether the inclusion of money changes the main results of the previous section. Secondly, we will briefly argue that the role of money in a general equilibrium model like our OLG model does not coincide with the role of money in Keynes's GT. This leads to the conclusion that the general equilibrium framework is still far too restrictive for analysing the role of money in a decentralized economy.

In the remainder of this section only those elements of our model are discussed that are relevant for the illustration of the peculiarities of money. Contrary to the real version of the model savings in period t may now also take the form of holding money balances (M), which has a price equal to one. Money now acts as the numéraire. Money balances do not enter the utility function; instead the use of money is rationalized by enabling agents to use money as a means to transferring purchasing power from the period when they are young to the period when they are old. Hence, there are now two vehicles for this transfer, namely bonds and money. The supply–side of our economy does not change (equation (5.6), the aggregate supply equation remains the same), neither does the analysis of the labour market (demand for labour determines level of employment, equation (5.5)). The relevance of including M comes from the demand–side of the economy. In contrast with the real version of our model there are now four markets in the economy: the goods market, the labour market, the bonds market, and the money market.

Given our assumption that households may be rationed in their supply of labour, there are three market clearing conditions left. Since the demand for bonds and the demand for money are assumed to be infinitely elastic with respect to the rate of return on bonds and money the equilibrium condition for the bonds and money market is given by the following arbitrage condition:

$$\frac{p(t)}{p(t+1)} = 1 + r(t+1) \tag{5.15}$$

In chapter 2 (section 2.5) we argued that Keynes developed a portfolio model in order to emphasize that only in equilibrium do the 'investment' rate of interest and the money rate of interest coincide. The real rate of return on captial, $r(t+1)$, and the rate of deflation (the rate of return on money) are proxies for this investment rate and money rate of interest, respectively. This idea of a portfolio equilibrium is only captured within the standard–LM equation as long as the return on non–money assets remains constant and as long as there is initially a stock equilibrium. Equilibrium on the goods market can be written as:

$$k(t+1) = \frac{\gamma_2(1-\alpha)}{\gamma_1+\gamma_2}\, y(t) - \frac{M}{p(t)} \tag{5.16}$$

This equation is very similar to the corresponding equation in the real version of the model except for the second term on the right–hand side, the dissavings of the old. The inclusion of real balances in the goods market equation and the inclusion of the arbitrage condition are the only differences between the present model and the model of the previous section. Again, the indeterminacy that characterizes our OLG model must be resolved by choosing variables that are determined from outside.[12] Using the same line of reasoning as in the previous section, the multi–sector extension reveals that the goods market equilibrium equation is characterized by a positive externality. It is important for our present purposes that in case of symmetric equilibrium the multi–sector version of the monetary model reduces to the following three equations ($i = 1,\ldots,n$)

$$y_i(t) = k_i(t)\left[(1-\alpha)\,\frac{p_i(t)}{W_i(t)}\right]^{(1-\alpha)/\alpha} \tag{5.17}$$

$$k_i(t+1) = \frac{\gamma_2(1-\alpha)}{\gamma_1+\gamma_2}y_i(t) \quad -\frac{\lambda M}{p_i(t)} \tag{5.18}$$

$$1+r_i(t+1) = \frac{p_i(t)}{p_i(t+1)} \tag{5.19}$$

Equation (5.17) is the aggregate supply equation and is equal to the aggregate supply equation in the real version of the model. Equation (5.18) represents the aggregate demand equation. Equation (5.19) is the above mentioned arbitrage condition. Except for the factor λ (the inverse of the number of sectors n) in equation (5.18), these three equations correspond exactly with the equilibrium conditions that hold in the one–sector version of our monetary model. The multi–sector model will be used to discuss the possibility of a fallacy of composition on the labour market.

If M is fixed, equation (5.18) shows that the relevance of the real balance effect depends upon the consequences of an increase in n (a decrease in λ) for the real cash balances per sector i. In order to bring out these consequences the question is how an increase in n influences the numerator M on the one hand and the denominator $p_i(t)$ on the other hand. Given $p_i(t)$ if the number of sectors tends to infinity M tends to zero. This implies that in case of a large value of n the impact of the real balance effect is mitigated and that the fallacy of composition on the labour market occurs under these circumstances. If, however, $p_i(t)$ can no longer be taken as given the impact of the real balance effect would not be mitigated if a decrease of λ to zero would imply that $p_i(t)$ also tends to zero. In that case a change in n would have the same effect on the numerator and denominator of $\lambda M/p_i(t)$ in equation (5.18). By substituting equation (5.17) in equation (5.18), it can rather easily be shown that, given M, $p_i(t)$ does *not* tend to zero as n becomes very large. We are therefore led to conclude that under the assumption of a fixed value of M the fallacy of composition on the labour market occurs if the number of sectors becomes very large. This conclusion is not surprising if one realizes that a large increase in the number of sectors, combined with the exogeneity of M means that the nominal cash balance *per sector* becomes very small. If M would increase as the number of sectors increases, our conclusion as to the fallacy of composition on the labour market would no longer be valid, however.

Under the assumption of a given value of M, our analysis in this section leads, therefore, to the conclusion that the results become qualitatively different from those in the previous section once M is included. In the version of the model with labour as the numeraire, we were not able to analyse the fallacy of composition on the labour market. Once M is included this is no longer the case and under the condition that the real balance effect does not work, the fallacy of composition does indeed arise.[13] As an aside it is interesting to observe that in the analysis of, for instance, Cooper and John (1988) these kinds of monetary problems, as with the real balance effect, do not occur because their analysis is wholly in terms of realia. It is therefore not surprising that Cooper and John conclude that a monetary version of their analysis needs to be extended with the menu–cost approach in order to rationalize nominal price stickiness and, more importantly, the non–neutrality of money.

This leads to the second issue of this section, the correspondence between the role of money in general equilibrium models like the OLG model and the role of money in the GT. Given the analysis in chapter 2 it will not come as a surprise that we do not consider these roles to be corresponding. Since the role of money in the GT cannot be separated from Keynes's analysis of the implications of the prevalence of uncertainty, the impossibility to capture Keynes's ideas on uncertainty and expectations in a general equilibrium framework implies that the role of and the rationale for money in this framework simply must be different from that in the GT. Instead of introducing money in a rather artificial way e.g. through a cash–in–advance constraint in this section it is better to abstract from the introduction of money in our model for at least the following two reasons. First of all, the introduction of money in our model would imply that the non–producible good money would act as a perfect vehicle for transferring purchasing power. This is in sharp contrast with the role of money in a world characterized by uncertainty, as for instance in Keynes's GT, in which money derives its utility from the fact that it functions as a hedge against the uncertainty surrounding future purchasing power. Though Keynes did not deny the theoretical possibility of intertemporal substitution (GT, p. 93) as such, he argued at length that the existence of uncertainty caused it to be of no importance for his theory. It is rather the other way around: due to uncertainty we are often completely in the dark as to the effects of intertemporal substitution (GT, chs. 2 and 16). Saving now does not tell us anything about future consumption:

> an act of individual saving means–so to speak– a decision not to have dinner to–day. But it does *not* necessitate a decision to have dinner or to buy a pair of boots a week hence or to consume any specified thing at any specified date.(...) It is not a substitution of future consumption–demand for present consumption–demand it is a net diminution of such demand (Keynes, GT, p.210).

Secondly, in a general equilibrium model like our OLG model it is the indeterminacy of the OLG model itself rather than the introduction of money that is a proxy for the indeterminacy of the GT, the role of uncertainty. Since indeterminacy is a main theme of this chapter we return to this point in the next section. The introduction of money does not add anything to the Keynesian content of our OLG model. What matters is the indeterminacy or the multiplicity result as such.

5.4 Indeterminacy, multiplicity and Keynes

The aim of this section is threefold. First of all, an analysis is made of the connection between the coordination failures literature (multiplicity of equilibria) and the literature which corresponds with our OLG model that focuses upon the indeterminacy result. It will appear that the role of expectations provides a link. Secondly, the indeterminacy feature of an OLG model is used to show how so called expectations driven business cycles may arise. Finally, the analyses developed and discussed in the present chapter are set against Keynes's framework as outlined in chapter 2 and the issue of 'macro'foundations for microeconomics.

It has been argued in the introduction to this chapter that a fruitful application of Keynes's ideas within a general equilibrium framework should start with the introduction of strategic behaviour and/or indeterminacy of equilibria. The analysis of strategic behaviour and of the resulting externalities enables the analysis of Keynesian issues like complementarity and increasing returns for the economy as a whole and of bootstrap equilibria. The introduction of indeterminacy of equilibria implies the analysis of the implications of indeterminacy and also of the role of self–fulfilling expectations. The emphasis in our OLG model has been upon the indeterminacy argument. Individual agents were assumed to treat prices and quantities as given. In this respect, we did not analyse strategic behaviour. We stuck to the case of perfect competition for firms and households (see also Geanakoplos and Polemarchakis (1986), p. 760, on the issue of parametric prices). In section 5.2.4 it has been shown that in the multi–sector version of our model there is a complementarity between sectors (an increase in the production of one sector leads to an increase in the demand in the other sector) but, and this must be stressed, there is no strategic complementarity[14] as is the case in the coordination failures literature. This does not mean, however, that the importance of multiplicity of equilibria as a building block has been neglected in our model. The starting point of the coordination failures literature is Keynes's proposition that demand is not a one–sided transaction for the economy as a whole. This idea led to Keynes's criticism of classical theory for neglecting complementarity and for solely relying on substitutability. Bulow, Geanakoplos and Klemperer (1985) were among the first to incorporate this complementarity/substitutability distinction in a game-theoretic framework.

At the end of section 5.2 it has been concluded that the indeterminacy which characterizes our model has important implications for the significance of expectations. Given the initial conditions on the capital stock and/or the money stock, expectations are of a self-fulfilling nature which becomes troublesome in case of the non–uniqueness of equilibria. Any perfect foresight expectation in period t concerning variables in $t+1$, which need to be fixed in order to establish equilibrium in t, is self-fulfilling. In period t equilibrium is unique given these expectations. But *any* level of market–equilibrium in period t is conceivable, given the appropriate expectations and the appropriate conditions on the state variables. Apart from the aforementioned complementarity in our model this self-fulfilling nature of expectations provides a second connection with the coordination failures literature. The bootstrap nature of equilibria is at the heart of this literature. In, for instance, the search–equilibrium framework mentioned in chapter 3 (see also chapter 7 on search and money), the probability of finding a trading partner increases if an agent increases its own production. The self-fulfilling nature of equilibria and, hence, of expectations in the search–equilibrium framework of Diamond (1982) is a consequence of the fact that the level of activity of agent i depends positively on the level of activity of agent j but that this positive interdependence cannot be communicated. Given some specific assumptions about the reaction functions,[15] this positive interdependency is the main reason for the existence of multiple, Pareto-ranked equilibria.

The fact that the concept of perfect foresight expectations and its stochastic equivalent rational expectations become troublesome in case of indeterminacy or multiplicity of equilibria, should come as no surprise for at least two reasons. First of all, both forms of expectations are ultimately equilibrium assumptions, as has already been argued in section 3.5. If the economy under consideration is no longer characterized by a unique equilibrium the rational (or perfect foresight) expectations assumption is of no use in diminishing the multiplicity/indeterminacy result since it sustains any equilibrium. Secondly, the bootstrap feature of equilibria in both the coordination failures framework and the Keynesian OLG model[16] is a consequence of the incompleteness of the theory (see also Kehoe (1989)). The bootstrap nature of equilibria and, equivalently, the self-fulfilling nature of expectations imply that

optimistic expectations *by themselves* can cause the economy's output to expand or contract. In short, the economy has an inherent volatility. The Keynesian story of animal spirits causing economic growth or decline can be told without invoking irrationality or non–market–clearing. Moreover, the Keynesian claim is that exogenous changes in expectations cannot be relied upon to increase output, and that therefore the government should actively intervene (Geanakoplos and Polemarchakis (1986) p. 759). Anticipating the discussion on the Keynesian content of these general equilibrium approaches at the end of this section, it can indeed be concluded in our view, that the impact of (exogenous) expectations in the OLG model of the previous section bears a clear resemblance with our discussion of the role of (long–term) expectations in Keynes's GT in chapter 2 of our study.

We now turn to the second topic of this section, i.e. the analysis of the relation between the indeterminacy feature of our OLG model and the dynamics of such a model. Despite the fact that the model of the previous two sections deals with important elements of the indeterminacy and multiplicity literature as outlined above it does address only the issue of dynamics in a rather restricted sense. It does analyse the effect of period $t+1$ expectations in period t for the behaviour of the economy in t but it remains silent on the development of the capital stock (or the money stock) over time. The question of convergence of the capital stock to a steady–state is not answered since the analysis stops at (the manipulation of) the derivation of equilibrium equations as such.[17] Since the main purpose of our model is to bring out the indeterminacy result, this derivation of the equilibrium equations suffices. If one is interested in the efficiency of equilibria, a one–period analysis as in section 5.2. does, of course, not yield any insights. Or, to be somewhat more specific, the fact that our model does not deal with the analysis of the state variables over time forecloses the analysis of what might be called expectations driven business cycles and thus of the theory of chaos and sunspots (see especially Grandmont (1985), (1989)). In order to shed some light on these issues, we will briefly digress on the dynamic behaviour of a very simple OLG model.

Following Cass, Okuno and Zilcha (1979) and Gale (1973) (see also Blanchard and Fischer (1989), pp. 246–250, Woodford (1984), Grandmont (1985), (1989), Kehoe (1989) and Weddepohl (1988)) assume the following simple OLG structure: each agent of generation t maximizes the utility function $U(c_t(t), c_t(t+1))$. Agents when young consume a part of their fixed first period endowment and they save the rest in the form of money holdings M_t. In the second period of their life agents use this money stock together with their fixed second period endowment for second period consumption. In period t the price level is p_t and in period $t+1$ it is p_{t+1}. This means that real savings for an agent when young are M_t/p_t and real dissavings for that agent when old M_t/p_{t+1}. The offer–curve gives all utility maximizing combinations of $c_t(t)$ and $c_t(t+1)$ when the slope of the budget–constraint $(-p_t/p_{t+1})$ changes. For our present purpose it is important that (p_t/p_{t+1}) represents the return on money and hence the return on savings. Changes in the rate of return on savings have an income– and a substitution effect. The relative importance of these two effects determines the slope of the offer curve and is the prime mover of the analysis of expectations driven business cycles in the context of the present OLG example. The standard textbook representation of the offer curve (see e.g. Varian (1984), pp. 118–119) of our example is in the $c_t(t)$, $c_t(t+1)$ space, but following Woodford (1984) this can also be done in terms of excess supply and excess demand. The savings of the young in period t $s_t(t)$ ($= M_t/p_t$) represent the excess supply of goods in that period. The dissavings of those same agents when old in period $t+1$ $s_t(t+1)$ ($= M_t/p_{t+1}$) represent the excess demand for goods in period $t+1$. Since goods markets clear in every period the savings of the young are necessarily equal to the dissavings of the old within a period. Hence, there is a relation between $s_t(t)$ and $s_{t+1}(t+1)$ through $s_t(t+1)$. This non–linear relation between the savings of the young in t and the savings of the young in $t+1$ is nothing but the offer curve in a different space. In a steady–state equilibrium we get:

$$s_t(t) = s_{t+1}(t+1) \tag{5.20}$$

or, equivalently:

$$M_t/p_t = M_{t+1}/p_{t+1} \tag{5.21}$$

We arrive thus at a relation between money holdings in period t and period $t+1$. Under the standard assumption that the substitution effect dominates the income effect, the offer curve OA as shown in Figure 5.2 results.

In case of the offer curve OA, the indeterminacy result in this example can be illustrated by tracing the perfect foresight equilibrium path once we start with the combination s_o and s_1 as representation of the savings in period 0 and 1 respectively. Indeterminacy arises in this example because these points are chosen arbitrarily. For any starting point on the offer curve OA between O and C there is a perfect foresight equilibrium and there are thus infinitely many of such equilibria (see Woodford (1984), pp. 8–9). In case one starts in point s_o, Figure 5.2 illustrates that one ends up in point O which is a non–monetary steady state. The monetary steady–state point C (which is Pareto–efficient) will be established only if we start with s_m as representation of savings in period 0.

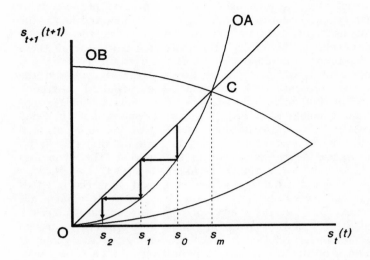

Figure 5.2 Indeterminacy and the offer–curve

More importantly for the issue of expectations driven cycles, however, is the assumed dominance of the substitution effect over the income effect. In case of the offer curve OA an increase in the rate of return on savings (p_t/p_{t+1} increases) implies that savings increase and it can be shown that cycles with a periodicity that exceeds 2 cannot exist. In terms of Figure 5.2, this implies that the slope of the offer curve must be greater than 1 in absolute value when it crosses the 45^0 line. Hence, a positive relationship exists between $s_t(t)$ and $s_{t+1}(t+1)$. The literature on deterministic chaos and sunspots, however, focuses upon the case that the income effect dominates. In our simple OLG example this means that an increase in the rate of return on savings leads to a *decrease* in savings. $s_t(t)$ and $s_{t+1}(t+1)$ are negatively related at point C, the offer curve is backward bending. For deterministic chaos to exist, the income effect must be so strong that the slope of the offer curve must be less than 1 in absolute value at point C, as is the case with the offer curve OB. Thus the fact that the offer curve is merely backward bending is not a sufficient condition for chaos to exist. Subsequently it can be shown that if the income effect is sufficiently strong so that the slope of the offer curve at C is less than 1 in absolute value cycles of periodicity 3 are possible and this means that cycles of any periodicity are possible and even that cycles with aperiodic behaviour can exist. If the latter is the case deterministic chaos results. Since we are primarily interested in the connection between the indeterminacy result and the development of the state variable(s) over time we will not go any further into the question as to how chaos may result from the backward bending offer–curve. Note that the indeterminacy feature of our OLG example is not a necessary condition for deterministic chaos to exist. The non–linearity of the offer curve creates the scope for chaos in our example.[18] The economy in our example with the offer curve *OB* may never converge to a steady state. If this would be the case the relevant economic variables are not subject to cyclical behaviour and behave in a (seemingly) erratic way and prediction becomes virtually impossible in that case. In the presence of chaos, economic variables are characterized by so–called sensitive dependence on initial conditions which means that very small changes in the parameters may lead to a very different time path for the economy.

The second example of expectations driven business cycles can be found in the theory of sunspots. This theory extends the indeterminacy result through the incorporation of the idea that a random variable (sunspot) can affect the equilibrium conditions of the economy with the result that multiple stochastic equilibria may exist. Sunspot equilibria are another illustration of equilibria characterized by self–fulfilling prophecies. In our example (given the assumption that expectations are now rational expectations instead of perfect foresight expectations) sunspot equilibria may exist if the same conditions with respect to income effects and slope of the offer curve apply as in the case of chaos. There will be a rational expectations equilibrium in period t if $s_t(t)$ equals the *expected* $s_{t+1}(t+1)$. The latter is the expected savings of the young in $t+1$ conditional on the information available in t, I_t. What drives the sunspot result is the composition of the information set I_t. If every agent believes that a random variable (the sunspot) that does not influence the fundamentals of that economy as such, does influence the equilibrium condition because every agent believes that other agents believe in this influence (see Grandmont (1989), pp. 282–283) this random variable will be part of I_t and will thus influence the equilibrium condition.[19] Sunspots may arise in a world in which agents must act upon their beliefs concerning the expectations of other agents, that is in a world in which the problem of higher–order expectations exists.

The question arises whether the dynamic behaviour of the OLG model as used in the previous two sections can be analysed along the same lines as the example derived from Woodford (1984). The answer is in the negative. The logarithmic specification of the utility function of the households in our model implies that changes in $r(t+1)$ do not influence the level of savings. Since our utility function is of the Cobb–Douglas type, this is not surprising because this implies that fixed shares are spent on $c_t(t)$ and $c_t(t+1)$ and that relative prices

126 *Keynes, Coordination and Beyond*

do not influence this allocation. The second implication of the log–linear utility function in our model is that the offer–curve can never be backward bending which forecloses the analysis of expectations driven business cycles.[20] A different specification of the utility function might have enabled us to discuss these issues. Using the above employed terminology in terms of our OLG model, $k(t+1)$ is the excess supply of goods of a generation when young and $\rho(t+1)k(t+1)$ is the excess demand for goods of that generation when old. Again, one should balance off the income effect of a change in the rate of return on savings against the substitution effect. It should be emphasized that the main objective of our OLG model has been to bring out the indeterminacy result and that this result does not hinge upon the specification of the utility function. In fact, adding a more general specification of the utility function to the model in section 5.2. would not provide any additional insights as far as the indeterminacy result is concerned.

In our view, the concepts of chaos and sunspots are related to Keynes's ideas on expectations formation and to his ideas concerning economics as a social and empirical science. In the GT, as well as in various pre– and post–GT writings, Keynes addresses some elements that are at the heart of, for instance, the theories of chaos and sunspots. In the former there are at least three important elements that were explicitly analysed by Keynes. First of all, there is the idea that non–linearities are important in economics. In his famous debate with Tinbergen on the use of econometrics (see for the point of non–linearities especially Keynes (1973B), p. 286 and pp. 311–314), Keynes criticized Tinbergen for assuming linearity in his econometric testing:

> One would have liked to be told emphatically what is involved in the assumption of linearity. It means that the quantitative effect of any causal factor on the phenomenon under investigation is directly proportional to the factor's own magnitude.(...) But this is a very drastic and usually improbable postulate to suppose that all economic forces are of this character, producing independent changes in the phenomenon under consideration which are directly proportional to the changes in themselves; indeed, it is ridiculous (Keynes (1973B), p.312).

Secondly, the issue of the changing content of economic variables through time constituted one of Keynes's major points against Tinbergen (see Keynes (1973B), e.g. pp. 296–297 and p.316). But the issue of non–homogeneity as a unifying feature of the social sciences in general can already be found in various pre–GT writings especially in his *Treatise on Probability* of 1921.[21] According to Keynes the issue of non–homogeneity is one of the main differences between physical sciences and social sciences like economics. With respect to the issue of 'macro'foundations for microeconomics this raises an interesting point. The quest for 'macro'foundations does precisely arise out of the recognition that the behaviour of the economy as a whole can not be understood if this behaviour is completely analysed according to the *interpretation*[22] of methodological individualism in mainstream economics in which for each agent the outside world is just a constraint and the coordination of economic activity is not an issue he or she need to bother about. Keynes argued that the atomic assumption, according to which the behaviour of the economy as a whole can be fully understood by neglecting the interaction between individual agents, 'is not valid for the world of social relations. The elements of that world do not function as legal atoms exerting their own independent effects in all circumstances, but might well obey different laws in each alternative configuration of the system' (Hamouda and Smithin (1988), p. 162).[23] Finally, the condition of sensitive dependence on initial conditions that is characteristic of the theory of chaos can also be found in Keynes's writings. This argument and much of what has been said above on Keynes and chaos come together in the following quotation which foreshadows his discussion with Tinbergen (see Keynes (1972), p. 262).[24] We certainly do not want to stretch Keynes's argument with respect to the theory of chaos too far but the resemblance between some elements of the theory of chaos and Keynes's writings is too interesting to leave unmentioned.

With respect to the theory of sunspots there is a clear resemblance with Keynes's view on expectations formation as outlined in, for instance, chapter 12 of the GT. The fact that sunspots can matter is due to the coordination problem that individual agents face in coordinating their beliefs about expectations. This argument is not only present in Keynes's example of the beauty contest as discussed in section 3.5, but also in his 1937 *General Theory of Employment* (Keynes (1973B)). In a world of uncertainty it may very well be rational for individual agents to react to seemingly irrelevant signals that do not bear any resemblance to economic fundamentals if only agent i believes that other agents j react to these signals. If it becomes conventional to react to these signals, every rational agent has no other choice than to follow this convention.[25] 'Knowing that our own individual judgment is worthless, we endeavour to fall back on the judgment of the rest of the world which is perhaps better informed. That is, we endeavour to conform with the behaviour of the majority or the average. The psychology of a society of individuals each of whom is endeavouring to copy the others leads to what we may strictly term a *conventional* judgment' (Keynes (1973B), p. 114).

This concludes our brief review of the possible implications of a backward bending offer curve in an OLG model as such and their connection, if any, with Keynes. In the third and final part of this section some concluding remarks will be made as to the relevance of the various approaches developed and discussed in this chapter for a foundation of Keynes's economics in general and for the quest for 'macro'foundations for microeconomics in particular.

Some observations in this respect have already been made in chapter 3 of our study. The literature on coordination failures, indeterminacy, chaos and sunspots does give a foundation for a number of important elements of Keynes's economics within a general equilibrium framework. The introduction of heterogeneity of agents, the emphasis on (self-fulfilling) expectations and the presence of bootstrap equilibria are in line with Keynes's ideas on the issue of coordination as outlined in chapter 2. This can be set against those mainstream attempts which rely above all on the rationalization of price or wage rigidities. For were it not for these rigidities, the classical propositions would come into play again. The theories which have been discussed in this chapter do not build on the existence of these rigidities in the first place. The Keynesian features of the theories in this chapter arise from the recognition that non-price interactions are important in decentralized economies (see also Howitt (1990)). The need to somehow coordinate these non-price interactions especially with respect to expectations, provides the link with one of the main objectives of our study, the necessity of 'macro'foundations for microeconomics. Pareto inefficiencies result because individual agents lack information on the actions and expectations of other agents and, hence, because full-price flexibility is not a solution to the coordination problem. The latter is true because the relevant information simply cannot be communicated through the market mechanism.[26] As far as the issue of 'macro'foundations is concerned, the approaches of the present chapter yield insights into the issue of equilibrium coordination. But as emphasized in section 5.3 and also at various points in the previous chapters the models developed and discussed in this chapter do not address all relevant aspects of the 'macro'foundations issue for at least the following two reasons.

First of all, the criticism raised against the choice-theoretic foundation of new-classical and new-Keynesian theories in section 3.5 can also be raised against these models. This holds especially for the assumption of market-clearing or, more generally, the equilibrium assumption.[27] This is important because the emphasis on problems of *equilibrium* coordination leaves the question unanswered how equilibria get established. The inability to answer this question becomes troublesome in the case equilibria are no longer unique. In order to avoid an 'anything goes' position one should therefore seek for mechanisms that restrict the range of equilibria. Keynes emphasized the importance of conventions and institutions in this respect. The issues of equilibrium selection and the role of conventions and institutions will be our main concern in chapter 8.

Secondly, as has already been mentioned in section 5.3, models like our own OLG model do deal with important elements of Keynes's GT but only as a proxy for, as we called it in chapter 2, the fundamental indeterminacy of the GT or, in other words, for the role of uncertainty. The fact that the treatment of (perfect foresight) expectations, money, intertemporal substitution (and, one may hasten to add, of time!) are clearly at odds with the GT is ultimately a consequence of the neglect of these general equilibrium approaches like our own model of an essential feature of Keynes's GT, the role of uncertainty.[28] This neglect is the reason for the different role of money in general equilibrium approaches or neo-classical theories in general as opposed to the GT. In the GT money is above all a coordinating device, a hedge against uncertainty. In the next chapter we will go into the problems that underly the inclusion of money in a general equilibrium framework, on the one hand, and the role of money and uncertainty in Keynes's theory, on the other hand.

5.5 To sum up: a pyrrhic victory?

Since the main conclusions of this chapter have already been stated in the last part of section 5.4, we will now only give a restatement of the basic conclusions that follow from the attempt to cast the Marshallian Keynes in terms of Walras without solely invoking the classical assumptions concerning price- or wage rigidities.

1. All those approaches that question the uniqueness or stability of equilibria do deal with the issue of equilibrium coordination but neglect an essential feature of Keynes's GT, the role of uncertainty with the result that important aspects of the coordination problem as analysed by Keynes (and Hayek for that matter) are not addressed.

2. Given the first conclusion, there is no proper place for money in these approaches. We take this conclusion as a starting point for chapter 6.

Ultimately, the analysis in chapter 5 does lead to the following important question in our view. Does the dismissal of the Walrasian auctioneer as an establisher of unique, stable, Pareto-efficient equilibrium prices and exchange arrangements and the resulting possibility of multiple or unstable equilibria turn out to be a Pyrrhic victory or not? Or, in other words, how can we reduce the degree of indeterminateness in these models?[29] It is one thing to address Keynes's micro-macro issue and indeterminacy issue within a general equilibrium framework but without an attempt to deal with the implications of the coordination problem for the behaviour of individual agents, this attempt is rather dissatisfying from a general equilibrium point of view. We will return to this issue in chapter 8.

Notes

[1]The indeterminacy in these models basically results because OLG models as opposed to the Arrow–Debreu model deal with an infinite number of agents and an infinite number of goods.

[2]The OLG model can be characterized as a general equilibrium model because it is based on the assumptions of rational behaviour and equilibrium that underly the general equilibrium framework as outlined in section 1.2.

[3]The initial attempt to develop the Keynesian OLG model of the present chapter can be found Garretsen and Janssen (1989B).

[4]There are, however, important differences. In our model the specification of the utility function is different for instance. Diamond uses a more general form $U(c_{t+1}, c_t)$ whereas we use a Cobb–Douglas specification. This has some implications for the dynamics of the model, as is shown in section 5.4. Also note that the exclusion of money in our model is an important difference with the Diamond model.

[5]Since we are primarily interested in the indeterminacy feature of the OLG model and not in the steady–state solution there is one equation to determine *three* unknowns. If we would derive the steady–state solution $(y(t) = y(t+1))$ the degree of indeterminacy would be one instead of two. The fact that we have one equation to determine three unknowns is obvious if we rewrite equation (5.7) as follows:

$$\alpha \frac{y(t+1)}{1+r(t+1)} = \frac{\gamma_2(1-\alpha)}{\gamma_1+\gamma_2} y(t)$$

[6]Assuming that the rates of return on the capital goods per sector are equalized: $\rho_h = \rho_i$. In fact, given our specification of the firm's capital stock (equation (5.3)) it is true that any price in sector i is equal to the corresponding price in sector j. This is just another way of saying that goods are identical across sectors.

[7]Note that there is no strategic complementarity in our model. This is because firms and households are assumed to behave competitively. In our model we simply have n equilibrium equations, which can be solved simultaneously. Cooper and John have n reaction functions and they compute the Nash equilibria of the models they consider. We return to this issue in section 5.4 on the relation between our OLG model and e.g. the coordination failures literature.

[8]In order to avoid confusion it is important to emphasize the assumption as to the numeraire. Labour from sector 1 is the numeraire which implies that by definition $W_1(t) = 1$. For $i = 2,...,n$ this means that W_i is endogenous and expressed in terms of W_1. All other prices in the multi-sector model are, of course, also expressed in terms of W_1. Under the Keynesian choice of the exogenous variables we thus assume that $W_i(t)$, with $i = 2,..,n$, is exogenous. Under the classical choice of the exogenous variables we assume that $w_i(t)$, with $i = 1,....n$, is exogenous. $w_i(t)$ is defined as $W_i(t)/p_i(t)$, in which $W_i(t)$ and $p_i(t)$ are both expressed in terms of W_1.

[9]As in the case of the one-sector model (see proposition 1) it can be shown that the multi-sector model is consistent over a large number of periods. For a general proof of this see for instance Kehoe (1989, pp. 380–381).

[10]The fact that $C = \alpha y_i(t+1)/(1+r_i(t+1))$ follows from the fact that

$$\Sigma_{i=j}^{n} \frac{k_i(t+1)}{n-1} = \Sigma_{i=j}^{n} k_i^j = \Sigma_{i=j}^{n} \frac{\alpha y_i p_i}{(1+r_j)(n-1)p_i} = \frac{\alpha y_i}{1+r_j}$$

[11]In the next section we show that in case real money balances are included in the model the fallacy of composition only arises if the nominal money stock is constant and has to be divided among a very large number of sectors.

[12]In the Keynesian case of the monetary version of the model the indeterminacy is resolved in period t by fixing the nominal wage rate, the real return on capital and the demand for goods in the next period.

[13]Of course, one can question the relevance and necessity of incorporating the real balance effect in a model like our OLG model but it is not the aim of this chapter to question the validity of the real balance effect. See for the issue of relevance for instance Stiglitz (1991), pp. 15–16 and for the issue of necessity chapter 1 of Johnson (1967) is probably still the best account.

[14]This concept refers to the phenomenon that a change in the strategy of an individual agent leads to a change in the optimal strategies of other agents. This concept has to be distinguished from the idea of spill-overs. The latter arise whenever a change in the activities of a particular agent leads to a change in the pay-off of the other agents.

[15]In Cooper and John (1988) it is shown that strategic complementarity is a necessary but not a sufficient condition for reaction functions (with a positive slope) to intersect more than once and thus for the existence of multiple equilibria.

[16]Again, the concept of a OLG model in this study does refer to a OLG model in which there is no such thing as a intergenerational bequest motive. The utility of future generations is of no importance in the decisions of the currently living agents. Moreover agents, whether old or young, are not able to borrow against the future generations.

[17]Besides one may wonder whether a *two − period* OLG model implies any interesting dynamics at all. Given the actions and expectations of the agents when young the subsequent actions of the same agents when old are predetermined.

[18]See also the surveys of Kelsey (1988) and Baumol and Benhabib (1989) who simply start with the following difference equation:

$$y_{t+1} = a \quad y_t(1-y_t)$$

This non–linear relation between y_t and y_{t+1} may give rise to chaotic behaviour for $a>3$ (see Baumol and Benhabib (1989), pp. 82–83) for the same reason as in our example, it crosses the $45°$ ray with a slope that in absolute value is less than one. For an in–depth analysis of the relevance of the theory of chaos for economic theory see Rosser (1991).

[19]In case of sunspots the condition on the slope of the offer curve is not as strict as in case of chaos. See Woodford (1988) for an example of sunspot equilibria in which the slope is greater than one in absolute value.

[20]A sufficient condition for this foreclosure is that second period utility is logarithmic; see Blanchard and Fischer (1989), p. 249.

[21]For recent attempts to analyse the influence of the *Treatise on Probability* see among others Lawson (1985), Carabelli (1988) Winslow (1989) and O'Donnell (1990). Our argument concerning the non–homogeneity and sensitive dependence on initial conditions (see below) builds upon Hamouda and Smithin (1988); see also de Cecco (1990). For a criticism of the 'organic' interpretation of Keynes's methodological position see Davis (1989).

[22]For an excellent analysis of the fact that methodological individualism does not exclude (coordinating mechanisms like) institutions and conventions see Agassi (1960).

[23]See also Hamouda and Smithin ((1988), especially p. 161) for some relevant quotes from the *Treatise on Probability* that support this conclusion.

[24]See Winslow (1986) who mentions this passage in Keynes's biography on Edgeworth, see also Hamouda and Smithin (1988) and de Cecco (1989).

[25]In this theory sunspots have only a subjective basis that is to say they are restricted to individual *beliefs*. In Keynes's theory these phenomena have also an objective basis which makes that they also depend on the institutions and conventions of a market economy (see Sen (1990)). Or, in other words, sunspot–like phenomena in Keynes's theory do not only depend on extrinsic uncertainty as in the case of the theory of sunspots but also on intrinsic uncertainty.

[26]Much of what is said here on information and coordination and the connection with Keynes goes, of course, back to Leijonhufvud (1968), (1981). Ribbers (1988) develops a similar point of view as to the necessity of the incorporation of the indeterminacy and the micro–macro issue in general equilibrium theory in order to be able to extend Keynes' analysis in a general equilibrium framework.

[27]It does not (or at least to a lesser extent) apply to the issue of rational expectations as an equilibrium assumption precisely because the underdetermination of expectations or the issue of higher order expectations in the analysis of multiple equilibria and sunspots, respectively, brings out this analytical weakness of the rational expectations hypothesis.

[28]For a similar conclusion as to the necessity of dealing with Keynesian uncertainty; see Grandmont (1989).

[29]One way out is to call for a satisfying empirical justification of the phenomena discussed in this chapter and to proceed along the line of (saddle–point) stable, unique equilibria as long as this verification does not exist. This position is for instance defended in Blanchard and Fischer (1989), p. 261. In our view this is a rather strange demand, for what is the empirical justification for relying solely on unique saddle–point stable equilibria?

6   Money, Prices and Uncertainty

6.1 Introduction

At various instances in the preceding chapters we have argued that mainstream interpretations of Keynes's GT do not address the question as to whether and how the fundamental indeterminacy that characterizes Keynes's analysis is responsible for the main conclusions of the GT. This neglect implies that Keynes's monetary theory becomes seriously crippled, as the fundamental indeterminacy, the role of uncertainty, appears to be an essential part of Keynes's analysis of the role of money in decentralized economies. In chapter 5 we have argued that once the issue of indeterminacy is taken into account in mainstream economics, analytical problems arise. The indeterminacy to which the approaches in chapter 5 have led is, however, nothing more than a proxy for the fundamental indeterminacy in the GT, the existence of uncertainty.   In the present chapter we take the monetary part of the GT as our starting point. In order to be able to do so, we must therefore build upon Keynes's own insights with respect to money on the one hand and upon the insights of the alternative approaches as discussed in chapter 4 on these matters on the other hand. The chapter elaborates in two important respects upon the analysis in chapter 4 on post–Keynesian and Austrian economics. In the first place, it takes seriously the notion of (some) post–Keynesian authors that Keynes's GT can only be understood by recognizing that a monetary production economy cannot be analysed by means of theories like the general equilibrium theory in which money is not essential; and also that the role which has to be assigned to money depends on the assumptions made with respect to the existence of uncertainty. In the second place, the analysis in this chapter incorporates Austrian insights with respect to the microfoundations of money and the pervasiveness of uncertainty in a decentralized economy.

The aims of this chapter are threefold. First of all, to shed some light on the question of why money is essential. Secondly, to make clear what Keynes had to say on this issue. Finally, to bring out the possiblity that our analysis of money and uncertainty may have implications for our search for 'macro'foundations for microeconomics and thus for the coordination problem.

The analysis of money, prices and uncertainty is not only the topic of chapter 6, but also of chapter 7. The present chapter deals with the nexus money and uncertainty and with the alleged special properties of money. One of the conclusions of chapter 6 is that the use of money is not compatible with full price flexibility. This conclusion serves as a starting point for the analysis in chapter 7 which deals with the trade-off between price rigidity and price flexibility. Keynes's criticism of classical theory on the role of money centres around two issues. In the first place, Keynes argues that the existing classical theory of money at that time could not address the role of money in decentralized economies as long as it neglected the importance of what we called the fundamental indeterminacy. In other words, the use of money and the existence of uncertainty are related. In the next section we will argue that the neglect of this relation is one of the main reasons why money is not essential in a general equilibrium framework. In the second place, Keynes criticizes classical theory for its failure to make clear whether and how the good money is different from other goods. In this respect Keynes tried to show the peculiarity of money in chapter 17 of the GT.

Chapter 6 is organized as follows. In the next section we will briefly discuss the various ways in which money is incorporated in neo-classical economics and compare this with Keynes's analysis. Section 6.3 contains an in-depth analysis of chapter 17 of the GT, *The Essential Properties of Interest and Money*, in wich Keynes not only sought to explain the essential properties of money but also tried to show how these properties may influence the determination of realia.

6.2 Is money essential?

As has been noticed in chapter 3, it is one of the declared objectives of the mainstream Keynesians that take part in the microfoundations debate (see, for instance, Blanchard (1987), p. 1), to rationalize the non-neutrality of money. Given the existence of price rigidities and/or incomplete or asymmetric information, money matters and may thus influence realia. At first sight this seems to settle the whole debate about the role of money in these theories as compared to the GT, since Keynes tried to show that money makes a difference and if money turns out to be non-neutral one could wonder what all the fuss is about. But, not surprisingly, things are not that simple. It was Keynes's aim in the GT to show that a monetary economy is fundamentally different from a barter economy.[1] The non–neutrality of money, which has been the focus of the mainstream microfoundations debate, does not imply that money or a monetary economy is fundamentally different from other goods and a barter economy, respectively. It only implies that given the restrictions placed upon the working of the price mechanism changes in the stock of the asset called money may have real effects. Or, in other words, in the terminology of Hahn (1973, p. 230) the non–neutrality result does not answer the question whether money is essential. Money is essential if it is not possible to describe equilibrium situations without referring to monetary factors. It turns out that in a standard general equilibrium framework of the Arrow–Debreu type money is in fact inessential.[2] In order to rationalize the use of money in general equilibrium based theories whether of the (new–) Keynesian or the (new–) classical type either the structure of the general equilibrium model has to be changed or money has to be superimposed upon the agents in the economy. An example of the former is the use of the OLG model in Samuelson (1958) to explain the use of money whereas the cash–in–advance constraint is an example of the latter. In both cases it remains however true that money cannot be distinguished from any other asset and the monetary economy functions therefore as a barter economy. The latter is reflected in the fact that of the three standard functions of money (medium of exchange, unit of account, and store of value) only the store of value function gets a foundation in neo–classical monetary theory with the result that money is just another asset among many other stores of value. This is rather dissatisfying to say the least because what really sets money apart from other assets is the combination of the three aforementioned functions in general and the role as a medium of exchange in particular.

The role of money as just another store of value raises the two following well–known questions. First of all, given the fact that money yields no return of its own in these models, why do people hold money in the first place?[3] Secondly, how can money come into play as a medium of exchange? Within mainstream economics there are three dominant approaches to answer these questions. First, the cash–in–advance approach (see for the original statement Clower (1967)), second, the legal frictions approach (see, for instance, Wallace (1988)) and, finally, the money–in–the–utility–function approach. This last approach in particular, is widely used but is in our view rather unsatisfactory for it begs the question of why money should have any kind of utility in the first place by simply putting real money balances in the utility function. A good example of this method is Blanchard's survey of the state of the art in macroeconomic theory (Blanchard (1987)). In most of the theories discussed in this survey the money–in–the–utility function approach is used. However, the only function money appears to have is to bring out the implications of shocks in aggregate demand on output. Blanchard's survey might therefore as well be entitled *Why does aggregate demand affect output?* instead of *Why does money affect output?* The cash–in–advance approach is subject to similar criticism (for the equivalence of this approach with the money–in–the–utility–function approach, see Feenstra (1986)) whereas in the legal frictions approach the use of money becomes a special case of government regulation (see Hoover (1988)).

In our discussion in the previous chapter on the inclusion of money in an OLG model, it became clear that the structure of an OLG model may give a foundation for money as a vehicle for the transfer of purchasing power between periods and rationalizes money as a store of value but that it remains unclear why (in the absence of a cash–in–advance constraint) money should be used in transactions within any period or even why it should be used as a store of value. In fact, the analytical difficulties that underly the various attempts to incorporate money in neo–classical theory are, to a considerable extent, due to the fact that the general equilibrium framework on which this theory is based lacks a theory of exchange. A given allocation of resources is compatible with any exchange rule. The approach of maximizing a utility function under some budget constraint does not place any restrictions on trade arrangements. In this respect, Clower's (1967) conclusion remains relevant

> any commodity, whether a good or money, can be offered directly in trade for every other commodity. But an economy that admits of this possibility clearly constitutes what any Classical economist would regard as a barter rather than a money economy. The fact that fiat money is included among the set of tradeable commodities is utterly irrelevant; the role of money in economic activity is analytically indistinguishable from that of any other commodity (Clower (1967), p. 83).[4]

The emphasis on money as a store of value leads to the conclusion that 'money had no unique role to play in coordinating economic activity...it was simply one asset among many, the market for which could be equilibrated along with those for everything else' (Laidler (1990A), p. 483).[5] The development of a theory of decentralized exchange is necessary in order to provide a role for money as a medium of exchange. This implies that the mere inclusion of a cash–in–advance constraint will not do. The question is how to endogenize this constraint.[6] This question will be discussed in chapter 7.

The analysis of the multi–sector OLG model with money in section 5.3 revealed that the inclusion of money leads to results that are clearly at odds with the role of money in Keynes's GT.[7] This

discrepancy between the role of money in neo–classical models like
the OLG model and the role of money in Keynes's GT is not only due to
a lack of a theory of exchange in the former but above all to an
incomplete interpretation of Keynes's liquidity preference theory in
the post–war development of monetary theory. This interpretation,
neo–classical portfolio theory, is incomplete for a number of
reasons. First of all, Keynes's analysis of uncertainty and the
impact of uncertainty on expectations formation is submerged since
uncertainty is replaced by risk. As we shall argue below, the
presence of uncertainty and especially that aspect of Keynes's
analysis of uncertainty that refers to a *lack of knowledge* of
individual agents[8] is a main building block of Keynes's theory of
liquidity preference. Secondly, in standard portfolio theory, money
thus only has a role as a store of value whereas in Keynes's theory
of liquidity preference the other two functions of money are also
important as the next section will show.

The main differences between standard portfolio theory and Keynes's
liquidity preference theory can be summarized as follows. In the
former, money is a substitute for all goods/assets but the utility of
holding money is solely derived from the possibility of (expected)
changes in the level of money prices leading to a movement into or
out of the money asset. This is in line with the GT but it is
incomplete. Subjects hold money in Tobin's portfolio model (Tobin
(1958)) because of the risk surrounding the level of the future
interest rates on bonds and other assets. The use of money can only
be indirectly rationalized. The problem that money is dominated with
respect to the rate of return by every other asset arises because the
importance of uncertainty in the analysis of money is neglected. The
very existence of uncertainty gives money a liquidity premium and a
role as medium of exchange and unit of account. The nexus
money–uncertainty also explains why the rate of interest is a
monetary phenomenon. In both Keynes's theory and neo–classical
portfolio theory a portfolio equilibrium will be reached because

> the effort to obtain the best advantage from the possession of
> wealth will set up a tendency for capital assets to exchange, in
> equilibrium, at values proportionate to their marginal
> efficiencies in terms of a common unit. That is to say, if l is
> the money–rate of interest (...) and R is the marginal efficiency
> of a capital asset A in terms of money then A will exchange in
> terms of money at a price such as to make $l = R$ (Keynes (1937A),
> p. 102).

It is in the explanation of the level at which portfolio equilibrium
will occur that Keynes's theory and the neo–classical theory diverge.
In the latter, l adjusts to R.[9] So when the demand for money shifts,
the subsequent change in the general price level guarantees that the
portfolio remains in equilibrium. The level of employment is not

affected. In Keynes's theory it is argued that R adjusts to l and that this may imply involuntary unemployment. We will show in the next section how Keynes reaches this conclusion.

The sole emphasis on money as a store of value in monetary theory nowadays reflects a more fundamental problem concerning the incorporation of money in a general equilibrium framework. Any attempt in that direction is doomed to fail because it tries to force one institution (money) upon a framework in which another institution (the Walrasian auctioneer) with the same purposes already exists. Following Laidler (1990B) we can therefore observe that with respect to the three standard roles of money 'competitive equilibrium analysis of the type that underlies the new monetary economics cannot comprehend these roles because the Walrasian market is an *alternative* social institution to money, not a complementary set of arrangements' (Laidler (1990B), p.106). The existence of uncertainty and lack of knowledge in the GT implies that Keynes's framework with respect to money is not reducible to the competitive equilibrium framework. Instead in Keynes's theory money should be conceived of as an institutional solution to a coordination problem. As Keynes explains (see, for instance, Keynes (1937B), pp. 114–117, in which he sums up why and how uncertainty and money are related) the lack of knowledge and the necessity for individual agents to act upon this lack of knowledge create scope for liquidity that is for money. As in a world in which uncertainty is significant, the possibility to redress economic decisions when conditions change exists if agents can hold their wealth in the form of liquid assets. As such this does not exclude other assets than money to fulfil this store of value function. But, as the lack of knowledge is not restricted to the future course of the economy, it also applies to the execution of actual transactions, that is to the coordination problem of finding a trading partner (see also chapter 7). Money as a medium of exchange is an institutional solution to the coordination problem of mutual trade. The same can be said about money as a unit of account. A common denominator in decentralized exchange facilitates trade and enables agents to economize on information requirements. In general equilibrium based theories the assumptions with respect to information dissemination exclude the analysis of liquidity and, hence, of money. The reason for this is stated most clearly by Shackle in his discussion of chapter 17 of the GT, 'insurmountable lack of knowledge, or the expense of gaining knowledge, lies at the root of liquidity preference. Were it not for a problem of lack of knowledge, there could be no need for liquidity. Liquidity is in some sense and degree, a *substitute* for knowledge' (Shackle (1972), p. 216). The analysis of money in the GT is an outstanding example of 'macro'foundations for microeconomics in our view. In a general equilibrium framework this role of money is superfluous and so is money because the Walrasian auctioneer is already assumed to perform this coordinating task.

Note that the role of money as a coordinating device is necessarily imperfect. It may reduce the disadvantages of the existence of uncertainty at the level of individual agents whereas at the same time this reduction at the micro level may increase the uncertainty for the economy as a whole. In answering the question that was posed at the beginning of this section (as to whether money is essential) part of the answer deals with the way expectations and knowledge are dealt with. But the essentiality of money in Keynes's GT does not only arise from the nexus money–uncertainty, it also arises because money is assumed to have some specific properties that distinguish it from all other goods. It is to the analysis of these properties and the implications of these properties that we now turn.

6.3 The essential properties of money

6.3.1 Introduction[10]

The inclusion of uncertainty is a necessary, but not a sufficient, condition for understanding Keynes's monetary theory in the GT. The incorporation of uncertainty does imply that Keynes's theory is fundamentally different from any perfect foresight type of analysis but Keynes also tried to show that irrespective of the inclusion of uncertainty money does possess some special properties of its own. A theory of a monetary economy along the lines of Keynes's GT should therefore start with a description of the characteristics of money, as Keynes did in chapter 17 of the GT. Such a description should then go on to analyse the implications of these characteristics for the functioning of the economy as a whole and for the use of utility functions as such instead of the reverse, as is the case in the money in the utility function approach. Something might, therefore, be learned from a consideration of this monetary aspect of the GT and its elaboration by the post–Keynesians (see chapter 4). Chapter 17 of the GT, *the Essential Properties of Interest and Money*, is a rather difficult and confusing chapter. But despite its rather complicated line of reasoning, the analysis contains some valuable insights, in our view.[11] Given the present muddled state in monetary theory (see also Laidler (1990A), p. 488), the neglect of chapter 17 in the mainstream literature seems unjustified.

More in particular, the aims of this section are twofold. First of all, to present an interpretation of Keynes's analysis of these essential properties of money and to give explicit definitions of the essential properties. Secondly, to offer a (preliminary) evaluation of the question whether money has the essential properties Keynes attributes to it, whether and how money's properties play a role in the explanation of unemployment and whether and to what extent the

(Neo-)Walrasian framework is compatible with the characteristics Keynes attributed to a monetary economy.

6.3.2 Money and portfolio equilibrium

In chapter 17 of the GT, Keynes focuses on money as an element of a (wealth) portfolio. Money is seen as an asset, the attractiveness of which is weighted against the attractiveness of other assets. Money's importance follows from its influence on the required yield of alternative assets and its consequent influence on the level of production of other assets. To explain this it has to be noted that the return on any asset, measured in terms of itself, over a given period follows from one or more of the following three sources:

'1. Some assets produce a yield or output q, measured in terms of themselves, by assisting some process of production or supplying services to a consumer.

2. Most assets, except money, suffer some wastage or involve some cost through the mere passage of time ..., they involve a carrying cost c measured in terms of themselves ....

3. Finally, the power of disposal over an asset during a period may offer a potential convenience or security, which is not equal for assets of different kinds, though the assets themselves are of equal initial value. There is, so to speak, nothing to show for this at the end of the period in the shape of output; yet it is something for which people are ready to pay something. The amount (measured in terms of itself) which they are willing to pay for the potential convenience of security given by this power of disposal ..., we shall call its liquidity premium l' (GT, pp. 225, 226).

The total yield of an asset i over a given period (measured in terms of itself) is equal to $q_i - c_i + l_i$. Measured in terms of money it is $q_i - c_i + l_i + a_i$, where a_i is the expected appreciation of the asset over the given period in terms of money. This total yield of an asset is also called its marginal efficiency by Keynes. As money has no carrying costs ($c = 0$) and does not produce any yield or output ($q = 0$), its marginal efficiency is equal to its liquidity premium. It may be argued that by attributing a liquidity premium to every asset and the highest liquidity premium to money Keynes was begging the question of why money should have any utility at all. In our view, such a criticism of Keynes's position is not justified since, as we argued in the previous section, Keynes underpins his analysis of money with an investigation into the uncertainty of decisions in a monetary economy and the consequent usefulness of money before addressing the issue of why money can have real effects.[12] In his view, every asset may have a liquidity premium. Even non-financial assets (may) offer some convenience or security. However, money has the highest liquidity premium of all assets, because of its role as a medium of exchange (and unit of account) and because of its being quickly convertible into other assets at any moment without much cost. The latter attribute is important, because the knowledge about the q's and c's of other assets may be small and variable over time, in other words because economic decisions have to be made under uncertainty. Again it must be emphasized that the rationale for the holding of money and the existence of uncertainty are closely related. The possession of money provides a feeling of safety, because it makes it possible to change, almost costlessly, the portfolio composition after acquiring new information about the marginal efficiencies of different assets. Possession of money does not commit an economic subject to the present composition of his balance sheet; it provides him room to manoeuvre.

A portfolio equilibrium requires all marginal efficiencies to be equal to each other and to the liquidity premium of money. So the condition for portfolio equilibrium is:

$$q_i - c_i + l_i + a_i = l_{money}; \quad i = 1, \ldots, n \text{ (all assets other than}$$

money).

In Keynes's view portfolio equilibrium will be established through the operation of basically two forces:

1. Expansion or contraction of the production of new assets. This influences the marginal efficiency, because it is assumed that the yield of an asset is decreasing while its stock increases, while its carrying costs are increasing in this event.

2. Changes in the relative prices of assets which clearly influence their marginal efficiencies in money terms if their expected future prices are unaffected.[13]

We can now turn to the question of the relation between portfolio equilibrium and the level of production and employment in the economy. First, we consider the level of production and employment in an economy, where money has no special properties, then we address the special properties of money and their influence on production and employment in a monetary economy.

6.3.3 Keynes's view of production and employment in an economy where money has no special properties

According to Keynes, if money has no special properties the requirement of portfolio equilibrium cannot prevent full employment. Full employment is defined as a situation in which the real wage rate is equal to both the marginal product and the marginal disutility of labour. When employment is below full employment, marginal productivity is higher and marginal disutility is lower than the full-employment real wage rate. Then, entrepreneurs are willing to employ more labour and workers are willing to supply more labour. The labour market does not constrain the expansion of production and employment. This is only the case, when full employment is reached.

However, as long as full employment is not reached an expansion of employment and production can only take place if there is no obstacle to a fall in the level of the marginal efficiencies at which portfolio equilibrium is reached. For as the marginal utility of consumption goods falls with their increased availability at least part of the increment in total production has to come from the production of investment goods if the marginal propensity to consume is less than one. Irrespective of the prevalence of uncertainty such production will only be consistent with maintaining portfolio equilibrium, in a world in which money has no special properties, if the marginal efficiencies of all assets (including money) can be made to fall simultaneously with the fall in the marginal efficiency of capital goods consequent upon extra production of capital goods. The economic process will automatically generate this adjustment process when all assets can be produced or when the marginal efficiency of an asset is reduced relative to the marginal efficiency of other assets as its price increases. Both conditions are fulfilled for producible assets. However, for the second condition it is required that future price expectations are less than unitary elastic. If money has no specific properties, they also hold for money. Even if it is assumed that money and some other assets cannot be produced but (otherwise) have no special properties, the second condition still holds if the non–reproducible asset is a substitute for at least one producible asset. Therefore, if money has no special properties production and employment tend to their full–employment levels supposed that the price–mechanism is functioning well (i.e. no permanent frictions occur).[14]

Through the same mechanisms shocks in the schedules of the marginal efficiencies of assets, the marginal utility of consumption and the liquidity premium of money can be absorbed in case of uncertainty without disrupting the tendency to full–employment. When, for instance, due to increased uncertainty the schedule of the liquidity premium of money is raised and the schedule of the marginal efficiency of capital goods is lowered, the general price level and the rate of interest will fall and less capital and more consumption goods will be produced. This restores portfolio equilibrium and preserves (the tendency to) full–employment. Thus, the introduction of uncertainty as such does not destroy the tendency to full–employment. In this respect we agree with Potestio (1989) who concludes that *in terms of chapter* 17 of the GT the prevalence of uncertainty is not a sufficient condition for the existence of an unemployment equilibrium.[15] We disagree, however, with Potestio's assertion that the existence of uncertainty is also not a necessary condition for the analysis of money in chapter 17 to hold.

6.3.4 The essential properties of money and the level of employment in a monetary economy

In Keynes's view, money has two essential properties which together may prevent a fall in the marginal efficiency of money and thus of capital goods although this is required for the attainment of full employment. As a result involuntary unemployment develops in his view. These properties are:

-- First, '... money has a zero, or at any rate a very small elasticity of production ..., elasticity of production meaning in this context, the response of the quantity of labour applied to producing it to a rise in the quantity of labour which a unit of it will command' (GT, p. 230). No additional money will be produced with the input of labour when the nominal wage falls. This characteristic is not essential to money alone; it applies to any non-reproducible asset.[16]

-- Second, money 'has an elasticity of substitution equal, or nearly equal to zero which means that as the exchange value of money rises there is no tendency to substitute some other factor for it; This follows from the peculiarity of money that its utility is solely derived from its exchange value, *so that the two rise and fall pari passu*' (GT, p. 231, emphasis added).

Thus, in Keynes's view, money being a medium of exchange implies that:

$$\frac{d\frac{\partial U}{\partial M^d}}{d\frac{1}{P}}\ \frac{\frac{1}{P}}{\frac{\partial U}{\partial M^d}} = 1 \tag{6.1}$$

(in which M^d is money demand, U is utility and $1/P$ is the exchange value of money[17]).

If we assume that the marginal utility for other assets (X^d) is independent of the exchange value of money, that is to say if we assume that money is the only asset with liquidity characteristics,

$$\frac{d\frac{\partial U}{\partial X^d}}{d\frac{1}{P}}\ \frac{\frac{1}{P}}{\frac{\partial U}{\partial X^d}} = 0 \tag{6.2}$$

then changes in the exchange value of money do not lead to substitution between money and other assets. In other words, because the marginal utility of money is reflected in its liquidity premium, changes in the exchange value of money call forth corresponding changes in the liquidity premium, so that an excess/deficient demand for money cannot be choked off through price changes. Note that a change in the exchange value is defined as an equiproportional change in *all* money prices, present and future hence we assume that money price expectations are unitary elastic. If an excess/deficient demand for money cannot be choked off through price changes, conditions (6.1) and (6.2) lead to the following (somewhat unorthodox) definition of Keynes's subsition elasticity in our view:

$$\text{elasticity of substitution} = \frac{d \ln X^d}{d \ln 1/P} = 0 \tag{6.3}$$

In Keynes's view this elasticity is zero (see also the appendix). Since condition (6.3) is based on conditions (6.1) and (6.2) any analysis of the substitution elasticity should address the meaning of (6.1) and (6.2). Especially (6.1) is essential, as it shows that Keynes's argumentation is ultimately based upon money being a medium of exchange, for only for a medium of exchange it is true that the marginal utility and the price of the good (the exchange value) are *positively* related. A zero substitution elasticity of money does not imply that money and other assets are no substitutes. It only means that changes in *money prices* do not lead to substitution between money and other assets. As long as any other price than P invokes substitution, M and X are still substitutes despite condition (6.3).[18] Replacing the exchange value of money by the marginal efficiency of X in condition (6.3) would imply in Keynes theory that the elasticity is no longer zero but goes to (minus) infinity meaning, that M and X are perfect substitutes. The bottom-line of our interpretation of the second essential property of money is that the demand for money and the demand for other assets are completely inelastic with respect to changes in the exchange value of money. Condition (6.3) implies that the macroeconomic demand curve for X in terms of $1/P$ is vertical. Changes in the exchange value of money $(1/P)$ do not lead to a change in the production of goods and assets (X^d). The question whether this (interpretation of the) zero elasticity makes sense in our view is addressed in the next subsection.

The following definition of the first essential property, a zero production elasticity, can be read from the quotation taken from chapter 17 of the GT at the beginning of this section

$$\text{elasticity of production} = \frac{d \ln L_m}{d \ln 1/W} = 0 \tag{6.4}$$

in which L_m = labour used to produce money
W = nominal wage

The importance of both properties[19] or more accurately of conditions (6.1), (6.2) and (6.4) for attaining portfolio equilibrium and employment can be explained by comparing the adjustment to shocks when all assets are both producible and have a non–zero elasticity of substitution with the adjustment to shocks when one of the assets has zero elasticities of production and substitution. Let us start with the first case. Suppose we have two assets x_1 and x_2 and let P be the price of x_2 in terms of x_1. The condition for utility maximization is:

$$U(x_1) = \frac{U(x_2)}{P}$$

(6.6)

in which $U(x_i)$ = the marginal utility of x_i

Notice that, in this case with only two goods, P stands for the general price level as well as for the relative price of x_1 and x_2. Suppose that initially condition (6.6) is fulfilled and that there is full employment.[20] Now the schedule of the marginal efficiency of x_1 is raised. This implies that given the initial values of x_1, x_2 and P: $U(x_1) > \frac{U(x_2)}{P}$. How is equality (6.6) restored? Recall that $\frac{\partial U}{\partial x_1}$ and $\frac{\partial U}{\partial x_2} < 0$. Therefore in a new equilibrium normally more of x_1 will be demanded, less of x_2 will be demanded and P will fall to choke off the demand for x_1.[21] This requirement yields a set of new portfolio equilibrium positions (x_1, x_2, P) which differ with respect to the amount of employment necessary to produce x_1 and x_2. Is the level of production of x_1 and x_2 necessary to maintain full employment an element of this set? This requires a definite relation between the increase in x_1 and the decrease in x_2. Given the non–zero substitution elasticity between x_1 and x_2, changes in P provoke changes in demand between x_1 and x_2 and therefore influence the proportion in which the increase in x_1 stands relative to the decrease in x_2. Therefore, full employment can be maintained by an appropriate change in P. In other words, if the price mechanism is allowed to function, full employment will be preserved in our simple 2–asset example.[22]

Let x_1 now be money with a *zero* elasticity of production and substitution. Again assume that (6.6) holds and that there is full–employment. Now the schedule of the marginal efficiency of money (= the liquidity premium) is raised. How is portfolio equilibrium restored in this case and what does it imply for employment? Contrary to the previous case, changes in the price level do not induce any substitution between x_1 and x_2, because a change in P calls forth an exactly offsetting change in $U(x_1)$. That is the consequence of the fact that a zero elasticity of substitution implies that (1) and (2) hold. Changes in P are not instrumental in restoring equilibrium[23]. Given our assumption that money price expectations are unitary elastic money's zero production elasticity implies that equilibrium can not be restored by producing extra money to reduce $U(x_1)$.[24] This leaves as the only equilibrating mechanism a reduction in the production of x_2 to increase $U(x_2)$. Thus, employment in the production of capital assets falls, which via the multiplier depresses total employment. Even if consumption would depend only on the rate of interest and not on income, it could fall with the fall in the production of capital assets, because in the new portfolio equilibrium the rate of interest is higher. Even in the case that the income effect of the increase in the interest rate dominates its substitution effect, there is no certainty that consumption will rise sufficiently to compensate the fall in investment. In Keynes's theory (with both elasticities zero), increases in liquidity preference *ceteris paribus* decrease employment, even if the price mechanism is allowed to do its job (i.e. prices are flexible), because 'not only is it impossible to turn more labour on to producing money when its labour-price rises, but money is a bottomless sink for purchasing power, when the demand for it increases, since there is no value for it at which demand is diverted – as in the case of other rent-factors – so as to slop over into a demand for other things' (Keynes (1936), p. 231). More generally, all shocks in the marginal efficiencies of assets and money have employment repercussions. According to Keynes, due to uncertainty these kinds of shocks do frequently occur and may be large (see also Keynes (1937B), p. 115).

Though we believe that this line of reasoning captures basic features of the monetary part of Keynes's GT, it is incomplete since it is static. As we saw in sections 1.2. and 2.6 in chapter 21 of the GT, Keynes made a clear distinction between the theory of static or stationary equilibrium and the theory of shifting equilibrium, 'meaning by the latter the theory of a system in which changing views about the future are capable of influencing the present situation...expectations concerning the future affect what we do to-day' (Keynes (1936), pp. 293–294). It is in the transition from a static or stationary equilibrium to a shifting equilibrium 'that the peculiar properties of money as a link between the present and the future must enter into our calculations...For the importance of money essentially flows from its being a link between the present and the future.' (Keynes (1936), p. 294). As soon as one takes these dynamic considerations into account the importance of the state of expectations becomes obvious. Thus far we have assumed that the substitution elasticity of money is zero. However, Keynes does not always assume this elasticity to be strictly zero. When this elasticity is no longer strictly zero, the price change required for full employment may be large relative to the disturbance (see also the appendix at the end of this chapter). These large price changes may invoke an increase in uncertainty and make price expectations more elastic and prevent the attainment of full employment. Wage and price changes may even be counter-productive (see chapter 2 and chapter 5 on the fallacy of composition). Although the chances for a tendency to full employment generated by wage and price changes may increase when money's elasticity of substitution is non-zero, it does not seem to be ensured as long as this elasticity remains low.

6.3.5 A preliminary evaluation of the essential properties of money

The elasticity of production

We have already argued that Keynes's assumption of a zero elasticity of production of money is a necessary, but not a sufficient, condition for unemployment even if it is joined with a zero elasticity of substitution. The point is that banks may create extra money, which *ceteris paribus*[25] may drive down the liquidity premium of money and/or the marginal efficiency of other assets given our assumption that money price expectations are unitary elastic. As a consequence, employment increases. The question is, of course, whether it is likely that banks will create this extra money or not.

A sufficient condition for the possibility of unemployment (in combination with the zero substitution elasticity of money) is that an exogenous shock does not automatically induce changes in the money supply so as to reduce money's liquidity premium or to increase the marginal efficiency of other assets to the required level for full employment. Although further research on this condition is required, at first sight it is likely to be fulfilled. For the factors that influence employment, either seem to influence the money supply hardly at all, or affect the money supply in the same, and thus wrong, direction as employment is affected. Notably changes in confidence of the non-banking sector will probably be positively correlated with confidence of the banking sector. Therefore, when private confidence falls the confidence of the banking sector will probably also fall. As a consequence, banks will reduce the money supply aggravating instead of eliminating unemployment. Summarizing, the banking sector has its own liquidity preference (*cf.* Kregel (1985)), which is probably positively correlated with the variables causing unemployment. A higher liquidity preference of the banking sector *ceteris paribus* reduces the supply of money. Therefore, it is unlikely that an automatic tendency to full employment results from the behaviour of the banking sector. Rather, the reverse will be true.[26]

The elasticity of substitution

With respect to the second property of money, a zero elasticity of substitution, there are two analytical difficulties in our view. First of all, the question of the (in)compatibility of this property with the concept of utility maximization. Secondly, the plausibility of the assumption of a zero elasticity of substitution as such. The question is whether conditions (6.1) and (6.2) and, hence, condition (6.3) are compatible with an analysis of utility maximization along traditional neo–classical lines. This is especially relevant in terms of the mainstream microfoundations debate. Incompatibility of conditions (6.3), and, hence, of (6.1) and (6.2) with the neo–classical principles of optimizing behaviour would mean that Keynes's analysis in chapter 17 of the GT cannot be captured by the mainstream literature. Conditions (6.1) and (6.2) imply that the utility function has to be strictly separable in M and P, on the one hand, and X, on the other hand. This implies:

$$ U = \frac{a \; (M^d)}{P} + b \; (X^d) \qquad (6.7) $$

with a and b denoting positive functions.

In all other cases except $a \; (M^d) = AM^d \; (A > 0)$ equation (6.7) implies that a given level of M/P generally yields a different level of utility, depending on M and P. There is no reason to expect this to be the case. Further, if $a(M^d) = AM^d$ the marginal utility of money does not fall with increases in the stock of money (nominal or real). This is implausible and at odds with the GT as will be explained below. In our opinion, Keynes's analysis with the production and substitution elasticities assumed zero, is hard to reconcile with the analysis of utility maximization along neo–classical lines. Given the above observations about the microfoundations debate and our analysis in section 6.2 we conclude that rational decision making under uncertainty and hence the use of money and liquidity in chapter 17 are difficult to reconcile with the neo–classical theory of value.

There are, therefore, two options to analyse and evaluate the theoretical contributions of Keynes in this respect. The first is, to start with the theory of value and adapt the analysis of the theory of money to the restrictions of the neo–classical theory of value. This is the line followed in the mainstream microfoundations debate, which has been discussed in chapters 3 and 5. The second option is to start with the characteristics of money and to analyse the differences with the theory of value and thus to analyse the differences with the first option. This route is taken by, for instance, (some) post–Keynesian economists as we have shown in chapter 4 of this study. Apart from the issue of the (in)compatibility of the concept of a zero substitution elasticity with utility maximization, there are also analytical problems with the concept as such. It seems implausible that the marginal utility of money should change proportionally with its exchange value. In our view a zero elasticity of substitution of money, which results in a utility function in which the ratio of the marginal utility of money and the value of money is constant, raises analytical difficulties. It is not plausible because Gossen's first law (the marginal utility of a good decreases if the available amount of the good increases) is applicable to other goods than money. Recall that in Keynes's view the utility of money is derived from it being (potentially) exchangeable for other goods. An increase in the exchange value of money (i.e. a fall in the price level) implies that additional goods can be acquired. Due to Gossen's first law the marginal utility of the goods falls. Consequently, when the exchange value of money rises the marginal utility of nominal money rises less than proportionally. Thus, there is no reason to assume that money's substitution elasticity can be assumed to be equal to zero. Changes in the price level *ceteris paribus* invoke substitution between money and other goods or assets. In case of the utility function $a(M^d) = AM^d$ in equation (6.7) Keynes's analysis implies that the marginal utility of *real* balances is constant since it equals A. If one conceives of the utility of money as resulting from its ability to provide a hedge against an uncertain future, the assumption of a constant marginal utility cannot stand close scrutiny. Increases in the individual money holdings will increase the amount of security provided but the utility of this additional security will probably rise less than proportionally.

The fact that a zero substitution elasticity of money is only compatible with utility maximizing behaviour as long as the utility function is linear in (real or nominal) money has the following interesting implication. Quasi–linear utility functions of which

$$ U = A \frac{M^d}{P} + b (X^d) \tag{6.7'} $$

is an example have the important feature that the demand functions that are derived from (6.7'), are characterized by the fact that demand is *in*dependent of (real) money balances and, hence, of income.[27] This is, of course, in contradiction with a major theme of Keynes's GT according to which income effects are of prime importance for the economy as a whole.

6.3.6 Conclusions

In this final section of chapter 6, we will come up with some conclusions following our interpretation and evaluation of the essential properties of money in the preceding sections. We will also compare our analysis with the post–Keynesian interpretation of these properties in general and with their interpretation of the substitution elasticity of money in particular.

Keynes's monetary analysis in its most extreme form (with the production and the substitution elasticity of money equal to zero) leads to inconsistencies unless Gossen's first law is rejected, which in our view, is not plausible. If these elasticities are no longer zero the real balance effect works.[28] Although we thus conclude that Keynes's analysis of the essential properties of money does not hold in its most extreme form at least two important insights can be derived from it.[29]

First of all, the marginal utility of an asset that acts as a medium of exchange increases with its exchange value, although less than proportionally. This implies that a given amount of substitution between this asset and other goods can only be invoked by larger price changes than when this asset were no medium of exchange. This point is illustrated in the appendix to this chapter.

Secondly, as the medium of exchange is a substitute for all other goods and assets, almost any change in economic conditions should lead to changes in money prices if all markets are to clear.

Both insights together imply that money prices may have to be very variable for continuous market clearing in a monetary economy. However, money as a medium of exchange, as a unit of account and as a hedge against uncertainty seems to be incompatible with too strongly fluctuating money prices. In the longer run a monetary economy is probably only viable if money prices show a limited degree of flexibility. Strong price flexibility may indeed be destabilizing. But contrary to what, for instance, DeLong and Summers (1986) postulate the destabilizing feature of price flexibility need not to be due to the fact that expectations of future prices are overly expansionary or contractionary but much more to the incompatibility of full price flexibility with the use of money as such. As Lerner already remarked long ago in his analysis of chapter 17: 'any money which was completely cured of wage and price rigidity would not be able to survive as money' (Lerner (1952), p. 191).[30] The warranted degree of flexibility may be too low for continuous market clearing. The possibility (or even the mere existence) of unemployment may be an inherent feature of a monetary economy. Insights derived from Keynes's analysis of a monetary economy seem, therefore, to open the possibility of giving a monetary foundation for nominal wage and price rigidities. This is very interesting in view of the present attempts to derive a microfoundation for such rigidities. Further research on the monetary foundation of nominal wage and price rigidities seems to be fruitful and we will give it a first shot in the next chapter. The main task will be to examine the factors that determine the permitted wage and price flexibility in a monetary economy, and the factors that determine the necessary wage and price flexibility for full employment in a monetary economy. The use of money would therefore imply that there is a conflict between the allocation improving function of price flexibility, on the one hand, and the requirement of monetary stability, on the other.

A monetary system – a sophisticated monetary system, with much 'fluidity' – is inherently unstable; it needs to have frictions imposed upon it to make it work. They will be frictions from the point of view of the arm's length 'price- mechanism', which I do not at all deny has a part – a great part – to play. From that point of view they are a nuisance. Still we need them.(Hicks (1982), p. 275).[31]

Monetary post–Keynesians in their analysis of chapter 17 of the GT also emphasize the necessity of limiting the degree of price flexibility in order for money to be able to fulfil its functions (see also chapter 4). Though we agree with their conclusion as to the desirability of restraining price flexibility in a monetary economy, we do not fully agree with their interpretation of the essential properties of money as such. In the remainder of this section it is argued why the post–Keynesian interpretation is untenable, in our view.

As noted in chapter 4, the analysis of the essential properties of money and of the necessity of nominal stickiness for monetary stability is at home in the monetary version of post–Keynesian economics. There are, however, some differences with our approach. First of all, despite Keynes's insistence on analysing money in terms of a utility concept in his portfolio analysis of chapter 17 of the GT the essential properties are *not* explicitly defined in post–Keynesian analyses of the essential properties. In our view, this does not only frustrate the comparison of Keynes's analysis with more neo–classical approaches on this issue but it may also lead to inconsistencies as we will try to illustrate below. Secondly, and related to the first point, the meaning of the substitution elasticity of money has been misinterpreted by some post–Keynesians. The main difference with the post–Keynesians concerns the meaning of a zero substitution elasticity of money. We will briefly digress on this difference.[32]

This misinterpretation of the elasticity of substitution is unfortunate since it distracts attention from the important conclusion in chapter 17 that the substitution mechanism applies to all goods but money or at least to a lesser extent to money. Some post–Keynesian authors, however, have taken this property to imply that money and reproducible assets are no (good) substitutes. Consider, for instance, the following quotation from Davidson, 'On the other hand, Keynes would reject the implications of the portfolio balance effect, namely the notion that resource–using reproducible durables are a good substitute for money as a component of one's portfolio– *for this would violate one of the essential properties of money*' (Davidson (1974), p. 105, see also Davidson (1978), p. 228). A similar line of reasoning is followed by, for instance, Kregel ((1980), p. 43).

For Keynes's theory to make sense, money and resource–using reproducible assets have to be substitutes. For how could the money rate of interest (or money's liquidity premium) prevent the production of investment goods if money and investment goods are no substitutes? The following argument by Keynes would not make much sense: 'the money rate of interest, by setting the pace for all other commodity rates of interest, holds back investment in the production of these other commodities' (GT, p. 235). But Keynes does not make the assumption post–Keynesians attribute to him. In chapter 17 of the GT, all assets are *perfect* substitutes. This is clear from the requirement that in portfolio equilibrium the marginal efficiencies of all assets (including money) have to be equal. Moreover, Keynes emphasizes that people in deciding to hold money or to buy resource using reproducible assets balance the attractivity of buying the assets now relative to the attractivity of waiting for some, presently unknown, better opportunity in the future. When the attractivity of buying assets now relative to postponing a decision to buy increases, less money will be held and vice versa. This implies that money and resource using reproducible assets are substitutes.

By focusing on the substitution possibilities in the portfolio, the post–Keynesians have interpreted the meaning of the zero substitution elasticity of money as

$$\frac{d \ln (M^d/X^d)}{d \ln i} = 0 \qquad (6.8)$$

in which X = producible assets and i = the yield on X.

In the discussion of post–Keynesians with adherants of the neo–classical portfolio theory, the attention is therefore unnecessarily focused upon the value of these elasticities which are often found to differ from zero. In our view, the misinterpretation of this essential property of money unduly weakens the post–Keynesian argument.

It should be emphasized that this brief digression on the meaning of the zero elasticity cannot hide that our analysis in the present chapter has much in common with the work of monetary post–Keynesians like Davidson, Kregel, Minsky, and Shackle with respect to the peculiarities of money and a monetary economy and also to the relation between nominal stickiness and monetary stability. In the next chapter, to which we now turn, this relation between nominal stickiness and monetary stability will be used in order to argue that in a monetary economy there is a conflict between the usage of money and price stickiness on the one hand, and price flexibility on the other hand.

Appendix: The required degree of price flexibility

To illustrate the relation between condition (1) and the required price flexibility to maintain full employment after some disturbance assume that:

$$\frac{\partial \ln \frac{\partial U}{\partial M^d}}{\partial \ln 1/P} = a \tag{A1}$$

in which $0 < a \leq 1$

Note that this version of condition (6.1) is somewhat more general than the one used in the main text for we now allow this condition to be less than one. A utility function satisfying this condition is:

$$U = b \left(\frac{M}{P}\right)^a + \beta (X^d);$$

with $a > 0$, $b > 0$ and β denoting a positive and increasing function. Assume M^d (hereafter M) to be given and X^d (hereafter X) to be the amount of producible goods.

The first–order condition for utility maximization in case of two goods is that the ratio of the marginal rates of substitution equals the relative price. This condition yields in our example with the two goods M and X, the relative price $1/P$ and the aforementioned utility function:

$$b \frac{1}{P} a \left(\frac{M}{P}\right)^{a-1} = \frac{\beta'(X)}{P} \tag{A2}$$

or $$P = [a \, b \, M^{a-1} \beta'(X)^{-1}]^{\frac{1}{a-1}} = Z.$$

Let us assume that initially there is full employment ($X = \bar{X}_f$) and consider how P has to change after a disturbance while maintaining full employment (i.e. while not changing X). As an example of a disturbance, we take an increase in liquidity preference, defined as an increase in b.

$$\frac{\partial P}{\partial b} = [a \ M^{a-1}\beta'(X)^{-1}b]^{\frac{1}{a-1}} \ \frac{1}{a-1}\frac{1}{b} = Z \ \frac{1}{a-1}\frac{1}{b} \qquad (A3)$$

The elasticity of the price level with respect to changes in liquidity preference ($E_{p,b}$) is:

$$E_{p,b} = \frac{\partial P}{\partial b}\frac{b}{P} = \frac{1}{1-a} \qquad (A4)$$

The elasticity increases, when a increases for:

$$\frac{\partial E_{p,b}}{\partial a} = \frac{1}{(1-a)^2} > 0 \qquad (A5)$$

Note finally that in the case $a = 1$, as assumed by Keynes in parts of chapter 17 of the GT, $E_{p,b}$ goes to infinity and the price mechanism cannot preserve full employment.

Notes

[1]See section 2.6 of our study and also, for instance, the introduction by Hoogduin (1991).

[2]This non–essentiality of money hinges upon the fact that in this framework it is not rational for agents to hold an intrinsically useless asset such as money.

[3]See also Keynes (1937B, pp. 115–116) for this question.

[4]The same point of view is expressed by Brunner and Meltzer (1971), Niehans (1978), Goodhart (1989) and Laidler (1990b).

[5]See also Hicks (1933) pp. 33–35 for an early statement along these lines; see also Hoogduin (1991), p. 3.

[6]The assumption of a cash–in–advance constraint is not a sufficient condition for a monetary economy to be analytically different from a barter economy. In Romer (1986), for instance, which is a general equilibrium version of the Baumol–Tobin model, the existence of transaction costs resulting from the conversion of bonds into money is a necessary condition for the difference between a monetary and a barter economy. In the absence of these transaction costs the cash in advance constraint only fixes the exchange arrangements and does not alter the real characteristics of the economy. In this respect Blanchard and Fischer's discussion of Romer (1986) is revealing: if the optimal time between trips to the bank to exchange bonds against money becomes very small Figure 4.7 in Blanchard and Fischer (1989), p. 173 shows that the money and barter economy coincide.

[7]The same holds true for the role of money in our discussion of Woodford (1984) in section 5.4.

[8]See also Hoogduin (1991) and O'Donnell (1990).

[9]Or, what amounts to the same, the market rate of interest adjusts to the natural rate of interest. This is, of course, the main building block of Wicksellian monetary theory. Wicksell's distinction between the market and the natural rate and his idea that the former adjusts to the latter has had an enormous influence on the development of neo–classical monetary theory. Leijonhufvud (1981) aptly refers to these theories as the *Wicksell Connection* (see also chapter 7). Keynes's theory of liquidity preference does not fit in with the Wicksell connection.

[10]Section 6.3 is a revised version of Garretsen, Hoogduin and Sprokholt (1988) and corresponds with sections 4.3–4.6 of Hoogduin (1991).

[11]See also the reference to chapter 17 on p. 294 of the GT where Keynes connects the analysis of the essential properties with the discussion about the stationary and the shifting model (see section 1.2. and section 2.6.).

[12]As to the origins of the use of money Keynes's theory bears some resemblance to certain aspects of Austrian monetary theory. In *The Theory of Money and Credit* Von Mises for instance concludes that 'money has no utility other than that arising from the possibility of obtaining other economic goods in exchange for it. It is impossible to conceive of any function, qua money, that can be separated from the fact of its objective exchange value.' (Von Mises (1953), p. 118). The idea that money derives its peculiarity from its role as a medium of exchange has a strong tradition in Austrian monetary theory and we will return to this issue in chapter 7. For our present purposes it is important to note that the conclusion of Von Mises is similar to Keynes's analysis of the substitution elasticity of money as will be outlined below.

[13]In line with Keynes's methodology (see section 2.6. of our study for an elaboration of this point) money price expectations will be treated as data in what follows, and frequently even as constants. In Keynes's view, expectations have a highly autonomous character. Economic theory does not allow us to say much about the contents of expectations. Fortunately, the essential features of the operation of a monetary economy can be described independently of the contents of expectations, although the precise course of the economy does depend on the contents of expectations.

[14]If money has no special properties as is argued in, for instance, Rogers (1989) the post–Keynesian analysis of Keynes's monetary theory seems to rest upon a given (or conventional) rate of interest. We return to this point in chapter 7.

[15]If money has no special properties Keynes therefore concludes that 'in the absence of money and in the absence –we must, of course, also suppose– of any other commodity with the assumed characteristics of money, the rates of interest would only reach equilibrium when there is full–employment' (GT, p. 235). A similar statement can be found on p.236 of the GT.

[16]In this respect Keynes writes that '... the above condition is satisfied (...) by all pure rent factors, the production of which is completely inelastic' (GT, p. 231).

[17]To allow for the application of price theory in our analysis, the term 'utility' in the quotation in the text is replaced by *marginal* utility in condition (6.1). As can easily be verified, in the utility function implied by Keynes's analysis in our terms (see section 6.3.5) Keynes's original definition (with utility instead of marginal utility) also holds.

[18]In fact, for Keynes' theory to make sense M and X must be substitutes. See also our criticism of post–Keynesian economics on this issue in section 6.5.

[19]Our definition of the substitution elasticity deviates from the definitions used in, for instance, the money–in–the–utility function approach for in the latter approach the elasticity of substitution of money would be defined as:

$$\frac{d\ \ln(\frac{M^d}{P}\ /X)}{d\ \ln\ r/l} \tag{6.5}$$

in which l, the liquidity premium, is the money rate of interest and r is the rate of return on the other assets X. Hence, in the standard definitions we get real instead of nominal money balances and r/l instead of the exchange value of money.

[20]For simplicity's sake, we assume the supply of labour to be fixed in the following argument.

[21]Supposing that the income effect plus the substitution effect of a fall in P on the demand for x_2 is smaller than the initial effect of the increase in the marginal efficiency of x_1 on the demand for x_2.

[22]In our analysis we only focused on the market for goods. Maintenance of full–employment also requires a fall in the wage rate in terms of x_1, smaller than the fall in the price level P. This ensures that more labour will be used to produce x_1 and less to produce x_2.

[23]One could argue that if price expectations are less than unitary elastic, changes in the exchange value of money (or, in this case, a fall in P) would lead to substitution between x_1 and x_2 irrespective of the existence of money's alleged essential properties.

[24]It might be argued that although no money will be produced to restore portfolio equilibrium, money can be created by banks with the effect that the marginal utility of x_1 will be reduced. A zero elasticity of production appears to be necessary, but not sufficient to eliminate the channel of equilibrium adjustment via $U(x_1)$. We return to this issue in the next subsection, where we will argue that the capacity of banks to create money does not imply that $U(x_1)$ will be sufficiently reduced to prevent changes in $U(x_2)$ and employment.

[25]Increases in money supply may reduce the confidence of the non-banking sector and may therefore even be counter-productive. We assume in the text that the confidence of the non-banking sector is unaffected by changes in the money supply. Not because we think these effects are unimportant, but because we intend to focus on the question of whether (without taking account of repercussions on other factors) the money supply process is capable of generating a tendency to full employment.

[26]For an analysis of the consequences of the fact that the banking-sector has a liquidity preference of its own, see for instance Minsky (1986).

[27]Given that $Y = M/P$ as is the case in much of the mainstream Keynesian microfoundations literature. See *e.g.* Varian (1984, ch. 3 and 7) for a brief analysis of quasi-linear or more general Gorman-type utility functions. This class of utility functions is often used in the mainstream literature because quasi-linearity is a necessary condition for *aggregate* demand functions to behave like individual demand functions. The assumption that utility is linear in income (see, for instance, Blanchard and Kiyotaki (1987), p. 650) does indeed facilitate welfare evaluations but it also implies that it neglects interdependencies between agents through the usual income-expenditure channel.

[28]See also Lerner (1952) and (1974) for this conclusion.

[29]Whether these insights constitute a challenge for the attempts to ground money upon a general equilibrium framework (section 6.2) remains an open question, as we have presented only the main arguments of Keynes's analysis of the essential properties in neo–classical terms and we did not develop a complete model. To mention just one example, we did not make an explicit distinction between stocks and flows in our account of Keynes's analysis and we did distinguish only two assets (M and X^d).

[30]See also chapter 21 of the GT: 'In fact we must have some factor, the value of which in terms of money is, if not fixed, at least sticky, to give us any stability of values in a monetary system.' (Keynes (1936), p. 304).

[31]See also Hicks (1935). This theme has remained important in Hicks's writings on the foundations of money, see also Hicks (1989).

[32]See also Hoogduin (1991), pp. 89–90 on this issue.

7 The Trade–off between Price Flexibility and Price Rigidity

7.1 Introduction

It has been concluded in section 6.2 that the rationale for the existence of money in a general equilibrium framework is not without its theoretical problems. This is especially relevant for those theories that try to provide macroeconomics with a microfoundation or for those theories which attempt to integrate the theory of money and the theory of value. Recently, however, there have been some interesting attempts to endogenize the medium of exchange function of money. These theories all start with the recognition that the explanation of money as a medium of exchange cannot do without a theory of decentralized exchange. In our view, the idea that the analysis of money should be based on a theory of exchange is very important. However, these theories are also characterized by a general neglect of the theory of value. From the point of view of the integration of the theory of money and the theory of value, this is rather unsatisfying. It is here that the analysis of this chapter comes in.

It is maintained in this chapter that an explanation of the three functions of money (medium of exchange, unit of account and store of value) in a world characterized by uncertainty must also address the question of the implications of this explanation for the theory of value. Building on the analysis of chapter 17 of the GT in the previous chapter it is argued that nominal price stickiness may be a necessary condition for money to fulfil these functions. The analysis of the link between money and nominal prices leads to the conclusion that changing nominal prices may be costly for the economy as a whole since it endangers price stability and, hence, the functioning of money as such. The idea that full price flexibility is not without its costs is a second main theme of this chapter. It implies that individual agents are faced with a trade–off between price flexibility and price rigidity. Price flexibility is warranted for the same allocative reasons as in a standard neo–classical model and (some degree of) price rigidity is needed to ensure stability in a monetary economy characterized by uncertainty and to enhance the functions of money. This implies that there may be a conflict between the social and private interests of price flexibility.

This chapter is organized as follows. In the next section recent theories of decentralized exchange are briefly discussed and criticized. The relation between money and nominal prices is set against the issue of coordination in general and the role of money as a unit of account and store of value in particular. Section 7.3 deals with the kind of model in which the trade–off between price flexibility and price inflexibility is relevant. Iwai (1981) is used as an example of how this question can be answered. Given the claim that such a trade–off exists the issue of whether and how a certain degree of nominal inertia may come about is the subject of section 7.4. It must be emphasized that the analysis in the sections 7.2– 7.4 does not deal with the analysis of money in the exchange process as such. Rather the hypothesis of a monetary foundation of nominal stickiness is used to rationalize the analysis of the trade–off between price flexibility and rigidity. In the remainder of this chapter, our discussion on money, prices and uncertainty will be briefly compared with the alternative approaches of chapter 4 (section 7.5). Section 7.6 concludes our inquiry into the nexus money, prices, and uncertainty.

7.2 Money and nominal inertia

As has been outlined in the previous chapter, one of the main reasons for the rather unsatisfactory foundation of money in the mainstream literature is the lack of a theory of exchange with the result that the feature that really distinguishes money from other goods, its role as a medium of exchange, does not follow from the analysis. The only way to analyse money as a medium of exchange is to superimpose this function on the economy. One of the objectives of a more developed monetary theory should, therefore, be to endogenize this function. Fortunately, there have been some recent attempts to rationalize the existence of money as a medium of exchange. These attempts have the following features.[1]

First of all, the aim is to arrive at a theory in which the medium of exchange function is endogenized. Individual agents deliberately choose to use a system of indirect exchange. The need to endogenize the medium of exchange function goes at least back to Menger (1892) (see also Nagatani (1978), pp. 113–131) and should be set against the legal restrictions approach which holds that the use of money is forced upon the individual agents by the government.

Secondly, the rationale for a good (or goods) to become a medium of exchange depends crucially upon the introduction of transaction or search costs. A good example of the former is Kiyotaki and Wright (1988) whereas Jones (1976) uses the concept of search costs. The assumption that exchange is not costless renders an indirect exchange arrangement (potentially) efficient in the sense that monetary equilibria are more productive than barter equilibria (see McCallum (1983), pp. 144–145). In the absence of these costs, all goods can be used as medium of exchange and this implies that the economic system becomes essentially one of barter (see Kiyotaki and Wright (1988), p. 32).

A third common feature of the recent literature on money as a medium of exchange concerns the use of a search equilibrium framework. The basic structure of these models is derived from Diamond (1982). Agents are typically paired randomly and are hence faced with the well-known double coincidence of wants. In such a set-up prices have no (allocative) role to play. In terms of the integration of the theory of money and the theory of value and in terms of the microfoundations debate this exclusion from the theory of value is rather dissatisfying. In these theories of decentralized exchange the emphasis is solely upon money and a Walrasian auctioneer is assumed to take care of the establishment of equilibrium prices (see, for instance, Jones (1976), p.760 and Ostroy (1989), p. 191).

This last remark implies a fourth common feature of the recent money in decentralized exchange models. The assumption of a given allocation of resources in these models means that individual agents have only to face one question, namely whom to trade with. Once equilibrium prices have been established the actual execution of trade can be improved upon by an indirect exchange arrangement.

In order to illustrate how the medium of exchange function of money may arise in these models, the basic framework of Iwai (1988A) and (1988B) will be briefly discussed. Suppose there are many individuals and many heterogenous goods in the economy and suppose that each individual is endowed with one unit of some good and that agents have the need to consume one unit of another good. Also assume that equilibrium prices are already somehow established. In line with the search equilibrium framework of Diamond (1982), this difference between endowments and needs induces search activity. Each individual with an endowment of one good i has two options in his or her attempt to exchange it for the consumption good j. The first option is direct exchange in which case the double coincidence of wants arises. The second option is indirect exchange in which endowment i is traded for good k and subsequently k for j. In this case, k is used as a medium of exchange. Taking q_{ji}, the supply–demand frequencies, as *given* the analysis on the level of the individual agent, is completed by denoting the following objective function for each agent that holds one unit of endowment i but wishes to consume one unit of good j.[2]

$$V_{ij} = \text{Max}_k \, [V_{kj} - b - c/q_{ki}] \qquad (7.1)$$

in which:

V_{ij} = maximum expected life–time utility of holding i and consuming j

V_{kj} = maximum utility of holding k and consuming j

b = exchange costs

c = search costs

Iwai uses thus both transaction costs and search costs. If utility is maximized when $k = j$ there is a system of barter and when V_{ij} is maximized for k is unequal to j, there is an exchange system in which k is used as medium of exchange.

Equation (7.1) describes the objective function of each agent *given* the supply–demand frequencies q_{ji}. Just as in Diamond's search equilibrium framework the peculiarity of the search model, the bootstrap character of the equilibria, arises if (7.1) is combined with the endogenization of q_{ji}. It can be shown that the supply–demand frequency is the *aggregate* outcome of the search activity, aimed at maximizing (7.1), of each agent. But the individual search activity depends on q_{ji}. Hence, the frequency of meeting a j-supplying, i-demanding agent is positively related to the level of search activity of each individual i-supplying, j-demanding agent whereas the level of individual search activity depends in turn positively on q_{ji}. Or, in other words, an increase in one's own effort of finding a trading partner increases the probability of actually doing so which in turn has a positive feedback on one's own search–activity. It can be shown that there exists an exchange equilibrium if the individual need to consume j given the possession of i is consistent with the aggregate behaviour (market behaviour) that leads to q_{ji}. Iwai then shows that given some assumptions the use of fiat and of commodity money characterize two of these exchange equilibria. This endogenization of the Clower constraint critically depends on the bootstrap nature of the equilibria, on the one hand, and on the existence of transaction/search costs, on the other hand.[3] The bootstrap quality of the equilibria provides a link with the coordination issue, as the failure to recognize that the probability of meeting a trading partner depends on the level of individual search activity may lead to equilibria which are Pareto–dominated by other equilibria, as has been argued in chapters 3 and 5.

In his discussion of the theories of decentralized monetary exchange, Warneryd (1990) points out that a commonly accepted medium of exchange is an institutional solution to a coordination problem.[4] The emphasis on money as a coordinating device in the exchange process is important in our opinion but it seems rather ambiguous to focus upon the coordinating properties of a medium of exchange while at the same time the Walrasian auctioneer is still around to equilibrate the various markets. In other words, in order to facilitate the analysis of money in the actual exchange process, the auctioneer is assumed to be non-existent but is still needed to establish equilibrium prices. This ambivalence with respect to the auctioneer assumption is also relevant for analysing the role of money as a unit of account and a store of value.

In the analysis of these two functions the role of prices cannot as easily be neglected. This holds, first of all, for the unit of account function. The rationale for the existence of one commonly accepted unit of account or one numeraire must be found in the possibility to economize on accounting costs (see Niehans (1978), pp. 120–121). In line with Niehans (1978), it can be argued that these accounting costs do not only depend on the number of traded goods but also on the *variability* of the prices of these goods in terms of the numeraire. The idea is that an increased variability in nominal prices leads to higher accounting costs. The choice of the good that could serve as a unit of account depends, therefore, *inter alia* on the variability that nominal prices display when they are expressed in terms of that particular numeraire. This line of reasoning can also be found in Lerner (1952) in his analysis of chapter 17 of Keynes's GT.[5] In the absence of a government that ensures price stability, individual agents can minimize on accounting costs and thus enlarge the efficiency of money as a unit of account by making institutional arrangements (*e. g.* contracts) that limit price variability. Note that the influence of the variability of prices on the efficiency of the unit of account only makes sense in a world that departs from the perfect foresight/rational expectations assumption. In case of perfect foresight (or rational expectations) a deliberate restriction of price flexibility cannot be rationalized and the choice of the numeraire is of no economic relevance at all.

The function of money as a store of value follows directly from the recognition that economic decisions take a certain amount of (historical) time to materialize. Once this is granted, a possible justification for money as a medium of exchange necessarily implies that money also serves as a store of value. The possibility to hold money enlarges the flexibility of individual agents or, in the terminology of Hicks (1974), it serves as a means of liquidity (see especially Hicks (1974), pp. 31–59).[6] Again, this view of money as a means of providing liquidity is only conceivable in an economy in which there is some form of uncertainty with respect to the future in general and to future prices in particular. This interpretation of the store of value function is not at home in a world in which perfect foresight or rational expectations are supposed to rule and where the store of value function of money can only be indirectly rationalized as occurs in the standard portfolio approach. The need for liquidity in the sense of Hicks (1974) or, what amounts to the same, in his version of Keynes's liquidity preference theory depends crucially on expectations with respect to the future value of money and thus on the expectations concerning future prices. As in the case of a unit of account, individual agents can influence the necessity of liquidity and thereby influence the uncertainty surrounding the economic future by making institutional arrangements that create a (endogenously determined) form of nominal price stickiness.

This brief sketch of money as a medium of account and a store of value and its implications for the theory of value is meant to illustrate that a meaningful explanation of money in all its functions cannot do without the introduction of uncertainty and hence of the coordination issue. In this way the theories of decentralized exchange could be extended by recognizing that both money and price setting behaviour can be means by which individual agents try to deal with the question of coordination.[7] In line with Heiner ((1983), see also chapter 8) it can be said that nominal price stickiness is one way of creating predictable behaviour in the presence of uncertainty.

The relation between the peculiarities of money and monetary stability, on the one hand, and nominal (wage) stickiness is explicitly addressed by Keynes at various instances in the GT (for instance pp. 303–304 of the GT; see section 6.3.5). In chapter 17, for instance, Keynes argues that 'the normal expectation that the value of output will be more stable in terms of money than in terms of any other commodity, depends of course, not on wages being arranged in terms of money, but on wages being relatively *sticky* in terms of money' (GT, p. 237) with the result that 'this expectation enhances money's liquidity premium and prevents the expectational correlation between the money–rate of interest and the marginal efficiencies of other assets which might, if it could exist, rob the money–rate of interest of its sting' (GT, p. 238).[8] Keynes concludes this section of chapter 17 with the observation that with respect to monetary stability it is nominal stickiness that matters for real (wage) stickiness may even be counterproductive, because in case of the latter 'every small fluctuation in the propensity to consume and the inducement to invest would cause money prices to rush violently between zero and infinity. That money–wages should be more stable than real wages is a condition of the system possessing inherent stability' (GT, p. 239).[9]

A second example of connecting monetary stability with price stickiness can be found in chapter 19 of the GT in the discussion of the pros and cons of changing nominal wages in case of unemployment. According to Keynes, the main result of decreasing wages would be 'to cause a great instability of prices, so violent as perhaps to make business calculations futile in an economic society functioning after the manner of that in which we live' (GT, p. 269). Or, in other words, the market mechanism would no longer function properly and the usefulness of money in its function of unit of account would decrease. It is, therefore, no surprise that Keynes concludes that 'the maintenance of a stable level of money wages is, on balance of considerations, the most advisable policy for a closed system; whilst the same conclusion will hold good for an open economy provided that equilibrium with the rest of the world can be secured by means of fluctuating exchanges' (GT, p. 279).[10]

We have concluded in section 6.3. on the essential properties of money that substitution between the good money and other goods can only materialize by means of larger price changes than when the good money would not fulfil the medium of exchange function. Too strongly fluctuating nominal prices hamper, however, the functioning of money. It is here that the need for nominal stickiness arises. If, for instance, the elasticity of future nominal price expectations with respect to current nominal prices exceeds unity the economy will be characterized by instability and money will cease to function properly. Exchange arrangements characterized by nominal stickiness are a means by which individual agents can influence this elasticity. Whether these exchange arrangements do in fact materialize depends on the particular institutional framework involved. Since general price stability can be looked upon as a public good, the individual decision to restrain price flexibility does involve an externality. The tension between money price flexibility (needed to react to disequilibrium situations) and money price stickiness will be further illustrated by means of Iwai (1981) in the next section.

From the analysis in the present section the hypothesis (and nothing more than that) can be derived that in a world in which agents have to cope with the coordination issue in the allocation and the actual exchange of goods, nominal stickiness is a necessary condition for money to fulfil its functions. Note the crucial difference with the analysis of nominal inertia in mainstream models in which increased price flexibility leads to outcomes that are more Pareto-efficient. In a standard maximization problem, individual agents only attach utility to the quantities of the various goods and not to the (variability of) prices of these goods. The analysis of this section can be summarized by the statement that in a monetary economy, in which the interaction between agents is essential, individual agents do also attach utility to the (movement of) money prices. The claim that some degree of nominal inertia is necessary for money to be able to fulfil its threefold purpose implies a trade-off between price flexibility and inflexibility. An increase in price flexibility allows agents to react better to shocks whereas the resulting decrease in inflexibility endangers the stability of the monetary economy and, hence, the working of the market mechanism as such. The analysis of money has to be grounded in a theory of exchange and the beneficial effects of price stickiness also follow from the characteristics of the exchange process under uncertainty. For it is in the interaction between individual agents that the importance of money and price stability arises. If agents also attach utility to the variability of money prices the neo–classical framework of maximizing a utility function under some budget constraint is of little use for the analysis of a monetary economy since that framework is based on the independency of utility and prices. In fact, the link between the utility of money and the variability of prices points to the existence of an externality because the variability of money prices depends on the weight other agents attach to money. By focusing solely on the theory of allocation the trade–off between nominal price flexibility and inflexibility does not exist in neo–classical models.

7.3 The trade-off between price flexibility and price stickiness: an example

In this section Iwai (1981) is used to illustrate the hypothesis that nominal inertia may be a necessary condition for stability in a monetary economy. Or, in other words, this section deals with the trade–off between price flexibility and price stickiness once price adjustment is no longer assumed to be costless. In the first part of this section, we will briefly digress on the main elements of Iwai's model and illuminate the relation with the analysis in the previous section. In the remainder of this section we will focus more explicitly on the trade–off between adjusting and fixing prices.

A model of cumulative price changes
The basic idea of Iwai's disequilibrium analysis is derived from Wicksell. A change in the general price level is thought to imply that on the aggregate level demand is (expected to be) unequal to supply. This implies that at least one firm is confronted with a situation of expected disequilibrium in the sense that its supply is not equal to its expected demand. According to Wicksell (1935), the reaction of firms to (expected) disequilibria tends to aggravate the inflationary or disinflationary situation, basically because individual firms try to influence relative prices by changing their nominal prices. This starts off a cumulative in- or deflationary process.

Iwai (1981) is, above all, an attempt to ground Wicksell's disequilibrium analysis in a model of price setting behaviour by individual firms. Of particular interest for our present purposes are the assumptions underlying this basic model. In the absence of a Walrasian auctioneer, firms set their own prices and in the absence of the behavioural assumption that markets are always cleared it becomes necessary to analyse the pricing decisions of individual firms in disequilibrium situations. Given the assumption that the various decisions of individual firms take a certain amount of time to materialize Iwai arrives at a sequential–analytical set–up in which firms have to decide on their nominal wage and price before the respective supply of labour and the demand for goods come about (see Iwai (1981), pp. 16–19). In deciding upon their wage and price offers firms take the wage and price decisions of other firms as given. Given this Nash assumption, firms try to maximize expected gross profits.

Since firms are uncertain about the state of labour supply and demand for goods the role of expectations is crucial in the model. In the case of a monetary economy,[11] aggregate demand may differ from aggregate supply on the labour and goods market and as a result expectations of at least one firm are bound to be disappointed. Those firms will adjust their nominal wage and price offers but these price changes will not establish a new equilibrium because the simultaneous attempts to change *relative* prices by means of *nominal* price adjustments ultimately result in changes in nominal prices whereas relative price adjustments do not take place.[12] The market mechanism does not ensure the establishment of a new equilibrium and, hence, instability reigns.[13] In the end the cumulative changes in the general price level will threaten the stability of the value of money and the functioning of money as such (Iwai (1981), p. 103). Iwai's conclusion as to the necessity of cumulative price changes depends on the fact that in his model expectations may be systematically disappointed. Disequilibria are assumed to cause errors in the expectations of firms which are not corrected by the price mechanism.

The Wicksellian model supports the analysis in this chapter with respect to the incompatibility between monetary stability and full price flexibility. It turns out that stable equilibria are nevertheless possible if prices are no longer fully flexible. The Wicksellian model then becomes a Keynesian model. Iwai chooses to analyse the case of nominal wage inflexibility.[14] In the extreme case of complete nominal wage rigidity firms are not able to use nominal wages as a policy instrument in an attempt to change relative wages. The quantity adjustments that are necessary if the labour market is in disequilibrium work in the same direction as changes in the product prices. An excess demand on the goods market causes an increase in product prices and employment. The latter leads to an increase in product supply with the result that both the increase in prices and employment tend to eliminate the excess demand. In the case of nominal wage flexibility, wages move in the same direction as prices thereby aggravating the disequilibrium situation. In short, with full price flexibility wages chase prices and vice versa. With nominal stickiness this is no longer true.

The trade–off between flexibility and rigidity
This brief discussion of the main elements of the basic model in Iwai (1981) serves as a prelude to the analysis of the decision individual firms face in Iwai's model whether to adjust their nominal wages or not. The assumption of complete nominal wage rigidity is untenable for it precludes a firm to react to any disequilibrium situation at all. The assumption of complete nominal wage rigidity implies that an individual firm has to accept any level of employment. Complete wage rigidity may create the possibility of stable equilibria but only at the cost of the dismissal of the allocative role of wages. There is, therefore, a trade-off between what Iwai calls the disequilibrium costs and the wage adjustment costs. The disequilibrium costs arise whenever a firm is confronted with a (subjective) disequilibrium on the labour market. This disequilibrium equals the difference between the nominal wage that maximizes expected profits and the actual nominal wage. If firms cannot adjust their nominal wages each firm has to accept any disequilibrium on the labour market and the resulting level of disequilibrium costs. In the case of nominal wage flexibility firms minimize these costs by trying to close the gap between the actual and the optimal money wage. Wage adjustment costs only arise whenever wages are actually changed and are assumed to exist because of some (ad hoc) characteristics of the labour market that need not concern us here. The disequilibrium costs represent the disadvantages of restraining price flexibility. These disadvantages are the same as in any neo–classical model. The foundation of the wage adjustment costs, however, is less clear cut. Though the introduction of nominal wage stickiness enables the establishment of stable equilibria in a monetary economy these costs are solely a function of certain institutional characteristics of the labour market and remain lump–sum throughout the analysis. Each firm tries to minimize these two types of costs by choosing an interval outside which wages are adjusted and inside which wages remain fixed.

In the absence of wage adjustment costs, the disequilibrium costs are minimized (and expected profits maximized) if the upper and lower boundary of the interval both equal zero. In other words, nominal wages should be as flexible as possible. The reasoning is essentially the same as in answering the issue of price flexibility in a neo–classical framework. But it should be kept in mind that this policy has its price since with full nominal wage flexibility the Keynesian model becomes the Wicksellian model in which full price flexibility implies instability.

In the presence of wage adjustment costs there is by definition a certain degree of nominal inertia. Given the aforementioned remarks about the theoretical foundation of the wage adjustment costs, Iwai's analysis can be extended, in our view, by making these costs a function of the variability of money wages. This is in line with our claim that individual agents do not only attach utility to quantities of goods but also to the variability in the prices. It should be remembered, however, that the issue of price stability and, hence, the issue of monetary stability is a *macro* issue. The public good nature of price stability necessitates the analysis of the interaction of individual firms in their decision whether to adjust nominal wages or not. In Iwai (1981), the decisions of other firms are taken as given and the particular use of the Nash assumption implies that individual firms have nothing to gain from a strategy in which they stick to nominal wage rigidity, given the expectation that other firms do not do so, or to a lesser extent. The important question whether and how individual firms voluntarily restrain their price flexibility once the actions of other firms are taken into account is taken up in the next section. In the context of Iwai's model of price setting behaviour the rationale for individual firms to attach costs to the variability of money wages is that (given the variability in goods prices) an increase in nominal wage flexibility frustrates the exchange process and the usefulness of money as such since in a world of cumulative inflation or deflation price signals can no longer be trusted.[15] If goods and labour are traded in money prices and money wages respectively traders have a common interest in the overall stability of prices. Given the abovementioned use of the Nash assumption in Iwai (1981), the remainder of this section elaborates upon the existence of the trade-off in Iwai's model. The Nash-assumption implies that Iwai does not deal with the interaction between various firms which means that the question how a certain degree of overall nominal stickiness comes about is left unanswered, but see section 7.4.

Each firm uses the following wage adjustment rule (all variables are logs).

$$W_t(i) = W_{t-1}(i) \quad \text{if} \quad |W_t^*(i) - W_{t-1}(i)| < S \qquad (7.2)$$

in which $\quad W_t(i)$ = actual nominal wage by firm i in period t

$W_{t-1}(i)$ = actual nominal wage by firm i in period $t-1$

$W_t^*(i)$ = optimal nominal wage for firm i in period t

$S > 0$ iff wage adjustments costs are positive

$S = 0$ iff wage adjustment costs are zero.

Note that the violation of the inequality in (7.2) may imply a wage increase as well as a wage cut. For our present purposes it is only relevant whether wages are changed or ·not. By assumption, each firm confronts at the beginning of period t the subjective disequilibrium on the labour market of the preceding period with the warranted change in the optimal wage. The optimal wage is mainly a function of the expected product demand and labour supply in period $t+1$. A change in this optimal wage, therefore, reflects a change in these expectations. The subjective disequilibrium in any period is defined as the difference between the optimal nominal wage in that period and the actual nominal wage in that period. As can easily be shown the summation of the subjective disequilibrium and the warranted change in the optimal wage equals the left hand side of the inequality in (7.2).[16] As long as this inequality holds wages are not adjusted. In other words, as long as the inherited disequilibrium z_{t-1} plus the warranted change in the optimal wage $[W_t - W_{t-1}]$ stays within a certain limit S, wages remain fixed.

Given the assumption that firms are following a satisficing approach and hence adhere to some form of bounded rationality the question is now, of course, what determines the choice of S for the individual firm. As argued above, the actual choice of S is determined by a trade–off between the disequilibrium costs and the wage adjustment costs. We follow Iwai (pp. 188–189) in that the disequilibrium costs D in period t are solely a function of the subjective disequilibrium $z_t = W_t - W_t$. An increase in z_t leads to an increase in D. If $W_t = W_t$ these costs equal zero. In the absence of wage adjustment costs (WA), expected profits are therefore maximized if $z_t = 0$. Using the standard first– and second order conditions this implies that expected profits are maximized if $D'(0) = 0$ and $D''(0) > 0$. It is obvious that the possibility to influence D only exists if the inequality in (7.2) does not hold. If considerations about monetary stability are of no importance at all, S should be set equal to zero.

As long as z_t differs from zero, D is positive irrespective of the fact whether wages are actually changed or not. Wage adjustment costs, however, only exist if wages are actually changed in period t. WA is therefore minimized if S goes to infinity. In the case of complete wage rigidity, WA is necessarily zero. In line with our analysis in the previous section and in contrast with Iwai, we conceive WA to be a function of the variability of money wages. This implies that the total cost function TC becomes:[17]

$$TC_t = D_t + WA_t = D(z_t) + WA\left(\frac{W_t - W_{t-1}}{W_{t-1}}\right) \qquad (7.3)$$

As will be argued in the next section in case of uncertainty (or, bounded rationality), all that can eventually be said about the actual choice of S given (7.3) is that the level of S lies somewhere between zero and infinity. In a neo–classical framework the trade–off between D and WA and, hence, the rationalization of nominal stickiness permits the determination of S, for instance, through the use of the envelope theorem as in Akerlof and Yellen (1985).[18]

Iwai (1981) is discussed here at some length because his analysis provides one of the few examples in which the claim of economists like Hicks and Keynes that price flexibility is not compatible with the stability of a monetary economy, is explicitly analysed. Moreover, the analysis could be strengthened, in our opinion, through a specification of the costs of wage adjustment function in which these costs depend directly on the variability of nominal wages and thus indirectly on the quest for price stability.

Nevertheless, the conclusion that it is possible to develop models in which there is a trade–off between money price flexibility and inflexibility does leave a number of questions unanswered. First of all, the analysis of the price setting behaviour in Iwai (1981) takes the decisions of other firms as given. This Nash assumption may be convenient but as to the issue of the overall stability of the economy the interaction between agents can not be neglected. Secondly, the question arises as to what can be said about the actual outcome of the trade–off. Is there an optimal degree of nominal inertia? It is to these questions that we now turn.

7.4 The degree of nominal inertia

It is important to separate the issue of a trade–off between price flexibility and price stickiness from the issue whether and how a certain degree of nominal inertia comes about. The former has been the major concern of this chapter up to now whereas the latter is the subject of this section.

In our view, there are basically two options to look upon the issue of the interaction between agents in their attempt to attain some degree of nominal inertia. Since the need for endogenous price stability is affected by the decisions of all economic agents, the realization of that objective does not solely depend on the decisions of a single agent. The problem of the actual choice of some degree of nominal inertia can be looked upon as the solution to a coordination problem. As Warneryd (1990) states, 'the crucial feature of such problems is that no action is individually dominant independently of what other people do' (Warneryd (1990), p.118). In the present context it depends on the institutional set–up whether this solution, the non–cooperative equilibrium, results in a situation in which all agents choose to maintain full price flexibility or in a situation in which nominal inertia exists. In the former case, each agent gets the highest pay–off if he sticks to full flexibility given that the other agents stick to some degree of nominal inertia. A coordinated solution in which some degree of stickiness is agreed upon is not an equilibrium since every agent has an incentive to deviate from that solution. The non–cooperative equilibrium will be one in which all agents remain fully flexible despite the fact that a Pareto–superior outcome exists. The need for an external agency (a Central Bank!) that takes care of the price stability requirement arises most clearly in this set–up.

In the latter case, the some degree of nominal inertia solution is a non–cooperative equilibrium meaning that solution can *not* be improved upon in terms of a higher pay–off for an individual agent through a deviation from that solution. This implies that the benefits of increased flexibility of agent i are off–set by the costs for agent i of increased uncertainty as a result of the fact that other agents may no longer feel obliged to stick to the convention.[19] It may even be the case that agents cannot, by definition, deviate from a nominal stickiness solution, however established. In Iwai (1988A) for instance, two agents wishing to trade money for goods and vice versa are not in a position to influence the terms of trade and have to take nominal prices as given. This result arises in the search–equilibrium framework of Iwai (1988A) because 'each individual is endowed with only one unit of a pre–determined good at birth and is able to store only one unit at a time', hence 'no degree of freedom is left for each trading pair to agree on the terms of their own trade by their own negotiation' (Iwai (1988), p. 23).[20]

Figure 7.1 illustrates these two options with respect to the interaction between agents. Both agents have two strategies at their disposal. The game is assumed to be symmetric. The first strategy is to remain as flexible as possible and the second strategy is to stick to some degree of nominal stickiness. The aforementioned first case arises if we assume the following pay–off structure:

$$D > B = C > A = 0 \text{ and } b_i > d_i \text{ and } c_j > d_j \text{ and } a_i = a_j = 0$$
$$\text{and } a_i > c_i \text{ and } a_j > b_j$$

The Pareto–efficient solution is not a non–cooperative equilibrium. Only solution A is a sustainable equilibrium.

The second case, nominal stickiness is a non–cooperative equilibrium, arises if for instance

$$D > B = C > A = 0 \text{ and } b_i < d_i \text{ and } c_j < d_j \text{ and } a_i = a_j = 0$$
$$\text{and } a_i < c_i \text{ and } a_j < b_j$$

agent *j*

flexible   sticky

flexible $A = a_i + a_j$ $B = b_i + b_j$

agent i

sticky $C = c_i + c_j$ $D = d_i + d_j$

Figure 7.1 Flexibility and stickiness in a static game

Even if the nominal stickiness solution is dominated in pay–off by strategies in which one or more agents can get a higher pay–off by remaining as flexible as possible as in the abovementioned first case, it can still be rational to restrain price flexibility. In the context of repeated games this will be the case if the equilibrium pay–off of the nominal stickiness solution D dominates the pay–off associated with the Nash–equilibrium A (see Schotter (1981)). In terms of figure 7.1, the dismissal of the assumption of one–shot or static games would mean in the first case that it is rational to restrict the strategies if the Nash–equilbrium A would yield a lower pay–off than the pay–offs associated with solution D.

The analysis of the choice of a *particular* degree of nominal inertia can be illustrated if one conceives this choice as choice between several conventions in the sense of Lewis (1986). This implies that any convention is conceivable as long as a sufficiently large number of agents stick to that convention. There is no mechanism that ensures that the most efficient convention will be realized unless it is assumed that one alternative 'always yields the highest pay–off for each individual agent, irrespective of the number of other agents that choose that particular alternative. But this contradicts the aforementioned definition of a coordination problem. The idea of a convention (and of a coordination problem) is illustrated in figure 7.2. Suppose there are two conventions with respect to the degree of nominal inertia with equal pay–offs that strictly dominate the other solutions. In fact, assume that for every set of chosen strategies pay–offs for agent *i* and agent *j* are equal and assume we have the following symmetric pay–off structure

$E = H > F = G$ and $e_x = h_x > f_x = g_x$. For $x = i, j$.

Whether solution E or H will get established as the actual equilibrium is not clear beforehand. Note, however, that neither agent *i* nor agent *j* has an incentive to deviate from the convention once this convention is established.

		agent j	
		sticky I	sticky II
agent i	sticky I	$E = e_i + e_j$	$F = f_i + f_j$
	sticky II	$G = g_i + g_j$	$H = h_i + h_j$

Figure 7.2 Stickiness in a coordination game

The issue of determining an *optimal* degree of stickiness points to a more fundamental problem, as the possibility of this determination is not compatible with the existence of uncertainty (and money) as such. The determination of an optimal degree would imply that agents would have a complete knowledge of (the variability of) future prices. In that case, however, the need for holding money disappears and uncertainty does not exist. This incompatibility is analogous to the problem of determining the optimal degree of information in case information is not costless (see also Hayek (1978) and Keynes (1921), pp. 83–84). The determination of an optimal degree of nominal stickiness is therefore only at home in a world in which agents have perfect foresight/rational expectations. Furthermore, since in such a world price stability is not an issue this optimal degree can in fact be determined easily for it equals, not surprisingly, zero. It is efficient for every single agent and also socially efficient to remain as flexible as possible irrespective of what other agents do. In the expected utility framework of Warneryd (1990) this can be illustrated as follows.[21]

Assume there is a continuum of individuals on the interval (0,1). n_s is the proportion of people who stick to the nominal inertia solution and $n_f = 1 - n_s$ is the proportion who choose to maintain full price flexibility. V_f is the expected utility for every agent of remaining as flexible as possible and this expected utility is a *de*creasing function of n_s. This assumption may be justified if the probability of finding someone to trade with also depends on the flexibility (stickiness) of the nominal prices of the potential trading partners. If other agents, for instance, wish to set up nominal contracts the expected utility for the individual agent of remaining as flexible as possible decreases as n_s increases. $V_f(n_s)$ is, therefore, the expected utility of being flexible when a proportion of the population does not do so. V_s is the expected utility of sticking to the nominal inertia convention and V_s is increasing in n_s for the same reason as V_f is decreasing in n_s.

The essence of figure 7.3 is that $V_f(1) > V_s(1)$.

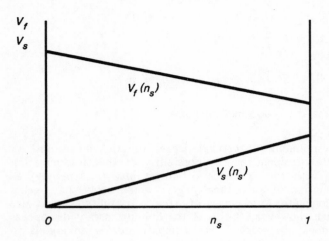

Figure 7.3 The optimal degree of price flexibility

This implies that even if everybody else would choose the stickiness
solution you would still be better off by maintaining full price
flexibility. As a result, every agent clings to full price
flexibility. The expected utility framework of figure 7.3, which is
based on Warneryd (1989, 1990), can also illuminate the problem of
choosing a particular convention of figure 7.2. In terms of this
framework there is a coordination problem if the V_e and the V_h
functions intersect. *Ex ante* it is not clear whether E or H will
actually be chosen but both solutions are stable equilibria since no
agent has an incentive to deviate from it as long as a sufficient
number of agents stick to the convention.[22] Before concluding this
chapter, we will briefly discuss how the analysis of this chapter
relates to our discussion of the alternative approaches in chapter 4
and to our analysis in chapter 6.

7.5 Money, prices, uncertainty and the alternative approaches

We saw in section 6.3.6 that our analysis of Keynes's essential
properties of money has important similarities with the monetary
post–Keynesians. We will not reiterate upon the differences between
our analysis of these properties and the interpretation by some
monetary post–Keynesians. For our present purposes it is especially
relevant that these post–Keynesians put great emphasis (see, for
instance Davidson (1978) and Kregel (1980) and Shackle (1972), pp.
218–219) on the necessity of some degree of nominal price inertia in

a monetary economy. Especially the existence of wage contracts is conceived of as a coordinating device that enhances monetary stability in a world characterized by uncertainty. The whole idea that full-price flexibility is not compatible with the existence of money lies at the heart of this branch of post-Keynesian economics. Both money and nominal stickiness are (imperfect) institutional solutions to the coordination problem.

This last conclusion also applies to the role of money in (neo-)Austrian economics. Money is not seen as an invention from the state but, on the contrary, as the outcome of the market process. The transformation from a barter to a money-using economy is not planned but only occurs because individual agents somehow recognize that the use of a common medium of exchange (and unit of account) is in their own interest, for it provides a means by which the coordination issue par excellence in Austrian economics, the dispersion of knowledge, can be (imperfectly) dealt with by agents. Money, especially money as medium of exchange, is, also in Austrian theory, an institutional solution to a coordination problem. The emphasis on the spontaneous emergence of money (or in the terminology of Menger (1892) the invisible hand explanation of money) not only implies that money is no state invention as in, for instance, the legal restrictions approach but also that governments should not intervene in a money-using market process. In its extreme version the latter means that the government monopoly of the (fiat) money supply should be dismissed and that there should be a privatization of money. The recent revival of the debate about free currency competition is probably due to Hayek (1976).[23] Monetary stability can be best guaranteed in this view if private banks can issue their own money. The Austrian ideas on competition and the market process imply that a private provision of money secures price and, hence, monetary stability: 'the past instability of the market economy is the consequence of the exclusion of the most important regulator of the market mechanism, money, from itself being regulated by the market process' (Hayek (1976), p. 79). The Austrian ideas on the emergence of money and the importance of price stability for the usage of money and the functioning of the market mechanism do, no doubt, have some resemblance with our analysis of Keynes on these matters in the previous sections, on the one hand, and with the monetary post-Keynesians, on the other hand. Keynes's emphasis on the nexus money-uncertainty, the indirect utility of money in decentralized exchange and the importance of monetary stability, for instance, illustrate this relation. There are, however, also important differences between the Austrians, on the one hand, and Keynes and the post-Keynesians, on the other hand, on these matters (see also section 4.4).

First of all, as to the provision of money by the private sector it is likely in our view that this creates coordination problems of its own. Using the line of reasoning of section 6.4. on nominal stickiness it can be argued that the privatization of money leads to externalities; see Vaubel (1977), (1984) and Laidler (1990B), pp. 108–109. The public good nature of money implies that the role of the government cannot as easily be dismissed as the Austrians seem to suggest. This points to a more fundamental difference between Austrians, on the one hand, and Keynes and the post–Keynesians, on the other hand. As noticed in chapter 4, Austrians emphasize the importance of the coordination problem but at the same time claim that the (unhampered) working of the market mechanism delivers a solution to this coordination problem. It is in their views on the beneficial effects of the price mechanism that the Austrians (Hayek) and Keynes (and post–Keynesians) diverge, as we saw in section 4.4. Applied to our analysis of the theory of a monetary economy in this chapter the difference boils down to what is known as the Wicksell connection (see section 6.2). In the remainder of this section, this connection is used to illustrate the main difference between the post–Keynesians and the (neo–) Austrians.

In Keynes's analysis in chapter 17 (but see also Keynes (1937A)), a portfolio equilibrium will be established if the money rate of interest equals the marginal efficiency of other assets. The same equilibrium condition holds for Keynes's version of classical theory. This equilibrium condition can be reinterpreted in terms of the Wicksellian monetary theory as the equality between the market rate of interest and the natural rate of interest in which the money rate of interest represents the former and the return on other assets the latter. In Keynes's liquidity preference theory the natural rate adjusts to the market rate whereas in the monetary theory of Hayek, which is in the Wicksellian tradition,[24] it is, of course, the other way around. Monetary disturbances (whether induced by the government or the commercial banks) lead to changes in the market rate and, hence, to a gap between the natural and the market rate of interest. Business cycles are, however, supposed to be self–correcting and in the long run the market rate adjusts to the natural rate and a new equilibrium results. The Austrian view of the business cycle ultimately depends on their assumptions concerning the working of the price mechanism in reestablishing equilibrium, on the one hand, and the existence of a natural rate that determines real variables, on the other hand. As Rogers (1989), who aptly summarizes the monetary post–Keynesian position, argues the natural rate has no theoretical foundation in Keynes's theory in the GT. As a matter of fact, the development of Keynes's monetary theory from the *Treatise on Money*, which is still in the Wicksellian tradition, to the GT can be looked upon as a dismissal of the Wicksellian approach. In Keynes's theory, there is no unique equilibrium but infinitely many equilibria since the market rate (the money rate of interest) sets the pace and the natural rate (the natural rate of interest) adjusts as we have argued in section 6.3. All this is just another way of saying that the rate of interest is a monetary phenomenon. Post–Keynesians often use Keynes (1937A) to support their interpretation of Keynes's liquidity preference theory. Keynes summarizes his position in this respect as follows.

> Put shortly, the orthodox theory [the Wicksellian approach, HG] maintains that the forces which determine the common value of the marginal efficiency of various assets are independent of money, which has, so to speak, no autonomous influence, and that prices move until the marginal efficiency of money, i.e. the rate of interest, falls into line with the common value of the marginal efficiency of other assets as determined by other forces. My theory, on the other hand, maintains that this is a special case and that over a wide range of possible cases almost the opposite is true, namely, that the marginal efficiency of money is determined by forces partly appropriate to itself, and that prices move until the marginal efficiency of other assets falls into line with the rate of interest (Keynes (1937A), p. 103).

According to Rogers (1989), these 'forces partly appropriate to itself' are precisely those forces that result from what we have called in our study the fundamental indeterminacy in Keynes's GT. Multiple monetary equilibria exist because for every state of expectations the market rate will be different (in other words there is no unique market rate) and the natural rate, the marginal efficiencies on real assets, adjusts to the money rate so to speak and realia are always influenced by monetary factors.

7.6 Conclusions

The analysis in the previous sections of this chapter suggests that it may be worthwhile to give some thought to the connection between the usefulness of money and nominal price stickiness. In our view, the existence of nominal inertia is a necessary condition for the usefulness of money as soon as the assumption of rational expectations (or perfect foresight) is dismissed as a behavioural hypothesis. The analysis does *not* deal with money in decentralized exchange as such, rather it analyses the supposed implications of money for price setting behaviour. The main part of the previous sections is, therefore, concerned with the rationale for restraining nominal price flexibility. A brief discussion of Iwai (1981) was meant to illustrate the theoretical possibility that full price flexibility is incompatible with the stability of a monetary economy and that nominal (wage) stickiness enhances this stability. It was furthermore concluded that the way nominal stickiness is actually realized depends on the institutional set-up. The idea that increased price flexibility may be destabilizing is neither new nor neglected in the recent theoretical literature. DeLong and Summers (1986), for instance, try to show that the impact of a change in price flexibility upon the stability of the economy crucially depends on the elasticity of expectations with respect to future price changes. Building on Keynes (GT, Ch.19) it can be shown that the expectations of future price changes may render the standard allocational role of prices ineffective, thus endangering the stability of the economy. The main difference between this line of reasoning and the analysis in the preceding sections is that the former is concerned with the development of expectations about prices over time whereas the latter emphasizes the incompatibility of nominal price flexibility, on the one hand, and stability of a monetary economy and the use of money as such, on the other hand.

A monetary foundation of nominal rigidities may be important for two reasons. First of all, the idea that a certain degree of nominal stickiness is a necessary condition for markets to work in a monetary economy has direct policy implications. It questions the rationality of those policies that are based on the assumption that more price flexibility is always to be preferred in terms of Pareto efficiency. At the same time it emphasizes the importance of price stability for a proper working of a decentralized monetary economy. Secondly, such a foundation makes clear that the integration of macro (theory of money) and micro (theory of value) is not a one-way process in the sense that macro should be founded necessarily on micro. On the contrary, the preceding analysis about money and nominal stickiness as coordinating devices is nothing but an example of the quest for 'macro'foundations for microeconomics. The main difference with this quest in the previous chapter is that the general equilibrium framework of chapter 5 is replaced by a framework in which uncertainty and lack of knowledge may shape individual decisions. Such a foundation of nominal stickiness may, therefore, also explain why the various attempts to give a foundation for nominal rigidities in mainstream economics are troublesome (see chapter 3, section 3.4).

Now that we have come to an end of our inquiry into the nexus money, prices, and uncertainty in chapters 6 and 7, it is important to compare the results of this inquiry with our analysis of money and coordination in a general equilibrium framework (chapters 3 and 5). In chapter 5 of this thesis it has been concluded that the difficulties underlying the incorporation of money in a general equilibrium framework like our OLG model can be traced back to a neglect of the significance of the role of the fundamental indeterminacy in the GT in analysing the coordination issue in general equilibrium based theories. It has been argued in chapters 6 and 7 that any useful analysis of a monetary economy should start with the recognition that the fundamental indeterminacy and the usage of money are related and that it should also address the question whether and how money is fundamentally different from other goods. The following conclusions follow from our investigation into these issues.

First of all, and opposed to the mainstream literature, money is not an independent cause, as in the mainstream debate on the non–neutrality of money (see chapter 3), but money is merely a consequence of the existence of uncertainty. Related to this conclusion is the conclusion that money is fundamentally different from other goods if one takes account of all of its functions in a world characterized by uncertainty. Secondly, and also opposed to the mainstream literature, it is not necessarily correct to argue that (nominal) price stickiness is a necessary condition for the non–neutrality of money. It may very well be the other way around: the use of money has implications for the degree of price flexibility. Finally, our analysis of the essential properties of money in section 6.3 and of nominal stickiness in the present chapter indicates that outside the general equilibrium framework it may be rational for individual agents to calculate in nominal terms.

It is, of course, well known that in the neo–classical world the concept of money–illusion is at odds with individual, rational behaviour. 'The type of behavior associated with money–illusion is the economist's prototype of irrational behavior' (Leijonhufvud (1968), p. 384). Keynes's monetary theory is about decision making under uncertainty. The charge of money–illusion may be misdirected for it does not capture an essential element of Keynes's theory namely that subjects calculate in money terms because the knowledge neo–classical theory assumes individual agents to possess is at least dispersed and often simply not yet available. Keynes is quite clear on the calculation of entrepreneurs in money prices. 'A process of production will not be started up, unless the money proceeds expected from the sale of the output are at least equal to the money costs which could be avoided by not starting up the process' or 'an entrepreneur is interested, not in the amount of product, but in the amount of money which will fall to his share' (Keynes (1933), p. 78 and 82). More generally, to assume the existence of an information set such that only calculation in real terms is conceived of as rational behaviour is rather misleading in our view[25]. The implication of Keynes's monetary theory is that, at least to some extent, rational choice does not exclude decision–making to be influenced by nominal variables.

No doubt the analysis in chapters 6 and 7 raises more questions than it answers. But, as has been argued in the introduction of our study, this may be a good thing. As to the main objective of this thesis, the search for 'macro'foundations for microeconomics, the preceding analysis shows that both money and (nominal) price stickiness can be conceived of as examples of (imperfect) coordinating devices. Apart from the vast differences in the analytical framework the main difference with the analysis on indeterminacy and multiplicity in chapter 5 is that in chapter 6 and the present chapter there does not only exist a coordination problem but agents also face the need to act upon (however imperfectly) this existence (compare with Keynes (1937B), p. 114). The usage of money and nominal stickiness (contracts) is one way of dealing with this coordination problem, in our view. The rather unsatisfactory conclusion concerning the multiplicity and/or instability of equilibria in a general equilibrium framework without the auctioneer in chapter 5 raises similar questions as to how to act upon the existence of the coordination problem. Again, the dismissal of the Walrasian auctioneer as an establisher of unique, stable Pareto–efficient equilibria implies that one should start to look for coordination devices that substitute for the coordinating device of the Walrasian auctioneer.[26] The next chapter will discuss the various ways in which general equilibrium analyses (should) deal with this issue as compared with other approaches.

Notes

[1]See, for instance, Kiyotaki and Wright (1988, 1989) and Warneryd (1989, 1990) and the references given in these papers. Niehans (1978) and Jones (1976) are two important forerunners of the recent literature. See also Laidler (1990B) for references of the microfoundations of money literature.

[2]The supply–demand frequency q_{ji} is defined by Iwai as 'the frequency (relative to the total population) of individuals who are willing to *supply* good j in exchange for good i' (Iwai (1988A), p. 4). The probability for our i-endowed, j-consuming agent to find a j-supplying, i-demanding agent is assumed to follow a Poisson process which implies that the meeting rate equals the frequency q_{ji}. It is furthermore assumed that each agent is always in expectational equilibrium (compare this with our discussion of Iwai (1981) in section 7.3. and note the difference!). Finally, the search process is not only represented by q_{ji} in Iwai's model but also by the supply–need and the endowment–need frequencies. For our present purposes the inclusion of the supply–demand frequencies suffices.

[3]More precisely, it also depends on the fact that these costs are assumed to be lower in case of a money equilibrium as compared to a barter equilibrium; see Iwai (1988A), p. 11.

[4]See also Brunner and Meltzer (1971) on this issue.

[5]See Scitovsky (1984) who also notes a similarity between Niehans (1978) and Lerner (1952) on this issue.

[6]For a recent assessment of the importance of this concept of liquidity see Hahn (1990); an interesting example of a recent attempt to elaborate on this concept of liquidity can be found in Jones and Ostroy (1984). In O'Driscoll (1986) this idea of liquidity is linked with the ideas of Menger (1892) on money in decentralized exchange. Our analysis of liquidity and uncertainty in Keynes' GT in section 6.2. is very similar to Hicks (1974). In fact, Hicks (1974) is an interpretation and amendation of Keynes's liquidity preference theory (and hence a dismissal of his early attempts in that direction in Hicks (1937)). See also Leijonhufvud (1984) on this issue. For a connection of Hicks' ideas on liquidity on the one hand and the role of transaction costs vis a vis uncertainty on the other hand see Kregel (1990).

[7]Whether they succeed in coordinating their activities or not is another issue; see section 7.4 below. See also Laidler (1990B).

[8]See also Davidson (1978).

[9]This conclusion can also be found on pp. 232–233 of the GT. Here Keynes states that the liquidity characteristics of money are enlarged by the nominal stickiness of wages (see also Shackle (1972), p. 218). At this point Keynes also connects his analysis of chapter 17 with the analysis of chapter 19 with respect to the effect of price expectations on the establishment of portfolio equilibrium.

[10]This does not mean that for Keynes's theory to hold nominal wage stickiness is a necessary condition as our analysis in chapters 2 and 5 with respect to the fallacy of composition shows. Note that for an open economy it may also be worthwhile in terms of monetary stability to peg its currency to a country with a high degree of monetary stability. In this case one has nominal exchange stickiness (see also Hoogduin (1991), p. 97).

[11]Iwai shows that the assumption of rational expectations is equivalent to the assumption of a barter economy in which Say's Law holds. Given the assumption of full price and wage flexibility the assumption of rational expectations would imply that every firm is always in expectational equilibrium. Since in that case the *aggregate* product and the labour market gap are zero the assumption of rational expectations boils down to assuming Say's law and hence to the negation of a monetary economy (defined as an economy in which labour and product market gaps may differ from zero). The difference between Iwai's analysis of expectations and the standard use of the rational expectations hypothesis concerns the fact that in Iwai's model the conditions of rational expectations only hold in case of an expectational equilibrium whereas the rational expectations hypothesis is normally used as a behavioural hypothesis. The latter excludes the issue of the non-existence of such an expectational equilibrium (see Iwai (1981), pp. 64–65). Note that this discussion of the rational expectations hypothesis as a behavioural hypothesis bears a striking resemblance to our discussion of the individualistic foundation of rational expectations in chapter 3 (see section 3.5.)

[12]See Iwai (1981), p. 92 and compare with Keynes's analysis of the fallacy of composition.

[13]Since Iwai's model is a model of firm behaviour the criticism has been raised that the neglect of consumer behaviour is essential for the conclusion of instability. As Iwai emphasizes, however, the inclusion of e.g. wealth effects does not automatically guarantee that a new equilibrium will be established (Iwai (1981), pp. 101–104).

[14]One could also pick the case of nominal stickiness of goods prices.

[15]Note that Iwai refers to chapter 17 of the GT in this respect, see Iwai (1981), p. 103.

[16]*Define* z_{t-1} as the subjective disequilibrium on the labour market of a firm i in period $t-1$ and $[W_t^* - W_{t-1}^*]$ as the warranted change in the optimal wage in period t. By definition $z_{t-1} = W_{t-1}^* - W_{t-1}$. Hence

$$z_{t-1} + [W_t^* - W_{t-1}^*] = W_t^* - W_{t-1}$$

and this last term equals the left–hand side of the inequality in (7.2).

[17]Iwai uses Taylor's theorem for a quadratic specification of the disequilibrium costs and, as noted above, the wage adjustment costs remain lump–sum. In our opinion a more detailed specification of the WA–function in (7.3) is not necessarily useful because in a world of uncertainty the determination of an *optimal* choice of S is beset with analytical difficulties, as will be argued in section 7.4. It should be noted, however, that if firms do take notice of the pricing decisions of other firms the WA–function of a individual firm should also be a function of the variability of money wages of other firms. The neglect of the interaction between firms in Iwai's model results in a WA–function of firm i such as (7.3) in which only the variability of the money wages of the firm itself is taken into account.

[18]Note that the concept of a monetary economy in Iwai's model only implies that Say's Law does not hold or what amounts to the same that markets do not clear. Money as a medium of exchange has no role to play.

[19]In the terminology of Langlois (1986) this is the case if the increase in behavioural entropy (i.e. the increase in flexibility) equals the increase in environmental entropy (i.e. the increase in uncertainty).

[20]To endogenize the terms of trade in the search model would imply that one has to take account of differences in bargaining positions which considerably complicates the analysis; see also Diamond (1984).

[21]The use of an expected utility framework is, of course, a far cry from Keynesian or Knightian uncertainty but it is only meant to illustrate the question of the determination of an optimal degree of nominal inertia.

[22]Note that the analysis underlying figure 7.2 and figure 7.3 (in case the V_f and the V_s function intersect) can not explain institutional transitions in terms of a change in equilibrium (see Boyer and Orléan (1991)) since any equilibrium is self–sustaining.

[23]See also White (1984) for this conclusion and for an account of the history of free banking in Britain.

[24]Our reference to the Wicksellian tradition refers to the textbook interpretation of Wicksell's monetary theory. We are aware of the fact that this interpretation does not necessarily correspond with Wicksell's own approach in, for instance, Wicksell (1935). See also section 7.3 in which we discuss Wicksell's approach of a cumulative disequilibrium process.

[25]Besides, who wants to be accused of using the concept of money–*illusion* or of any illusion in economics? The word money–illusion is a nice illustration of the use of rhetoric in economics in the sense of McCloskey (1983).

[26]Given our preoccupation with the issue of coordination the criticism that our analysis concerning the coordinating properties of money and nominal prices is not built upon first principles is misdirected to the extent that the coordinating device par excellence in a general equilibrium framework, our friend the Walrasian auctioneer, is also in need of choice theoretic foundations. See also Laidler (1990B) for a similar point of view.

8 Implications of the Coordination Problem

8.1 Introduction

Chapter 1 of this study defined a 'macro'theory as a theory of the economy as a whole that does not take the coordination issue for granted in the sense of not assuming that the unhampered working of the price mechanism guarantees a unique, stable Pareto–superior equilibrium. Given this definition, the quest for 'macro'foundations for microeconomics must be looked upon as the analysis of the implications of the coordination issue for the behaviour of individual agents in our view. This rather broad definition of a 'macro'theory and our plea for methodological pluralism made it possible to analyse the coordination issue within a general equilibrium framework (chapters 3, 5) as well as within an alternative framework (chapters 4, 6, 7). Irrespective of the analytical framework 'macro'theories cannot do without 'macro'foundations since the coordination issue needs to be endogenized if there is no longer a *deus ex machina* that imposes a unique, stable Pareto–efficient equilibrium upon a decentralized economy. The relevance of the search for 'macro'foundations arises from the absence of such a coordinating device because in that case one should look for mechanisms that enable individual agents to establish some (imperfect) degree of coordination in the economy.

We showed in chapter 2 that Keynes's GT deals with the coordination problem for the economy as a whole. In chapter 5 it was concluded that a useful extension of Keynes's analysis of the micro–macro and the indeterminacy issue within a general equilibrium framework should focus on the coordination failures approach in which bootstrap equilibria prevail and on the indeterminacy of equilibria in Keynesian OLG models, respectively. Though the analysis in chapter 5 deals with 'macro'theory it has not much to say on 'macro'foundations. In the next section of the present chapter we briefly discuss whether and how 'macro'foundations can be dealt with within a general equilibrium framework. In chapters 6 and 7 we concluded that the analysis of the coordination problem associated with the fundamental indeterminacy in the GT, the existence of uncertainty, results in a role for money and nominal price stickiness as coordinating devices. In section 8.3 the connection between 'macro'foundations and uncertainty is put in a somewhat broader perspective. The (need for the) analysis of 'macro'foundations in mainstream and non–mainstream economics shows some similarities as will be explained in section 8.4 which rounds up the theoretical part of our study. Section 8.5 concludes this study.

8.2 Implications of the coordination problem for individual behaviour (I): non-uniqueness of equilibria

In section 5.5 the important question arose how the analysis of Keynes's micro–macro and indeterminacy issue within a general equilibrium framework can be extended in order to diminish the degree of indeterminateness. In the case of the OLG model, the fact that indeterminacy implies that one is dealing with an open system has implications for the underlying assumptions concerning the formation of expectations. The use of perfect foresight expectations in the OLG model is of no use in arriving at determinate solutions. On the contrary, perfect foresight expectations sustain any equilibrium path and 'if there is a continuum of perfect foresight paths, the theory is incomplete' (Kehoe (1989), p. 392). Given our analysis of Hayek's criticism of the perfect foresight assumption, this conclusion does not come as a surprise, as it has been observed in section 4.3. that assuming perfect foresight boils down to assuming equilibrium. Hence, in case indeterminacy prevails this assumption becomes troublesome because it shows that perfect foresight does not represent a *theory* of expectations formation. We agree, therefore, with Kehoe (1989) who concludes that from a general equilibrium point of view 'indeterminacy is symptomatic of an incompleteness of the model. What is needed is a serious theory of expectations formation' (Kehoe (1989), p. 393). Or, in the terminology of our study, the lack of 'macro'foundations in the OLG model causes the indeterminacy to remain.

Similar observations can be made with respect to the analysis of Keynes's micro–macro issue within a general equilibrium framework. The coordination failures approach and its main feature of multiple Pareto–ranked equilibria do address the coordination issue but without dealing with 'macro'foundations the multiplicity result is ultimately unsatisfactory. The assumption of rational expectations that underlies the coordination failures approach is of no use in this respect because it is also essentially an equilibrium assumption (see section 3.5). The rational expectations hypothesis does not give any clue as to which equilibrium will be established. With respect to the use of rational expectations in models with multiple equilibria, Howitt (1990) observes that 'in such models the assumption that the economy is in a rational expectations equilibrium is not enough to make empirical predictions. And without some explicit adjustment assumptions that describe how people behave and interact when they are not in an equilibrium, we have no way of knowing which equilibrium they will go to, if any, or how fast, or by what route' (Howitt (1990), p. 17). The question thus becomes how to model expectations (or even *dis*equilibrium behaviour) when perfect foresight and rational expectations will not do.

One approach followed in the recent literature on this subject within a general equilibrium framework is to fall back on the assumption of adaptive expectations. With adaptive expectations, agents are no longer assumed to know the structural model of the economy. This means that some form of bounded rationality is introduced but, as is of course well-known, adaptive expectations may lead agents to make systematic errors. The assumption of adaptive expectations is, therefore, supplemented with a particular learning rule. It is assumed that agents are able to learn that their forecasts are not correct and that they may revise their expectations accordingly. Given the appropriate assumptions on the parameters of the reduced form estimation of the underlying structural model,[1] this process of expectations revision or, in other words, this learning process may eventually lead to convergence to a rational expectations equilibrium. For our present purposes it is not the assumption of adaptive expectations that is relevant, but the specification of the learning process. While it is no longer assumed that agents know the structural model, agents are still supposed to be able to distil the reduced-form equations of the structural model. This is somewhat less demanding in terms of information dissemination but it is still based on a number of rather restrictive assumptions in our view.[2] First of all, the specific learning rule(s) is (are) assumed to be given to each agent and also to be the same for all agents. Secondly, agents are somehow supposed to know that (all agents know that) the specific learning rule used by all agents leads to convergence to a rational expectations equilibrium. Finally, it is typically assumed that there are no costs of information gathering and processing. The first two assumptions imply that the recent work on learning within a general equilibrium framework presupposes individual agents to possess a substantial amount of what Pesaran (1987) calls common knowledge. In the absence of these two assumptions, problems of infinite regress arise because of the existence of higher-order expectations. The third assumption, information is costless, is important because in the presence of information costs 'it is less likely that learning will ever be complete. Given agents' subjective beliefs it may not be worthwhile to learn the true model even if it were in fact possible' (Pesaran (1987), p. 45). Furthermore, following our discussion of knowledge and the role of markets in section 4.3.1., *costless* information is difficult to reconcile with learning in a *market* economy. We will return to the issues of common knowledge and information costs in the final part of this section.

A second example of dealing with the non–uniqueness of equilibria can be found in Cooper (1987). The aim of the analysis is to show that in case of multiple Pareto–ranked equilibria the Pareto–dominant equilibrium is not a natural focal point (in the sense of Schelling (1960)). It is obvious that Pareto dominance cannot be reconciled with the coordination failures approach. Cooper (1987), therefore, develops an equilibrium selection criterion in which equilibria are history–dependent.[3] The details of his approach need not concern us here but the main idea is that 'agents' conjectures about the actions chosen by other agents move slowly. If the economy reaches an equilibrium in period t then agents believe that the equilibrium outcome will be close by in period $t+1$. Actions taken based on these beliefs are correct in equilibrium' (Cooper (1987), pp 20–21). Since these conjectures are in principle unobservable, Cooper, DeJong, Forsythe and Ross (1990) use an experimental framework in order to be able to test for the relevance of this idea and especially for the relevance of the Pareto–dominance criterion. In a controlled experiment players participate in a number of games with multiple Pareto–ranked equilibria.[4] The main result of this experiment is that the Pareto dominant outcome is indeed not (always) selected and this supports the analysis in Cooper (1987). In our view, however, this conclusion leaves an important question unanswered, namely why a particular Nash equilibrium in period t became established to begin with. The idea of history– or path dependency of equilibria does not solve this issue for it can only explain the established equilibrium in period t by referring to the equilibrium in $t-1$ etc. In fact, this points to a more general problem in game theory, the selection of equilibria in the case of multiple equilibria given the standard assumption that players' behaviour is solely determined by strategies and pay–offs. If behaviour is assumed to be solely determined by strategies and pay–offs and if players have full knowledge of each other's stategies and pay–offs, the existence of multiple equilibra is worrying, for this standard assumption does not give a clue as to which equilibrium will get established.

This brief discussion of two examples which try to cope with endogenous expectations formation and equilibrium selection, respectively, indicates that agents are still assumed to have (too) much knowledge about the model of the economy and/or about the game, with the result that these examples are as yet rather inconclusive in terms of 'macro'foundations. In the rest of this section we will argue that probably (further) changes in the notions of rational behaviour and equilibrium within the general equilibrium framework are called for in order to deal with the analytical implications of the coordination problem. For instance, in the example of the learning process the common knowledge assumption with respect to the optimal learning rule and the existence of a rational expectations equilibrium begs the question of how such a rule and a particular rational expectations equilibrium get established. A way out of these kinds of infinite regress problems might be to broaden the rather narrow interpretations of rationality (maximizing under a given set of constraints) and equilibrium. In that case, learning behaviour can be conceived of as (at least partly) determined by conventions[5] which implies that the need to explain the optimality of a learning rule and the knowledge of a rational expectations equilibrium disappears. If learning behaviour or behaviour in general is governed by bounded rationality and by past experience, the question of convergence to a rational expectations equilibrium loses much of its relevance.[6]

A similar observation can be made with respect to the issue of information costs. Not only is the assumption of costless information difficult to reconcile with the existence of markets, it also forecloses the analysis of other institutions.[7] If information costs are not negligible, the degree of indeterminateness may very well diminish since agents may be reluctant to change their actions in case information gathering and processing is costly. Lack of knowledge may *increase* predictable behaviour (see also the next section). The existence of information costs may also explain the existence of various non–market institutions. This notion or, more accurately, the idea of transaction costs lies at the heart of the so–called new–institutional economics in which various forms of economic organization (firms, contracts, property rights, etc.) are seen as resulting from the incompleteness of markets. Incomplete markets basically exist because the use of the price system is not without its (transaction) costs.[8] Institutions are thus conceived of as substitutes for missing markets. Langlois (1986, pp. 5–6) mentions the following three unifying themes of the new–institutionalist approach that bear a resemblance with the main theme of this section. First of all, adherence to some form of bounded rationality, secondly, emphasis on processes instead of static equilibria, and, finally, the recognition that 'the coordination of economic activity is not merely a matter of price–mediated transactions in markets, but is supported by a wide range of economic and social institutions that are themselves an important topic of theoretical economic inquiry' (Langlois (1986), p. 6). A survey of this approach is beyond the scope of this chapter but in terms of our search for 'macro'foundations it is important to note that the assumption of information/transaction costs may help to explain why it is rational for individual agents to restrain their flexibility and to resort to non–market institutions. The analysis of money as a medium of exchange in chapter 7 is a good example of this approach.

With respect to the issue of multiple equilibria in a game theoretic framework like Cooper and John (1988), the analysis of 'macro'foundations can also be improved in a game theoretic framework, in our view, once it is recognized that the standard notion of rationality in game theory (the behaviour of each player completely determined by knowledge of pay–offs and strategies) hinders instead of helps the attempts to solve the problem of (too) many equilibria.[9] Particular equilibria may act as a focal point merely because a particular convention, however established, to act in a certain way exists or even because agents think they ought to stick to a certain convention. Though the explanation of the origin of a *particular* convention or institution is probably not very useful, the idea of a convention or institution can be rationalized in case of coordination problems in a game theoretic framework as is shown by Schotter (1981).[10] The basic idea is that in the context of repeated games it may be rational for individual agents to restrict their strategies because of the possibility of a higher equilibrium pay–off for each player. This deliberate restraint on the part of the players can be looked upon as the adherence to a certain rule.

The main point of this brief discussion of the two abovementioned attempts[11] to model learning behaviour and history dependency of equilibria is that the analysis of 'macro'foundations calls for important deviations from the standard notions of rationality and equilibrium behaviour upon which general equilibrium theory is based.[12] In our view, less demanding assumptions as to both notions in terms of knowledge and information dissemination will enlarge our understanding of the implications of the coordination problem and will, hence, decrease the analytical 'anything goes' position associated with the indeterminacy or multiplicity of equilibria as discussed in chapter 5. Following DeVroey (1990), we can conclude that what is actually called for is a shift away from the analysis of the existence of equilibrium towards the process analysis of the establishment of equilibria. The approaches discussed in chapter 5 still focus upon the issue of existence, perhaps without realizing that the dismissal of the Walrasian auctioneer eventually calls for the analysis of market exchange and price formation. The inclusion of conventions and institutions does, of course, not provide a solution to the aforementioned problem of the economic system being an open system. But contrary to the idea that an open system is a feature of the incompleteness of the economic theory, the incorporation of conventions and institutions takes this feature as its starting point and thereby illustrates that the recognition of the inevitably open character of economic theories does not necessarily lead to analytical nihilism.

8.3 Implications of the coordination problem for individual behaviour (II): dealing with uncertainty

In chapter 4 we argued that Keynes's analysis in the GT of the fundamental indeterminacy, i.e. the role of uncertainty, is elaborated upon in some branches of post–Keynesian and Austrian economics. The inclusion of uncertainty in the analysis brings the coordination problem to the fore as in, for instance, the post–Keynesian analysis of the usage of money and the Austrian analysis, following Hayek, of dispersed knowledge. However, as we observed in the previous section, emphasizing the importance of the coordination problem and analysing the implications of this problem for individual behaviour are really two separate issues. This observation is also relevant with respect to the alternative approaches discussed in chapter 4. If one takes the pervasiveness of uncertainty to the extreme, logical difficulties arise because complete indeterminacy and individual actions are difficult to reconcile.

The question thus arises whether and how individual agents act upon the recognition that they somehow need to coordinate their activities in the face of uncertainty. In mainstream economics the implications of the existence of uncertainty for the coordination problem are not taken into account mainly because the inclusion of uncertainty is thought to lead to analytical nihilism (see, for instance, Lucas (1981), p. 224). Two remarks are here in order. In the first place, and in line with our plea for methodological pluralism, the fact that uncertainty is at odds with the general equilibrium framework does not imply that uncertainty is only compatible with irrational behaviour (see Coddington (1982) for this view) because it overlooks the possibility that the analysis of uncertainty may be at home in an alternative analytical framework.

In the second place, the exclusion of uncertainty increases rather than decreases the difficulties that mainstream economics faces in rationalizing the role of money or nominal price stickiness. In fact, both money and nominal stickiness can be looked upon as two examples of 'macro'foundations in the presence of uncertainty. If the fundamental indeterminacy of decentralized market economies is taken into account or, what amounts to the same (see Lawson (1985)), if the lack of knowledge of agents is taken into consideration, it may very well be the case that the degree of indeterminateness may be diminished if one focuses upon the implications of uncertainty for individual behaviour. The need to coordinate economic activity under uncertainty may lead agents to stick to conventional behaviour and may clarify the existence of various social institutions. In this respect the analysis of money and nominal price stickiness in chapters 6 and 7 illustrate the conclusion of the last section that less demanding assumptions as to the knowledge of agents may increase the usefulness of the analysis in terms of the quest for 'macro'foundations.

The idea that conventional behaviour is a dominant strategy once uncertainty is allowed for is aptly summarized by Keynes in his Galton Lecture of 1937. In his view, the incompleteness of our knowledge implies that

> we do not know what the future holds. Nevertheless, as living and moving beings, we are forced to act. Peace and comfort of mind require that we should hide from ourselves how little we foresee. Yet we must be guided by some hypothesis. We tend, therefore, to substitute for the knowledge which is unattainable certain conventions, the chief of which is to assume, contrary to all likelihood, that the future will resemble the past (Keynes (1973B), p. 124).

It is important to emphasize that conventions and institutions are imperfect coordinating devices. Unforeseen events may lead to the dismissal of certain conventions and institutions and may upset the formation of expectations. The idea that uncertainty *in*creases predictable behaviour is the main building block of Heiner (1983) in which it is shown why this is the case once the neo–classical assumption that 'there is no gap between an agent's competence and the difficulty of the decision problem to be solved' (Heiner (1983), p. 562) is dropped. If such a gap does exist, Heiner shows that more flexibility on the part of individual agents is not necessarily to be preferred. The existence of a gap between the competence of the decision maker and the complexity of the decision problem means that agents face the risk that allowing for more flexibility, in terms of selecting a new action, may turn out to be counter–productive, for they may choose the wrong action at the wrong time. An increase in the abovementioned gap will, in general, lead to an increase in inert behaviour. In our view Heiner's study is important for it provides a choice–theoretic foundation for decision making under uncertainty that rationalizes the existence of conventions and institutions as analysed by post–Keynesian and Austrian authors.

As has been outlined in section 4.3, Hayek's analysis of the coordination problem boils down to the question as to how individual agents acquire knowledge. The initial Austrian answer was that the price mechanism (somehow) takes care of this issue. It remained unclear, however, how prices influence the amount of knowledge agents possess. As a result, the attempt to 'solve' the coordination problem along these lines failed, basically because Hayek *et al.* did not develop a theory of expectations formation and information acquisition that would validate their claim as to the coordinating properties of the price mechanism.[13] In his later work, Hayek[14] comes up with a different answer to the extent that it is argued that rules and institutions are (imperfect) coordinating devices in a world in which knowledge is dispersed. The core concept is spontaneous order. The behaviour of individual agents is thought to be governed by rules and institutions inherited from the past that coordinate economic activity in the sense that these rules and institutions influence (but not determine) individual decision making. The resulting order is spontaneous, for these rules and institutions are often not a product of rational design and the history–dependency of this order ensures that certain rules that somehow came into existence in the past are carried over to the present.[15] The idea that these rules and institutions (laws, property rights and a system of markets) only influence and not fully determine decision making is important, for it illustrates that analysing the coordination issue in terms of arriving at a unique, determinate outcome is at odds with the subjectivistic principles of Austrian economics as discussed in chapter 4. The existence of dispersed knowledge implies by definition that individual agents (and economists for that matter) are at any moment neither in a position to plan economic activity like the Walrasian auctioneer nor are they in a position to fully explain the existing order.

> Concerning our modern economic system, understanding of the principles by which its order forms itself shows us that it rests on the use of knowledge (and of skills in obtaining relevant information) which no one possesses in its entirety, and that it is brought about because individuals are in their actions guided by certain rules. Certainly, we ought not succumb to the false belief, or delusion, that we can replace it with a different kind of order, which presupposes that all this knowledge can be concentrated in a central brain, or groups of brains of any practicable size (Hayek (1978), p. 13).

The attempt to combine the analysis of the coordination issue along these lines with uncertainty is known as pattern coordination. Rules and institutions constitute a pattern for the economy as a whole that serves as a guide line for (unique) individual decisions.[16]

In recent Austrian work on the issue of how individual agents cope with the coordination problem these insights are supplemented with the issue of expectations formation. With respect to the latter, the work of Lachmann is probably one of the main influences (see also Wubben (1991), pp. 26–29). The main idea is that expectations formation under uncertainty implies that agents lack the knowledge to change their expectations accordingly every time the economic environment changes. As a result agents will develop relatively simple 'rules of thumb' to deal with this lack of knowledge. With respect to expectations formation this means that expectations will tend to be fairly inelastic. This inelasticity of expectations may in turn contribute to a certain amount of price stickiness. In normal circumstances, prices will be fairly inflexible (see Lachmann (1977), pp. 65–81).

This brief discussion of Austrian ideas with respect to the need to act upon the coordination problem under uncertainty revolves around the incorporation of rules and institutions into the analysis. The same holds true for those post–Keynesian economists whose work has some similarities with our discussion of money and price stickiness in chapters 6 and 7, respectively. Following Keynes's observation that notwithstanding the prevalence of uncertainty we are forced to act, money and price stickiness are nothing but two examples of acting upon the coordination problem. In the absence of conventions and institutions any individual action becomes troublesome in a world characterized by uncertainty; hence 'notions of the active subject and social practices presuppose each other' (Lawson (1985), p. 919). Since the main elements of chapters 6 and 7 are at home with the monetary strand of post–Keynesian economics we do not need to reiterate its main conclusions. The discussion of money in chapter 6 and, subsequently, of nominal price stickiness in chapter 7 is precisely meant as an illustration of 'macro'foundations under uncertainty. The discussion of price setting behaviour under uncertainty in the appendix to chapter 4 also provides an example of the implications of uncertainty and hence of the coordination problem for individual behaviour. Given the analysis in chapters 4, 6 and 7 the following remarks are in order. First of all, despite important differences in the analytical framework both Austrian and post–Keynesian economics deal with the implications of the coordination problem for individual behaviour. These analytical differences cannot hide the essential point that at least some Austrian and post–Keynsian economists recognize that the incorporation of uncertainty into the analysis does not imply that economic theory has next to nothing to say on expectations formation and decision making. The need for coordination and hence for some degree of determinacy still exist if one allows for the role of uncertainty. Secondly, post–Keynesians stress the potential instability of conventions and institutions. The existence of these coordinating devices does not necessarily mean that the stability of the economy as a whole increases. Money may act as a hedge against uncertainty from an individual point of view but an overall increase in liquidity preference may increase the degree of uncertainty for the economy as a whole.[17] Minsky's financial instability hypothesis (see Minsky (1986)) also shows that certain (financial) institutions may enlarge the instability of decentralized market economies. Finally, the post–Keynesian case illustrates that the analysis of conventions and institutions does not automatically imply that equilibrium analysis as such should be discarded. The analysis of market institutions and of actual market exchange may be hard to reconcile with the Walrasian equilibrium concept but is at the heart of Marshallian economics on which much of monetary post–Keynesian economics is based (see, for instance, Davidson (1978) or Hicks (1989)). The need for a reassessment of Marshallian economics in order to extend Keynes's analysis has already been suggested by Clower (1975, pp. 203–204) but it has only been recently that the analysis of market exchange and the actual process of price formation have gained a renewed interest among mainstream economists.[18]

The discussion of the implications of the coordination problem in the previous and in the present section will be compared in the next section.

8.4 To sum up (I): facing the coordination problem[19]

Given our analysis in the previous chapters, we are now in a position to state that the differences between alternative approaches and general equilibrium theories are in some cases to be found mainly in methodology and not so much in the object of theoretical research. In a way mainstream economic theory starts to deal with the kind of coordination problems that were already a main focus in the work of Keynes more than fifty years ago but that have long been neglected in the post–war development of mainstream economics in our view.

The discussion in chapter 5 on multiplicity and indeterminacy of equilibria makes clear that nowadays the neo–classical framework of methodological individualism no longer mandates determinate solutions as the only legitimate practice (see also Ferri and Minsky (1989) for this conclusion and compare with Samuels (1989), p. 531). The question now arises whether the substitution of particular assumptions (non–cooperative behaviour, indeterminacy of equilibria, missing markets, non–linearities) for the assumption of the Walrasian auctioneer makes a difference in the foreclosure of the analysis of processes and of the particular way in which these processes determine economic reality by means of conventions, institutions, etc. In other words, does the possibility of indeterminate or multiple solutions constitute a sufficient condition for the analysis of processes? Not surprisingly, as we saw in section 8.2, this is not the case. The result of indeterminacy and/or the analysis of strategic complementarity does not imply that *dis*equilibrium behaviour is analysed. Only equilibrium positions are analysed. In the theory of coordination failures, for instance, the assumption of cooperative equilibrium behaviour is simply replaced by the assumption of non–cooperative equilibrium behaviour. The question why and how a particular equilibrium comes about is mostly left unanswered (see also De Vroey (1990), pp. 243–244). The idea of evolutionary economics cannot be analysed in theories in which the *interaction* of economic agents is absent.[20] In our opinion, however, the extension of the abovementioned developments with the analysis of (learning) processes is a logical and necessary next step in these theories in order to limit the degree of indeterminateness of these models. It is necessary in order to avoid an 'anything goes position' once the possibility of indeterminate solutions is no longer excluded.[21] The resulting degree of indeterminateness in general equilibrium theories without the auctioneer is highly unsatisfactory. In Hahn (ed.) (1989), which serves as a good survey of the state of the art in general equilibrium theory, the general message is clear. The lack of determinateness is a necessary and fruitful extension of the Walrasian model without the auctioneer but it raises many difficult issues. It raises especially the question of how the number of equilibria in the various models can be reduced. The general feeling is that this can only be done by formulating a *theory* of expectations formation in which it is recognized that the informational abilities between individual agents are bounded and that the analysis of the interaction of individual agents is essential. With a few exceptions this question is mainly raised and not answered yet. Whether future research in the general equilibrium framework will be able to provide an answer at all, remains of course to be seen. The indeterminacy of particular models forces general equilibrium theorists to face issues like the acquisition of knowledge by individual agents, the necessity to model processes (and hence the importance of history–dependency) and, eventually, the role of conventions and institutions in decentralized economies. The latter is already the subject of those neo–classical economists who use the standard choice theoretic paradigm to analyse institutions and conventions by means of transaction costs and property rights.

Notwithstanding the major differences between orthodox and non–orthodox economics, the recent work on indeterminacy and multiplicity is in sharp contrast with the tradition in mainstream economics to circumvent the coordination issue. The dominance of the quest for unique, stable equilibria in mainstream economics lies at the heart of neo–classical economics. The reductionist research strategy of neo–classical economics is mainly directed towards the individualistic foundation of this particular equilibrium for specific markets or for the economy as a whole. To a large extent, this research does not deal with the issue of how equilibria come about, it only explains the rationality of these equilibria as such. The majority of economic theorists have been using a variety of metaphors to circumvent the coordination issue. The invisible hand of classical economists became the Walrasian auctioneer in neo–classical economics and this in turn became the representative agent, Robinson Crusoe, in new–classical models. The coordination problem is either assumed to be taken care of by some force outside the economic system or is not an issue at all. The coordination problem and the implications of the coordination problem for individual behaviour are central issues in, for instance, (neo-) Austrian economics and post–Keynesian economics. This is hardly surprising because these two schools build directly upon the original contributions by Keynes and Hayek in which this issue is essential. The recent attempts in mainstream economics to take the coordination issue no longer for granted are no more than a first step. As we argued above, future research in non–Walrasian general equilibrium theory has to focus upon diminishing the degree of indeterminateness in models without the auctioneer. In so far as this does lead to a reorientation of economic research, economic theory is back where it started beccause mainstream economics than starts to deal with those aspects of decentralized economies that were the focal point for economists like Keynes and Hayek in the 1930s but that were submerged in the post–war development of economic theory. Take, for instance, the following quotation from Hahn's own contribution to Hahn (ed.) (1989).

> Current economic theory by and large avoids dynamics. This has the virtue of allowing orderly argument and conclusion...dynamics should be viewed as a learning process, both about demand conditions and about the strategies of near competitors. Once again, when an equilibrium is defined relatively to such processes, it seems that they are indeterminate unless history– that is information– is explicitly modelled and known. The path of history is the outcome of individual decisions and in turn helps to fix the latter. This is really the main message: the information available to agents at any time is determined by the particular path followed. The economy could have followed a different path and generated quite different information. There is something essentially historical in a proper definition of equilibrium and of course in the dynamics itself. (Hahn (ed.) (1989) pp. 125–126).

This quotation might also have been taken from an article by Joan Robinson on historical time (see, for instance, Robinson (1974)). In my view adherents to the different schools in economic theory mostly tend to emphasize the mutual differences. Undoubtedly there are good reasons for doing so. But to some extent these differences are more apparent than real.[22] In line with methodological pluralism one should analyse the differences in substance and discard the differences in elegance.

8.5 To sum up (II): extending Keynes's analysis

The following objectives of this study were formulated in chapter 1. First of all, to argue that the coordination problem[23] is at the heart of Keynes's economics. Secondly, to show that what we consider to be Keynes's main theoretical message got lost in the post-war development of mainstream economics with the result that the microfoundations debate does not address the right issue. Finally, given these first two objectives we have tried to come up with some answers to the question of what constitutes a more useful extension of Keynes's ideas within both a general equilibrium framework and an alternative framework. Irrespective of the analytical framework and in agreement with our methodological position, such an extension ultimately calls for a search for 'macro'foundations for microeconomics in our view. Once the need to coordinate economic activity becomes an endogenous one, as in the case of the non-uniqueness of equilibria or of uncertainty, it becomes clear that the standard way of dealing with issues like expectations formation and price flexibility will no longer do. The question of the proper analytical framework to deal with the (implications of the) coordination problem is not only beyond the scope of this study, it is also not a very relevant one, given the remarks on methodological pluralism in the introductory chapter.

Now that we have come to the end of our inquiry, two final remarks must be made. First of all, it must again be emphasized that we do *not* claim that the present study shows what Keynes really meant, nor do we wish to claim that 'it's all in Keynes'. This study deals with what we consider and what we think Keynes considered to be the central question of economic theory: whether and how economic activities are coordinated in a decentralized market economy. We do discard the question whether Keynes did develop a full-fledged theoretical answer to that question. Secondly, the aforementioned central question also lies at the heart of Adam Smith's use of the Invisible Hand. The title of our thesis is therefore not a rejection of any invisible hand explanation of economic phenomena or of equilibrium analysis as such. Rather it is meant to criticize the use of the Invisible Hand assumption as a means to circumvent the coordination issue. Whereas Smith was interested in the way market institutions function, the invisible hand gradually became a short-cut for the dismissal of the question of coordination. In the GT, Keynes criticized the validity of this use of the invisible hand assumption for the economy as a whole. In the post-war development of economic theory Keynes's analysis and hence Keynesian theory mainly became associated with the view of frictions on the part of the price mechanism. The question of the coordination of economic activity once again disappeared. As has been outlined in the previous chapters, a useful extension of Keynes's economics should not start with the allocative characteristics of various markets but should address the issue of coordination of activities in a market economy. The real challenge in elaborating upon Keynes's GT lies therefore in the recognition that once the highly centralized institution of the Walrasian auctioneer has left the stage or, even more far-reaching, once uncertainty is allowed for, it is no longer possible to circumvent the question as to how individual agents in a decentralized economy are able to achieve some level of coordination for the economy as a whole.

Notes

[1] See Blanchard and Fischer (1989), pp. 257–260 or Bullard (1991) for a comprehensive model of learning behaviour and for references to the relevant literature.

[2] The following discussion of learning behaviour is largely based on Pesaran (1987), chapter 3.

[3] The idea of connecting history–dependency of equilibria with the Cooper and John (1988) framework of expectations driven equilibria in order to cope with the existence of multiple equilibria can also be found in Krugman (1991A). For an interesting example of history–dependency of equilibria see Krugman (1991B).

[4] For a similar experiment see also VanHuyck *et al.* (1990) in the same issue of the *American Economic Review*.

[5] Following Sugden (1989) a convention can be defined as an established pattern of behaviour in case there are several other solutions to a coordination problem. The analysis of conventions does also have to face the issue of history–dependency.

[6] In fact the substitution of adaptive expectations for rational expectations can be looked upon as increasing rather than decreasing predictable behaviour. The rationality of adhering to adaptive instead of to rational expectations in terms of enhancing the stability of the economy is for instance well–established in the literature on hyperinflation. See also Kuipers (1981), p. 99.

[7]For a definition of a social institution and a social convention see section 1.1 of our study.

[8]As is well known this idea was first analysed by Coase (1937). As the various contributions to Langlois (ed.) (1986) reveal the label 'new–institutionalist economics' covers a variety of approaches but the transaction cost approach is probably the most influential one. For a good survey of the latter see Eggertson (1989); the work of Williamson (1975), (1985) is especially important.

[9]This is a main theme of Kreps (1990), chapter 6. See also Sugden (1989), pp. 89–90.

[10]In this respect one can distinguish coordination games from non–cooperative equilibrium games. In the former a particular player does not only not want to change his own behaviour he or she also does not want the other players to do so (check figure 7.2 in section 7.4.). In the latter a particular player may benefit if other players change their strategies (check figure 7.1 in section 7.4.); the Prisoner's Dilemma is, of course, a classic example of a non–cooperative game.

[11]It should be emphasized that these are just two examples. On how to deal with the issue of multiple Pareto–ranked Nash equilibria and a critique of the concept of Nash–equilibrium see, for instance, Janssen (1990), pp. 148–163) on rationalizable strategies. Haltiwanger and Waldman (1985) show how the rationality postulate can be amended by allowing for heterogeneity in expectations formation. The various contributions to Hahn (ed.) (1989) are to some extent all dealing with the topics touched upon in this section.

[12]Following Howitt (1990, p. 82) it is good to remember that these standard notions are after all nothing but mere conventions themselves, they are devoid of any analytical superiority. For a similar viewpoint on the necessity of changing the core assumptions of general equilibrium theory see Leijonhufvud (1981, pp. 340–345) and Clower (1975, pp. 187–209). For an excellent analysis of the deficiencies of neo–classical choice theory in case strategic considerations are important see Sugden (1991).

[13]From our discussion of the basic tenets of Austrian economics in chapter 4 it will probably be clear why the recent approaches to model learning processes in mainstream economics, as briefly discussed in the previous section, are not suited as a theory of learning behaviour along Austrian lines. See also O'Driscoll and Rizzo (1985), pp. 37–38.

[14]See, for instance, Hayek (1967), chapter 3, Hayek (1973), chapter 2 and Hayek (1978), chapter 1.

[15]For a connection between the problem of equilibrium selection in game theory mentioned in the previous section and Hayek's ideas on the establishment of rules see Sugden (1986) and (1989).

[16]See also the contributions by O'Driscoll and Rizzo and by Langlois in Kirzner (1986). Pattern coordination or pattern equilibrium can be defined as follows, 'plans are in a pattern equilibrium if they are coordinated with respect to their typical features, even if their unique aspects fail to mesh' (O'Driscoll and Rizzo (1985), p. 85).

[17]Compare this with Keynes's remark that the desire of investors to hold their resources in 'liquid' securities overlooks the fact that 'there is no such thing as liquidity of investment for the community as a whole' (Keynes (1936), p. 155).

[18]In this respect it interesting to note that Marshallian ideas pop up in a number of contributions to the special issue of *The Economic Journal* (vol. 101(1), 1991) on future developments in economic theory. See for instance the contribution by Morishima (pp. 48–49) on the future of general equilibrium theory and his plea to build upon Okun (1981) and Hicks (1989) both of which analyse the actual process of market exchange. See also Okun (1981), p. 22   for a link with Marshall and the connnection between micro and macro.

[19]This section is based upon Garretsen (1991).

[20]Of course, there are notable exceptions. In Langlois (ed.) (1986) for instance the process nature of economics is analysed from both alternative (neo–Austrian economics) and neo–classical (the transaction costs approach) viewpoints. In Pheby (ed.) (1989) various contributors point to the similarities between post–Keynesian economics and the so–called new–institutional economics in, for instance, Langlois (ed.) (1986). A comparison of these approaches is beyond the scope of our study but see for instance Hodgson (1988) for a critical assessment of the transaction cost approach. We also abstract from the important and well–known debate as to the origin and rationalization of institutions that exists between those institutional economists that work in the tradition of Veblen as opposed to those following the lead of Menger.

[21]Given this quest for analytical control the incorporation of concepts that have their origin in the process nature of economics is either truncated or totally absent. An example of the former is the neo–classical theory of hysteresis in the natural rate of unemployment in which the path–dependency of this rate is only used in order to get rid of the Phillips–curve effect. Recognition of the path–dependency of *all* economic variables, as in for instance Joan Robinson's concept of historical time, is difficult to reconcile with a standard neo–classical model in which the concept of logical time is used.

[22]See, for instance, the contribution by Makowski in Hahn (1989) and compare this with our discussion of money and uncertainty in section 6.2. Or see Akerlof and Yellen (1987) on the fairness of wages and compare this with our discussion of nominal price stickiness in chapter 7. For some evidence as to the importance of conventional behaviour in wage and price setting behaviour along the lines of Akerlof and Yellen (1987), see Blinder and Choi (1990) and Blinder (1991).

[23]In this study the coordination problem refers to the economy as a whole andthe analysis of the implications of the coordination problem refers to individual households and firms. It is, of course, also possible to refer to the coordination problem *within* a particular household or firm and to deal with the implications for the participants within that household or firm; see Leibenstein (1979) and (1982) for the coordination problem on the level of the individual firm.

References

Agassi, J. (1960), 'Methodological Individualism', *British Journal of Sociology*, pp. 244–270.

Agliardi, E., (1988), 'Microeconomic Foundations of Macroeconomics in the Post–Keynesian Approach', *Metroeconomica*, 39, pp. 275–297.

Akerlof, G.A. and J. Yellen, (1985), 'A Near–Rational Model of the Business Cycle with Wage and Price Inertia', *Quarterly Journal of Economics*, 100, Supplement, pp. 823–838.

Akerlof, G.A. and J. Yellen, (1987), 'Rational Models of Irrational Behavior', *American Economic Review, Papers and Proceedings*, 77, pp. 137–142.

Andrews, P.W.S., (1964), *On Competition in Economic Theory*, London.

Arrow, K.J., (1959), 'Toward a Theory of Price Adjustment', in M. Abramowitz (ed.), *The Allocation of Economic Resources*, Stanford U.P., pp. 41–51.

Aschheim, J. and C. Hsieh, (1969), *Macro‑economics: Income and Monetary Theory*, Columbus.

Asimakopulos, A., (1977), 'Profits and Investment: A Kaleckian Approach', in G.C. Harcourt (ed.), *The Microeconomic Foundations of Macroeconomics*, London and Basingstoke, pp. 328–343.

Ball, R. and D. Romer, (1987), 'Sticky Prices as Coordination Failure', *NBER Working Paper*, No. 2327.

Barro, R.J., (1974), 'Are Government Bonds Net Wealth?', *Journal of Political Economy*, 81, pp. 1095–1117.

Barro, R.J., (1976), 'Rational Expectations and the Role of Monetary Policy', *Journal of Monetary Economics*, 3, pp. 1–32.

Barro, R.J., (1980), 'A Capital Market in an Equilibrium Business Cycle Model', *Econometrica*, 48, pp. 1393–1417.

Baumol, W.J., (1952), 'The Transactions Demand for Cash: An Inventory Theoretic Approach', *Quarterly Journal of Economics*, 66, pp. 545–556.

Baumol, W.J. and J. Benhabib, (1989), 'Chaos, Significance, Mechanism and Economic Applications', *Journal of Economic Perspectives*, 3, pp. 77–107.

Bausor, R., (1983), 'The Rational Expectations Hypothesis and the Epistemistics of Time', *Cambridge Journal of Economics*, 7, pp. 1–11.

Bernheim, D., (1984), 'Rationalizable Strategies', *Econometrica*, 52, pp. 1007–1028.

Blanchard, O.J., (1987), 'Why does Money affect Output?', *NBER Working Paper*, nr. 2285.

Blanchard, O.J., (1989), 'Comment on McCallum', *Scandinavian Journal of Economics*, 91, pp. 259–279.

Blanchard, O.J. and S. Fischer, (1989), *Lectures on Macroeconomics*, MIT Press Cambridge.

Blanchard, O.J. and N. Kiyotaki, (1987), 'Monopolistic Competition and the Effects of Aggregate Demand', *American Economic Review*, 77(4), pp. 647–666.

Blinder, A.S., (1991), 'Why Are Prices Sticky? Preliminary Results from an Interview Study', *American Economic Review Papers and Proceedings*, 81, pp. 89–97.

Blinder, A.S. and D.H. Choi, (1990), 'A Shred of Evidence on Theories of Wage Stickiness', *Quarterly Journal of Economics*, 105, pp. 1003–1016.

Blinder, A.S. and S. Fischer, (1981), 'Inventories, Rational Expectations and the Business Cycle', *Journal of Monetary Economics*, 8, pp. 277–304.

Boland, L.A., (1986), *Methodology for a New Microeconomics*, Boston.

Boyer, R. and A. Orléan, (1991), 'Why Are Institutional Transitions So Difficult?', *Rapports et Documents du CREA*, 9105A, Paris.

Brady, M.E., (1990), 'The Mathematical Development of Keynes' Aggregate Supply Function in the General Theory', *History of Political Economy*, 22, pp. 167–173.

Brunner, K. and A.H. Meltzer, (1971), 'The Uses of Money: Money in the Theory of an Exchange Economy', *American Economic Review*, 61, pp. 784–805.

Buiter, W.H., (1989), *Macroeconomic Theory and Stabilization Policy*, Manchester.

Bullard, J.B., (1991), 'Learning, Rational Expectations and Policy: A Summary of Recent Research', *The Federal Reserve Bank of St. Louis Review*, 73, pp.50–60.

Bulow, J.I., J. Geanakoplos and P. Klemperer, (1985), 'Multimarket Oligopoly: Strategic Substitutes and Complements', *Journal of Political Economy*, 93, pp. 448–511.

Caldwell, B., (1982), *Beyond Positivism*, London.

Caldwell, B., (1988), 'Hayek's Transformation', *History of Political Economy*, 20, pp. 513–543.

Caldwell, B., (1989), 'Post–Keynesian Methodology: An Assessment', *Review of Political Economy*, 1, pp. 43–65.

Caldwell, B, (1991), 'Clarifying Popper', *Journal of Economic Literature*, 29, pp. 1–34.

Carabelli, A.M., (1988), *On Keynes's Method*, London, Macmillan.

Carson, C., (1990), 'Kalecki's Pricing Theory Revisited', *Journal of Post-Keynesian Economics*, 13, pp. 146–152.

Carvalho, F., (1985), 'Alternative Analyses of Short and Long Run in Post–Keynesian Economics', *Journal of Post-Keynesian Economics*, 7, pp. 214–234.

Casarosa, C., (1981), 'The Microfoundations of Keynes' Aggregate Supply and Expected Demand Analysis', *Economic Journal*, 91, pp. 188–194.

Cass, D., M. Okuno and I. Zilcha, (1979), 'The Role of Money in

Supporting the Pareto Optimality of Competitive Equilibrium in Consumption–Loan Type Models', *Journal of Economic Theory*, 20, pp. 41–80.

Cecco, M. de, (1990), 'Keynes Revived, A Review Essay', *Journal of Monetary Economics*, 26, pp. 179–191.

Chatterjee, S. and R. Cooper, (1989), 'Multiplicity of Equilibria and Fluctuations in Dynamic Imperfectly Competitive Economies', *American Economic Review Papers and Proceedings*, pp. 353–358.

Chick, V., (1983), *Macroeconomics after Keynes: A Reconsideration of the General Theory*, Deddington.

Clower, R., (1965), 'The Keynesian Counter–Revolution: A Theoretical Appraisal', in F. Brechling and F.H. Hahn (eds.): *The Theory of Interest Rates*, London, Macmillan, pp. 103–125.

Clower, R., (1967), 'A Reconsideration of the Microfoundations of Monetary Theory,' in D.A. Walker (ed.), (1984), *Money and Markets. Essays by Robert Clower*, Cambridge.

Clower, R., (1975), 'The Coordination of Economic Activities: a Keynesian Perspective', in D.A. Walker (ed.), (1984), *Money and Markets. Essays by Robert Clower*, Cambridge.

Coase, R.H., (1937), 'The Nature of the Firm', *Economica*, 4, pp. 386–405.

Coddington, A., (1982), 'Deficient Foresight: A Troublesome Theme in Keynesian Economics', *American Economic Review*, 72, pp. 480–488.

Cooper, R., (1987), 'Dynamic Behavior of Imperfectly Competitive Economies with Multiple Equilibria', *NBER Working Paper*, No. 2388.

Cooper, R. and A. John, (1988), 'Coordinating Coordination Failures in Keynesian Models', *Quarterly Journal of Economics*, 103, pp. 441–465.

Cooper, R., D.V. DeJong, R. Forsythe and T.W. Ross, (1990), 'Selection Criteria in Coordination Games', *American Economic Review*, 80, pp. 218–233.

Cowling, K., (1983), *Monopoly Capitalism*, London.

Cukierman, A., (1984), *Inflation, Stagflation, Relative Prices, and Imperfect Information*, Cambridge University Press, Cambridge.

Davidson, P., (1974), 'A Keynesian View of Friedman's Theoretical Framework for Monetary Analysis', in R. Gordon (ed.), *Milton Friedman's Monetary Framework. A Debate with Critics*, Chicago, pp. 90–110.

Davidson, P., (1978), *Money and the Real World*, 2nd edition, London.

Davidson, P., (1982), *International Money and The Real World*, London.

Davidson, P., (1983), 'The Marginal Product Curve is not the Demand Curve for Labor and Lucas' Labor Supply Function is not the Supply Curve for Labor in the Real World', *Journal of Post–Keynesian Economics*, 6, pp. 105–117.

Davidson, P. and E. Smolensky, (1964), *Aggregate Supply and Demand Analysis*, New York.

Davis, J.B., (1989), 'Keynes on Atomism and Organicism', *Economic Journal*, 99, pp. 1159–1172.

DeLong, B.J. and L.H. Summers, (1986), 'Is Increased Price Flexibility Stabilizing?', *American Economic Review*, 76, pp. 1031–1045.

DeVroey, M., (1990), 'The Base Camp Paradox', *Economics and Philosophy*, 6, pp. 235–253.

Diamond, P., (1965), 'National Debt in a Neoclassical Growth Model', *American Economic Review*, 55, pp. 1126–1150.

Diamond, P., (1982), 'Aggregate Demand Management in Search Equilibrium', *Journal of Political Economy*, 51, pp. 881–894.

Diamond, P., (1984), *A Search Equilibrium Approach to the Micro–Foundations of Macroeconomics*, Cambridge.

Dickson, H., (1983), 'How did Keynes Conceive of Entrepreneurs' Motivation', *History of Political Economy*, 15, pp. 229–249.

Dow, S., (1985), *Macroeconomic Thought: A Methodological Approach*, Basil Blackwell, Oxford.

Dow, S. and A. Dow, (1985), 'Animal Spirits and Rationality', in T. Lawson and M. Pesaran (eds.), *Keynes' Economics: Methodological Issues*, London, pp. 46–66.

Earl, P., (1983), *The Economic Imagination*, Brighton.

Ees, H. van, (1989), 'An Explanation of Unemployment through an Integration of the Efficiency Wage Theory and the Kinked Demand Curve Approach', *Jahrbuch für Sozialwissenschaft*, 40, pp. 82–94.

Ees, H. van, (1990), *Macroeconomic Fluctuations and Individual Behaviour. The Implications of Real and Nominal Inertia*, PhD–disseration, Groningen.

Ees, H. van and H. Garretsen (1990), 'The Right Answers to the Wrong Question? An Assessment of the Microfoundations Debate', *De Economist*, 138, pp. 123–145.

Eggertson, T., (1989), 'The Role of Transaction Costs and Property Rights in Economic Analysis', *paper presented at the 1989 EEA convention*, Augsburg.

Eichner, A.S., (1976), *The Megacorp and Oligopoly*, Cambridge.

Eichner, A.S., (1983), 'The Post Keynesian Paradigm and Macro Dynamic Modelling', *Thames Papers in Political Economy*, No. 26.

Eichner, A.S. and J.A. Kregel, (1975), 'An Essay on Post–Keynesian Theory: A New Paradigm in Economics', *Journal of Economic Literature*, 12, pp.1293–1315.

Eijgelshoven, P. J., (1982), *De kritiek op de neo–klassieke allocatie–en verdelingstheorie*, Wolters–Noordhoff, Groningen.

Feenstra, R.F., (1986), 'Functional Equivalence between Liquidity Costs and the Utility of Money', *Journal of Monetary Economics*, 17, pp. 271– 290.

Ferri, P. and H.P. Minsky, (1989), 'The Breakdown of the IS–LM Synthesis: Implications for Post–Keynesian Economic Theory', *Review of Political Economy*, 1, pp. 123–144.

Fischer, S., (1988), 'Recent Developments in Macroeconomics', *Economic Journal*, 98, pp. 293–340.

Friedman, B., (1978), 'The Theoretical Non Debate about Monetarism' in T. Mayer (ed.), *The Structure of Monetarism*, New York.

Frydman, R. and E. Phelps (eds.), (1983), *Individual Forecasting and Individual Outcomes*, Cambridge.

Gale, D., (1973), 'Pure Exchange Equilibrium of Dynamic Economic Models', *Journal of Economic Theory*, 6, pp. 12–36.

Garegnani, P., (1978), 'Notes on Consumption, Investment and Demand', *Cambridge Journal of Economics*, 2, .

Garretsen, H., (1990), 'Pricing, Uncertainty and the Economics of Keynes: a Comment', *Metroeconomica*, 41, pp. 89–95.

Garretsen, H., (1991), 'Some Remarks on Determinate Solutions and the Foreclosure of Process', *Journal of Post–Keynesian Economics*, 13, pp. 414–424.

Garretsen, H., L.H. Hoogduin and E. Sprokholt, (1988), 'The Essential Properties of Money?', *IER Researchmemorandum* no. 271, University of Groningen.

Garretsen, H. and M.C.W. Janssen (1989A), 'Indeterminacy in Macroeconomics. On the Method of Keynes' General Theory', *IER Researchmemorandum*, no. 319, University of Groningen.

Garretsen, H. and M.C.W. Janssen (1989B), 'Two Fallacies of Composition in a Keynesian OLG Model', *IER Researchmemorandum*, no. 317, University of Groningen.

Geanakoplos, J.D. and H.M. Polemarchakis, (1986), 'Walrasian Indeterminacy and Keynesian Macroeconomics', *Review of Economic Studies*, 53, pp. 755–779.

Gerrard, B., (1991), 'Keynes' General Theory: Interpreting the Interpretations', *Economic Journal*, 101, pp. 276–288.

Goodhart, C.A.E., (1989), *Money, Information and Uncertainty*, London.

Gordon, R.J., (1990), 'What is New–Keynesian Economics?', *Journal of Economic Literature*, 28, pp. 1115–1171.

Grandmont, J.M., (1985), 'On Endogenous Competitive Business Cycles', *Econometrica*, 53, pp. 995–1045.

Grandmont, J.M., (1989), 'Keynesian Issues and Economic Theory', *Scandinavian Journal of Economics*, 91, pp. 265–293.

Greenwald, B. and J.E. Stiglitz, (1987), 'New–Keynesian, New–Classical and Keynesian Economics', *Oxford Economic Papers*, 39, pp. 119–132.

Hahn, F.H., (1973), 'On the Foundations of Monetary Theory', in M. Parkin (ed.), *Essays in Modern Economics*, Parkings, pp. 230–242.

Hahn, F.H., (1978), 'On Non–Walrasian Equilibria', *Review of Economic Studies*, 45, pp. 1–17.

Hahn, F.H., (1983), 'Comment' in: D. Worswick and J. Trevithick (eds.), *Keynes and the Modern World*, Cambridge, pp. 72–75.

Hahn, F.H, (1984), 'Keynesian Economics and Equilibrium Theory: Reflections on Some Current Debates', in F. Hahn, *Equilibrium and Macroeconomics*, Oxford.

Hahn, F.H. (1988), 'On Monetary Theory', *Economic Journal*, 98, pp. 957–973.

Hahn, F.H. (ed.), (1989), *The Economics Of Missing Markets, Information and Games*, Clarendon Press, Oxford.

Hahn, F.H. (1990), 'John Hicks the Theorist', *Economic Journal*, 100, pp. 539–550.

Haltiwanger, J. and M. Waldman, (1989), 'Limited Rationality and Strategic Complements: The Implications for Macroeconomics', *Quarterly Journal of Economics*, 104, pp. 463–483.

Hamouda, O.F. and G.C. Harcourt (1989), 'Post–Keynesianism: from Criticism to Coherence', in J. Pheby (ed.), *New directions in Post–Keynesian Economics*, Aldershot, pp. 1–35.

Hamouda, O.F., and J.N. Smithin (1988), 'Some Remarks on Uncertainty and Economic Analysis', *Economic Journal*, 98, pp. 159–165.

Harcourt, G.C., (1985), 'Post Keynesianism: Quite Wrong and/or Nothing New?' in Arestis and Skouras (eds.), *Post Keynesian Economic Theory*, New York, pp. 125–145.

Hausman, D.H., (1989), 'Economic Methodology in a Nutshell', *Journal of Economic Perspectives*, 3, pp. 115–127.

Hayek, F.A., (1937), 'Economics and Knowledge', reprinted in F.A. Hayek, *Individualism and Economic Order*, 1949, London, pp. 33–54.

Hayek, F.A., (1945), 'The Use of Knowledge in Society', *American Economic Review*, 35, pp. 519–530.

Hayek, F.A., (1946), 'The Meaning of Competition' in F.A. Hayek, *Individualism and Economic Order*, 1949, London, pp.92–107.

Hayek, F.A., (1967), *Studies in Philosophy, Politics and Economics*, London.

Hayek, F.A., (1973), *Law, Legislation and Liberty*, London.

Hayek, F.A., (1976A), *Denationalization of Money*, London.

Hayek, F.A., (1976B), 'The Pretence of Knowledge', in F.A. Hayek, (1978), London, pp. 23–35.

Hayek, F.A., (1978), *New Studies in Philosophy, Politics, Economics and the History of Ideas*, London.

Heiner, R.H., (1983), 'The Origin of Predictable Behavior', *American Economic Review*, 73, pp. 560–596.

Heller, W.P., (1986), 'Coordination Failure under Complete Markets with Applications to Effective Demand" in W.P. Heller, R.M. Starr and D.A. Starrett (eds.), *Equilibrium Analysis. Essays in Honour of Kenneth J. Arrow, Volume ii*, Cambridge U.P., pp. 155–175.

Hicks, J.R., (1933), 'Equilibrium and the Cycle', reprinted in J.R. Hicks (1982), *Money , Interest and Wages. Collected Essays on Economic Theory, Vol. II*, Oxford, pp. 28–41.

Hicks, J.R., (1935), 'A Suggestion for Simplifying the Theory of

Money,' reprinted in J.R. Hicks (1982), *Money, Interest and Wages, Collected Essays on Economic Theory, Vol. II*, Oxford, pp. 46–64.

Hicks, J.R., (1937), 'Mr. Keynes and the Classics', reprinted in J.R. Hicks, *Money, Interest and Wages, Collected Essays on Economic Theory, Vol. II*, Oxford, pp. 100–115.

Hicks, J.R., (1974), *The Crisis in Keynesian Economics*, Basil Blackwell, Oxford.

Hicks, J.R., (1979), *Causality in Economics*, Oxford.

Hicks, J.R., (1982), *Money, Interest and Wages, Collected Essays on Monetary Theory, Vol. II*, Oxford.

Hicks, J.R., (1989), *A Market Theory for Money*, Oxford.

Hodgson, G.M., (1985), 'Persuasion, Expectations and the Limits to Keynes' in T. Lawson and M. Pesaran (eds.), *Keynes' Economics: Methodological Issues*, London, pp. 10–45.

Hodgson, G.M., (1988), *Economics and Institutions*, Oxford.

Hodgson, (1989), 'Post–Keynesianism and Institutionalism, The Missing Link', in J. Pheby (ed.), (1989), *New Directions in Post–Keynesian Economics*, Aldershot, pp. 94–124.

Hoogduin, L.H., (1991), *Some Aspects of Uncertainty and the Theory of a Monetary Economy*, PhD–dissertation, Groningen.

Hoogduin L.H. and J. Snippe, (1987), 'Uncertainty in/of Macroeconomics: An Essay on Adequate Abstraction', *De Economist*, 135, pp. 429–442.

Hoover, K.D., (1988A), 'Money, Prices and Finance in the New Monetary Economics', *Oxford Economic Papers*, 40, pp. 150–168.

Hoover, K.D., (1988B), *The New Classical Macroeconomics*, Oxford.

Howitt, P., (1990), *The Keynesian Recovery and Other Essays*, New York.

Iwai, K., (1981), *Disequilibrium Dynamics*, New–Haven, Yale University Press.

Iwai, K., (1988A), 'Fiat Money and Aggregate Demand Management in a Search Model of Decentralized Exchanges', *Caress Working Paper*, 88–16, University of Pennsylvania.

Iwai, K., (1988B), 'A Bootstrap Theory of Money', *Caress Working Paper*, 88–03, University of Pennsylvania.

Janssen, M.C.W., (1990), *Micro and Macro in Economics. An Inquiry into their Relation*, PhD–dissertation, Groningen.

Janssen, M.C.W., (1991), 'The Alleged Necessity of Microfoundations', *Journal of Macroeconomics*, forthcoming.

John, A., (1988), 'Imperfect Competition, Keynesian Dynamics and the Paradox of Thrift', *Mimeo*, Michigan State University.

Johnson, H.G., (1967), *Essays in Monetary Economics*, London.

Jones, R.A., (1976), 'The Origin and Development of Media of Exchange', *Journal of Political Economy*, 84, pp. 757–776.

Jones, R.A. and Ostroy, J.M., (1984), 'Flexibility and Uncertainty', *Review of Economic Studies*, 51, pp. 13–32.

214 Keynes, Coordination and Beyond

Kaldor, N., (1956), 'Alternative Theories of Distribution', *Review of Economic Studies*, 23., pp.83–100.

Kaldor, N., (1972), 'The Irrelevance of Equilibrium Economics', *Economic Journal*, 82, pp. 1237–1255.

Kaldor, N., (1983), 'Keynesian Economics after Fifty Years', in D. Worswick and J. Trevithick (eds.), *Keynes and the Modern World*, Cambridge, pp. 1–28.

Kalecki, M., (1938), 'The Determinants of Distribution of National Income', *Econometrica*, 6, 1938, pp. 97–112.

Kalecki, (1971), *Selected Essays on the Dynamics of the Capitalist Economy*, 1933–1970, Cambridge.

Kehoe, T.J., (1989), 'Intertemporal General Equilibrium Models', in F.H. Hahn (ed.), (1989), *The Economics of Missing Markets, Information and Games*, Oxford, pp. 363–394.

Kelsey, D., (1988), 'The Economics of Chaos', *Oxford Economic Papers*, 40. pp. 1–19.

Kelsey, D., (1989), 'An Introduction to Nonlinear Dynamics and its Application to Economics' in F.H. Hahn (ed.), (1989), pp. 410–437.

Keynes, J.M., (1921), *Treatise on Probability*, The Collected Writings of John Maynard Keynes, vol. 8, London, 1973.

Keynes, J.M., (1930), *Treatise on Money*, The Collected Writings of John Maynard Keynes, vol. 5 and 6, London, 1971.

Keynes, J.M., (1933), *The Collected Writings of John Maynard Keynes*, vol. 29, London, 1979.

Keynes, J.M., (1936), *The General Theory of Employment, Interest and Money*, The Collected Writings of John Maynard Keynes, vol. 7, London, 1973.

Keynes, J.M., (1937A), 'The Theory of the Rate of Interest', *The Collected Writings of John Maynard Keynes*, vol. 14, London, 1973, pp. 101–108.

Keynes, J.M., (1937B), 'The General Theory of Employment', *The Collected Writings of John Maynard Keynes*, vol. 14, London, 1973, pp. 109–124.

Keynes, J.M., (1939), 'Relative Movements of Real Wages and Output', *The Collected Writings of John Maynard Keynes*, vol. 7, London, 1973, pp. 394–412.

Keynes, J.M. (1972), *The Collected Writings of John Maynard Keynes*, vol. 10, London, 1972.

Keynes, J.M. (1973A), *The Collected Writings of John Maynard Keynes*, vol. 13, London, 1973.

Keynes, J.M. (1973B), *The Collected Writings of John Maynard Keynes*, vol. 14, London, 1973.

King, R., (1981), 'Monetary Information and Monetary Neutrality', *Journal of Monetary Economics*, 7, pp. 195–206.

Kirman, A.P., (1989), 'The Limits of Modern Economic Theory', *Economic Journal*, 99, pp. 126–139.

Kirzner, I.M., (1973), *Competition and Entrepreneurship*, Chicago.Kirzner, I.M. (ed.), (1986), *Subjectivism, Intelligibility and Economic Understanding*, New York University.
Kiyotaki, N. and R. Wright, (1988), 'Fiat Money in Search Equilibrium', *SSRI Working Paper* 8825, University of Wisconsin.
Kiyotaki, N. and R. Wright, (1989), 'On Money as a Medium of Exchange', *Journal of Political Economy*, 97, pp. 927–954.
Klundert, Th. van de, (1987), 'Coordination Failure in an Industrial Society', *De Economist*, 135, pp. 467–487.
Kregel, J.A., (1973), *The Reconstruction of Political Economy*, London.
Kregel, J.A., (1976), 'Economic Methodology in the Face of Uncertainty', *Economic Journal*, 86, pp. 209–225.
Kregel, J.A., (1977), 'Some Post Keynesian Distribution Theory' in S. Weintraub (ed.), *Modern Economic Thought*, Oxford, pp. 421–441.
Kregel, J.A., (1980), 'Markets and Institutions as Features of a Capitalistic Production System', *Journal of Post Keynesian Economics*, 3, pp. 32–48.
Kregel, J.A., (1982A), 'Money, Expectations and Relative Prices in Keynes' Monetary Equilibrium', *Economie Appliquee*, 35, pp.449–466.
Kregel, J.A., (1982B), 'Expectations and Rationality within a Capitalist Framework', *Diskussionsbeiträge zur gesamtwirtschaftlichen Theorie und Politik*, 4, Universität Bremen.
Kregel, J.A., (1983), 'Post Keynesian Economics: An Overview', *Journal of Economic Education*, 14, pp. 32–43.
Kregel, J.A., (1985), 'Constraints on the Expansion of Output and Employment: Real or Monetary?,' *Journal of Post Keynesian Economics*, 7, pp. 139–152.
Kregel, J.A., (1987), 'Rational Spirits and the Post Keynesian Macrotheory of Microeconomics', *De Economist*, 135, pp. 520–533.
Kregel, J.A., (1990), 'The Formation of Fix and Flex Prices and Monetary Theory: An Appraisal of Hicks' A Market Theory of Money', *Banca Nazionale del Lavoro Quarterly Review*, 175, pp. 475–486.
Kreps, D.M., (1990), *Game Theory and Economic Modelling*, Oxford.
Kriesler, P., (1987), *Kalecki's Microanalysis*, Cambridge.
Krugman, P., (1991A), 'History versus Expectations', *Quarterly Journal of Economics*, 106, pp. 651–668.
Krugman, P., (1991B), 'History and Industry Location: The Case of the Manufacturing Belt', *American Economic Review Papers and Proceedings*, 81, pp. 80–84.
Kydland, F.E. and E.C. Prescott, (1977), 'Rules Rather than Discretion: The Inconsistency of Optimal Plans', *Journal of Political Economy*, 85, pp. 473–492.
Kydland, F.E. and E.C. Prescott, (1982), 'Time to Build and Aggregate Fluctuations', *Econometrica*, 50, pp. 1345–1370.

216 Keynes, Coordination and Beyond

Kuipers, S.K., (1981), 'Keynesian and Neo–Classical Growth Models: a Sequential Analytical Approach', *De Economist*, 129, pp. 58–104.

Lachmann, L.M., (1977), *Capital, Expectations and the Market Process*, Kansas City.

Laidler, D., (1982), *Monetarist Perspectives*, Oxford. Laidler, D., (1990A), 'Hicks and the Classics', *Journal of Monetary Economics*, 25, pp. 481–489.

Laidler, D., (1990B), *Taking Money Seriously*, New–York.

Langlois, R.N. (ed.), (1986A), *Economics as a Process. Essays in the New Institutional Economics*, Cambridge University Press.

Langlois, R.N. (1986B), 'Coherence and Flexibility: Social Institutions in a World of Radical Uncertainty', in I. Kirzner (ed.), *Subjectivism, Intelligibility and Economic Understanding*, New York University, pp. 171–192.

Lawson, T., (1985), 'Uncertainty and Economic Analysis', *Economic Journal*, 95, pp. 909–927.

Leibenstein, H., (1979), 'A Branch of Economics is Missing: Micro–Micro Theory', *Journal of Economic Literature*, 17, pp. 477–503.

Leibenstein, H., (1982), 'The Prisoners' Dilemma in the Invisible Hand: An Analysis of Intrafirm Productivity', *American Economic Review Papers and Proceedings*, 72, pp. 92–96.

Leijonhufvud, A., (1968), *On Keynesian Economics and the Economics of Keynes*, Oxford.

Leijonhufvud, A., (1981), *Information and Coordination*, New York.

Leijonhufvud, A., (1984), 'Hicks on Time and Money', *Oxford Economic Papers*, 36, pp. 26–46.

Lerner, A.P., (1952), 'The Essential Properties of Interest and Money,' *Quarterly Journal of Economics*, 46, pp. 172–193.

Lerner, A.P., (1974), 'From *The Treatise on Money* to *The General Theory*', *Journal of Economic Literature*, 12, pp. 38–42.

Lewis, D.K., (1986), *Convention, A Philosophical Study*, Oxford.

Long, J.B. and I. Plosser (1983), 'Real Business Cycles', *Journal of Political Economy*, 91, pp. 39–69.

Lucas, R.E., (1972), 'Expectations and the Neutrality of Money', *Journal of Economic Theory*, 4, pp. 103–124.

Lucas, R.E., (1973), 'Some International Evidence on Output–Inflation Trade–Offs', *American Economic Review*, 63, pp. 326–334.

Lucas, R.E., (1975), 'An Equilibrium Model of Business Cycles', *Journal of Political Economy*, 83(6), pp. 1113–1144.

Lucas, R.E., (1981), *Studies in Business – Cycle Theory*, Oxford.

Lucas, R.E. and L. Rapping, (1969), 'Real Wages, Employment and Inflation', *Journal of Political Economy*, 77, pp. 721–754.

Mankiw, N.G., (1991), *The Reincarnation of Keynesian Economics*, paper presented at September 1991 meeting of the European Economic Association in Cambridge, England.

Makowski, L., (1989), 'Keynes' Liquidity Preference Theory: A Suggested Reinterpretation', in F. Hahn (ed.), (1989), pp. 468–477.

Marglin, S.A., (1984), *Growth, Distribution and Prices*, Harvard University Press.

Markowitz, H., (1959), *Portfolio Selection*, New York.

McCallum, B.T. (1979), 'The Current State of the Policy Ineffectiveness Debate', *American Economic Review Papers and Proceedings*, 69, pp. 240–246.

McCallum, B.T., (1983), 'The Role of the Overlapping Generations Model in Monetary Economics', *Carnegie–Rochester Series on Public Policy*, 18, pp.9–44.

McCallum, B.T., (1988), 'Real Business Cycle Models', *NBER Working Paper*, no. 2480.

McCloskey, D., (1983), 'The Rhetoric of Economics', *Journal of Economic Literature*, 21, pp. 481–517.

Meltzer, A.H., (1988), *Keynes's Monetary Theory*, Cambridge.

Menger, K., (1892), 'On the Origin of Money' in R.M. Starr (ed.), *General Equilibrium Models of Monetary Economics. Studies in the Static Foundations of Monetary Theory*, 1989, San Diego, pp. 67–83.

Minsky, H.P., (1975), *John Maynard Keynes*, New York.

Minsky, H.P., (1986), *Stabilizing an Unstable Economy*, Yale U.P.

Morishima, M., (1991), 'General Equilibrium Theory in the Twenty–First Century', *The Economic Journal*, 101, pp. 69–75.

Nagatani, K., (1978), *Monetary Theory*, Amsterdam, North–Holland.

Nell, E.J., (1983), 'Keynes after Sraffa: The Essential Properties of Keynes' Theory of Interest and Money: Comment on Kregel,' in: J.A. Kregel (ed.), *Distribution, Effective Demand and International Economic Relations*, London, pp. 85–104.

Nentjes, A., (1977), *Van Keynes tot Keynes*, PhD–dissertation, Groningen.

Niehans, J., (1978), *The Theory of Money*, Baltimore.

O'Donnell, R., (1990), 'An Overview of Probability, Expectations, Uncertainty and Rationality in Keynes' Conceptual Framework', *Review of Political Economy*, 2, pp. 253–267.

O'Driscoll, G.P., (1977), *Economics as a Coordination Problem: The Contributions of Friedrich A. Hayek*, Kansas City.

O'Driscoll, G.P., (1986), 'Money: Menger's Evolutionary Theory', *History of Political Economy*, 18, pp. 601–608.

O'Driscoll, G.P. and M.J. Rizzo, (1985), *The Economics of Time and Ignorance*, Oxford.

O'Driscoll, G.P. and M.J. Rizzo, (1986), 'Subjectivism, Uncertainty and Rules', in I.M. Kirzner (ed.), *Subjectivism, Intelligibility and Economic Understanding*, London, MacMillan, pp. 252–268.

Okun, A., (1981), *Prices and Quantities*, Oxford.

Ostroy, J.M., (1989), 'Money and General Equilibrium Theory', in J. Eatwell, M. Milgate and P. Newman (eds.), *General Equilibrium*, The

New Palgrave, London, pp. 187–194.

Panico, C., (1988), *Interest and Profit in the Theories of Value and Distribution*, London, Macmillan.

Pasinetti, L.L., (1977), *Lectures on the Theory of Production*, New York.

Patinkin, D., (1956), *Money, Interest and Prices*, New York.

Patinkin, D., (1976), *Keynes' Monetary Thought*, Durham.

Patinkin, D., (1982), *Anticipations of the General Theory?*, Oxford.

Patinkin, D., (1990), 'On Different Interpretations of the General Theory', *Journal of Monetary Economics*, 26, pp. 203–205.

Peeters, M., (1987), 'A Dismal Science; An Essay on New Classical Economics', *De Economist*, 135, pp. 442–467.

Pen, J., (1971), *Income Distribution*, London.

Pesaran, H., (1987), *The Limits of Rational Expectations*, Oxford.

Pheby, J. (ed.), (1989), *New Directions in Post–Keynesian Economics*, Aldershot, Edward Elgar.

Phelps, E.S., (1968), 'Money Wage Dynamics and Labor Market Equilibrium', *Journal of Political Economy*, 76, pp. 687–711.

Potestio, P., (1989), 'Alternative Aspects of Monetary Theory in the 'General Theory': Significance and Implications,' *Recherches Economiques de Louvain*, 55, pp. 257–273.

Reynolds, P.J., (1987), *Political Economy, A Synthesis of Kaleckian and Post–Keynesian Economics*, Brighton.

Ribbers, J.A., (1988), *Onvrijwillige Werkloosheid*, Groningen.

Richardson, G.B., (1960), *Information and Investment, A Study in The Working of a Competitive Economy*, Oxford.

Roberts, J., (1987), 'An Equilibrium Model with Unvoluntary Unemployment at Flexible Competitive Prices and Wages', *American Economic Review*, 77, pp. 856–874.

Robinson, J., (1974),'History versus Equilibrium', *ThamesPapers in Political Economy*, No.1, London.

Robinson, J., (1977), 'What are the Questions?', *Journal of Economic Literature*, 15, pp. 1318–1339.

Rogers, C., (1989), *Money, Interest and Capital. A Study in the Foundations of Monetary Theory*, Cambridge, Cambridge University Press.

Romer, P.M., (1986), 'Increasing Returns and Long-run Growth, *Journal of Political Economy*, 94, pp. 1002–1038.

Rosser, J.B., (1991), *From Catastrophe to Chaos: A General Theory of Economic Discontinuties*, Boston.

Rotemberg, J.J., (1987), 'The New Keynesian Microfoundations', *NBER Macroeconomic Annual* 1987, Cambridge, Massachusetts, pp. 69–104.

Rotheim, R., (1981), 'Keynes' Monetary Theory of Value', *Journal of Post–Keynesian Economics*, 3, pp. 568–586.

Rousseas, S., (1985), *Post Keynesian Monetary Economics*, New York.

Rymes, T.K., (1989), *The Keynes' Lectures: 1932–1935*, University of

Michigan Press.

Samuels, W.J., (1989), 'Determinate Solutions and Valuational Processes: Overcoming the Foreclosure of Process', *Journal of Post Keynesian Economics*, 11, pp. 531–547.

Samuelson, P.A., (1958), 'An Exact Consumption Loan Model of Interest with or without the Social Contrivance of Money', *Journal of Political Economy*, 66, pp. 1002–1011.

Sargent, T.J. and N. Wallace, (1975), 'Rational Expectations, The Optimal Monetary Instrument and the Optimal Money Supply Rule', *Journal of Political Economy*, 83, pp. 241–254.

Sargent, T.J and N. Wallace, (1976), 'Rational Expectations, and the Theory of Economic Policy', *Journal of Monetary Economics*, 2, pp. 169–183.

Sawyer, M., (1985),'Towards a Post–Kaleckian Macroeconomics' in Arestis and Skouras (eds.), *Post Keynesian Economic Theory*, Oxford, pp. 146–180.

Schelling, T., (1960), *The Strategy of Conflict*, Yale.

Schotter, A., (1981), *The Economic Theory of Social Institutions*, New York.

Scitovsky, T., (1984), 'Lerner's Contributions to Economics', *Journal of Economic Literature*, 4, pp. 1547–1572.

Sen, K.K., (1990), 'The Sunspot Theorists and Keynes', *Journal of Post–Keynesian Economics*, 12, pp. 564–572.

Shackle, G.L.S., (1967), *The Years of High Theory*, Cambridge.

Shackle, G.L.S., (1972), *Epistemics and Economics*, Cambridge.

Shackle, G.L.S., (1974), *Keynesian Kaleidics*, Edinburgh.

Snippe, J., (1987A), 'Monetary Equilibrium Versus the Wicksell Connection,: On Method and Substance in Monetary Controversy', *Banca Nazionale del Lavoro Quarterly Review*, 161, pp. 197–212.

Snippe, J., (1987B), 'An Invisible Hand without Foresight and Hindsight: Comment on Garrison', *History of Political Economy*, 19, pp. 329–334.

Solow, R.M., (1980), 'On Theories of Unemployment', *American Economic Review*, 70, pp. 1–12.

Solow, R.M., (1986), 'Unemployment: Getting the Questions Right', *Economica*, supplement, 53, pp. 23–35.

Sraffa, P., (1926), 'The Laws of Return under Competitive Condition, *Economic Journal*, pp. 535–550.

Sraffa, P., (1932), 'Dr. Hayek on Money and Capital', *Economic Journal*, vol. 42.

Sraffa, P., (1960), *Production of Commodities by Means of Commodities*, Cambridge.

Stiglitz, J.E., (1991), 'Alternative Approaches to Macroeconomics: Methodological Issues and the New Keynesian Economics', *NBER Working Paper*, No. 3580.

Sugden, R., (1986), *The Economics of Rights, Cooperation and Welfare*,

Oxford.

Sugden, R., (1989), 'Spontaneous Order', *Journal of Economic Perspectives*, 3, pp. 85–97.

Sugden, R., (1991), 'Rational Choice: A Survey of Contributions from Economics and Philosophy', *Economic Journal*, 101, pp. 751–786.

Tarshis, L., (1980), 'Post–Keynesian Economics: A Promise that Bounced?', *American Economic Review Papers and Proceedings*, 70, pp. 10–15.

Taylor, J.B., (1980), 'Aggregate Dynamics and Staggered Contracts', *Journal of Political Economy*, 88, pp. 1–23.

Tobin, J. (1956), 'The Interest Elasticity of the Transactions Demand for Cash', *Review of Economics and Statistics*, 38, pp. 241–247.

Tobin, J., (1958), 'Liquidity Preference as Behaviour towards Risk', *Review of Economic Studies*, 25, pp. 65–86.

Tobin, J., (1978), *Asset Accumulation and Economic Activity*, Chicago

Townshend, H., (1937), 'Liquidity Premium and the Theory of Value', *Economic Journal*, 47, pp. 321–326.

VanHuyck, J., R. Battalaio, and R. Beil, (1990), 'Tacit Coordination Games, Strategic Uncertainty and Coordination Failure', *American Economic Review*, 80, pp. 234–248.

Varian, H.R., (1984), *Microeconomic Analysis*, Norton.

Vaubel, R., (1977), 'Free Currency Competition', *Weltwirtschaftliches Archiv*, 37, pp. 435–461.

Vaubel, R., (1984), 'The Government's Money Monopoly: Externalities or Natural Monopoly?', *Kyklos*, pp. 27–58.

Von Mises, L., (1953), *The Theory of Money and Credit*, Indianapolis, Liberty Classics, edition 1981.

Wallace, N., (1988), 'A Suggestion for Oversimplifying the Theory of Money,' *Economic Journal*, Supplement, Conference Papers, Vol. 98, pp. 25–36.

Warneryd, K., (1989), 'Legal Restrictions and the Evolution of Media of Exchange', *Journal of Institutional and Theoretical Economics*, 145, pp. 613–626.

Warneryd, K., (1990), 'Legal Restrictions and Monetary Evolution', *Journal of Economic Behavior and Organization*, 13, pp. 117–124.

Weddepohl, H.N., (1988), *Overlappende Generatie–Modellen*, Amsterdam.

Weintraub, E.R., (1977), 'The Microfoundations of Macroeconomics: A Critical Survey', *Journal of Economic Literature*, 15, pp. 1–23.

Weintraub, E.R., (1979), *Microfoundations*, Cambridge.

Weintraub, E.R., (1985), *General Equilibrium Analysis: Studies in Appraisal*, Cambridge.

Weintraub, S., (1958), *An Approach to the Theory of Income Distribution*, Westport.

Weintraub, S., (1961), *Capitalism's Inflation and Unemployment Crisis*, Reading.

Weintraub, S., (1978), 'The Missing Theory of Money Wages', *Journal* of *Post – Keynesian Economics*, 1, pp. 59–79.

Weitzman, M.L., (1982), 'Increasing Returns and the Foundations of Unemployment Theory', *Economic Journal*, 92, pp. 787–804.

Wells, P., (1978), 'In Review of Keynes', *Cambridge Journal of Economics*, 2, pp. 315–326.

Wicksell, K., (1935), *Lectures on Political Economy*, vol. 2, London.

Williamson, O.E., (1975), *Markets and Hierarchies: Analysis and Antitrust Implications*, New York.

Williamson, O.E.,(1985), *The Economic Institutions of Capitalism*, New York.

Winslow, E.G., (1986), 'Human Logic and Keynes' Economics', *Eastern Economic Journal*, pp. 413–430.

Winslow, E.G., (1989), 'Organic Interdependence, Uncertainty and Economic Analysis', *Economic Journal*, 99, pp. 1173–1183.

White, L.H., (1984), 'Competitive Payments System and the Unit of Account', *American Economic Review*, 66, pp. 699–712.

Woodford, M., (1984), 'Indeterminacy of Equilibrium in the Overlapping Generations Model: A Survey', *Mimeo*, New–York, Columbia University.

Woodford, M. (1988), 'Self–Fulfilling Expectations and Fluctuations in Aggregate Demand', *Mimeo*, Chicago, University of Chicago.

Wubben, E.F.M., (1991), 'Austrian Economics and Uncertainty: On a Non–Deterministic but Non–Kaleidic Future', *Discussion Paper* 9105–G, Erasmus University, Rotterdam.

Index

indeterminacy (cont)
  in labour market, 22–4
  and money, 139, 140, 141, 144, 183
  in OLG model, 103–16, 120–27
  in post–Keynesian theories, 70–71,
    76, 90, 91
information costs, 193
institutions, 4–5, 70, 91–2, 174, 193,
  198
interest rates
  in classical theory, 25–6, 28, 29
  Keynes on, 26–7, 28, 30, 154, 181
intertemporal substitution, 119
investment
  in classical theory, 24, 26–7
  Keynes on, 24–8, 119
  and paradox of thrift, 25, 113–15
  in post–Keynesian theories, 72–3
IS/LM model, 45
Iwai, K., 61, 163, 164–5, 168, 169–74,
  175, 181

Janssen, M.C.W., 60
John, A., 57, 58, 59, 103, 104, 111,
  119, 194
Jones, R.A., 164

Kaldor, N., 54, 73
Kalecki, M., 12, 71–2, 73, 80
Kaleckian post–Keynesians, 69, 70,
  71–4, 79–81, 93
Kehoe, T.J., 121, 122, 190
Keynes, John Maynard, (principal
  references only)
  on competition, 54
  on effective demand, 21, 24, 33, 34,
    79
  on expectations, 7, 9, 27–8, 29,
    30–37, 91, 126, 127
  on indeterminacy, 11, 22–37, 79,
    88, 89, 102, 104, 139, 140
  on interest rates, 26–7, 28, 30, 154,
    181
  on labour market, 21, 22–4
  on liquidity preference, 29, 32, 88,
    94–5, 139, 142–3
  on macro/micro issue, 6–8, 11,
    126–7
  and microfoundations debate, 43–5
  on money, 2, 7, 28–9, 88, 119,
    135–6, 138–51, 154, 180–81

on saving and investment, 24–8,
  119
theoretical legacy of, 1–5, 19
on unemployment, 2, 21, 23
on wages, 21, 22–3, 167–8
Keynesian Cross, 34
King, R., 51
Kirman, A.P., 10
Kiyotaki, N., 55, 164
Klemperer, P., 121
Klundert, Th. van de, 54
Kregel, J.A., 31, 34, 35, 70, 73, 78, 94,
  95, 149, 154, 178
Kriesler, P., 71, 73, 80
Kydland, F.E., 49, 51

labour market, 11, 48
  in classical theory, 22–3
  Keynes on, 21, 22–4
  in OLG model, 107
  in post–Keynesian theory, 74
Lachmann, L.M., 197–8
Laidler, D., 45, 84, 138, 140, 141, 180
Langlois, R.N., 193
Lawson, T., 32, 89, 195, 198
learning process, 191, 193
Leijonhufvud, A., 47, 48, 59, 183
Lerner, A.P., 152, 166
Lewis, D.K., 4, 176
liquidity preference, 29, 32, 88, 94–5,
  139, 142–3, 149, 180–81
Long, J.B., 51
Lucas, R.E., 49, 51, 82, 84, 195

McCallum, B.T., 49, 52, 164
macro–micro issue, 4–8, 10, 11, 22,
  126–7, 128
  see also microfoundations debate
Mankiw, N.G., 54
marginal efficiency of capital, 27
Marglin, S.A., 80
market(s), 2–3
  in Austrian economics, 83–6
  failure of, in new–Keynesian
    theories, 53–60
  in new–classical theories, 49–53
  in OLG model, 107–8
  in post–Keynesian theories, 70
  see also goods market; labour
    market
Markowitz, H., 45